ABBREVIATIONS DICTIONARY

A practical compilation of today's
acronyms and abbreviations

ROBERT S. WACHAL

Houghton Mifflin Company
BOSTON · NEW YORK

Library of Congress Cataloging-in-Publication Data

Wachal, Robert S.
  Abbreviations dictionary : a practical compilation of today's
  acronyms and abbreviations / Robert S. Wachal.
      p.   cm.
  ISBN 0-395-92691-2
  1. Abbreviations, English.   I. Title.
PE1693.W34   1999
423'.1–dc21   99-33430
                                                        CIP

Manufactured in the United States of America
QWT 10 9 8 7 6 5 4 3

PREFACE

We live in an abbreviated age. All around us, in all forms of communication, from advertisements to business reports, the world is teeming with abbreviations. And they seem to be proliferating. With the number of computer users rising every month, increasingly sophisticated digital devices, global communications, and rapid exchanges on the Internet, the occasions for using abbreviations are as plentiful as they are multifarious.

Many abbreviations are created as expediencies by people working in specialized fields who want to avoid repeating strings of polysyllables many times a day. Quite often nonspecialists encounter these abbreviations in their everyday lives and are at a loss to interpret them.

Still other abbreviations are common and familiar but are not easy to decipher. Reading classified ads can be a bewildering experience for people unaccustomed to their clipped mode of expression. Jumping to the wrong conclusion about the meaning of an abbreviation in an ad describing an apartment, used car, or prospective date can turn into a disappointment, if not an embarrassment.

For all these reasons, I have compiled the *Abbreviations Dictionary*. With roughly 13,000 entries it not only lists common terms that you will encounter in newspaper ads, but it also includes many truncations and initialisms used in specialized fields, whose language is often underrepresented in general dictionaries. My goal was simply to offer quick and easy reference for abbreviated terms that Americans may encounter in a multitude of situations.

This book will help you decipher the conversations of medical personnel in your HMO, the specifications printed on the box of your computer, and the ratings in your television listings. It will help you navigate the shorthand names of hundreds of important organizations and government agencies. If you need to place a want ad, it will help you save money by reducing the amount of text you have to pay for. It will familiarize you with the conventions of

Internet chat rooms and the two-letter geographic Internet domains used to identify each country, so you can understand what people are saying and where they are coming from.

This collection is more comprehensive, more inclusive, and more up-to-date in its selections than other dictionaries of its type, not only in its wide coverage of spheres of interest but also in its broad range of abbreviation types. The following are examples of the kinds of abbreviations found in the *Abbreviations Dictionary*:

acronyms
radar radio detecting and ranging

blends
Chunnel (Channel Tunnel)

clippings
dorm dormitory
roo kangaroo

defined terms
ABC's the basics

foreign terms
loc. cit. *loco citato* (in the place cited)

initialisms
FBI Federal Bureau of Investigation

mnemonic devices
HOMES (Huron, Ontario, Michigan, Erie, Superior)

numericals
L8R later

phonetic initialisms
EZ easy

respellings
biz business

symbols
Na sodium

truncations
adj. adjective

As this list shows, abbreviations are not only essential to modern living but interesting in their own right. They reflect the fast-paced, highly productive way in which we live. They are, in short, a reflection of who we are.

STYLING Abbreviations vary widely in their style of punctuation, capitalization and internal spacing. Following the contemporary trend toward less-frequent use of periods, entries in the *Abbreviations Dictionary* are generally shown without periods, except for academic degrees, truncations, and terms that require or almost always appear with punctuation. Abbreviations used in Internet domain names are listed with a preceding period (.com, .edu, .br, .ne).

SOURCES The resources of the Reference Department at Houghton Mifflin Company, including *The American Heritage® Dictionary, Third Edition*, were made available for this publication.

The New York Times was a major source of contemporary abbreviations, especially the sections on science and computing. Classified ads, personal or dating ads, and crossword puzzles from nearly two dozen newspapers across the country were reviewed. Other publications and texts examined include computer magazines (*PC World, PC Novice, Net*), news magazines (*Business Week, Time, U.S. News and World Report*), general magazines (*The Atlantic Monthly*, the *New Yorker, Readers' Digest*), numerous books concerning computer and Internet technology, and hundreds of Web sites.

ACKNOWLEDGMENTS

The completion of this project would not have been possible had it not been for the excellent facilities of the University of Iowa's Obermann Center for Advanced Studies, at which I was fortunate enough to have an appointment. I am very grateful to the director of the center, Jay Semel, and his superb technical support staff, Lorna Olson and John Robert Gardner, and to editorial assistance from Rachel Warden.

There are times when the reference specialists at a good academic library are indispensable. I thank the University of Iowa Librarian, Sheila Creth, and two of her able staff members, Mary Monson and George Mullally, for their help and thereby proving the World Wide Web doesn't know everything.

I am also in the debt of Iowa's Department of Linguistics and its chair, William Davies, for providing me, its one emeritus member, with a computer account and for suggesting some abbreviations used by linguists.

The work on this dictionary would have been far less pleasurable and efficient were it not for the good offices of my editor, Steve Kleinedler. I am extremely grateful for his assistance, for his encouragement and unfailing goodwill and for his editorial touch. I would also like to thank Ben Fortson, David Pritchard, and Jacquelyn Pope for their review of foreign entries; the production department, especially Beth Rubè and Chris Leonesio; the proofreader, Janet Bond Wood; and the designer, Melodie Wertelet.

A number of people have provided me with entries or pointed me to places where I might find them. Author and political scientist Lyell Henry provided me with 150 items and much encouragement. Others who have helped by supplying items or giving indispensable advice are Kit Austin, Jill Beckman, John Bergstrom, Jean and Douglas Boatman, Gareth Branwyn, Maureen Burke, Ronald R. Butters, Frank Camp, Alice Chindblom, Christopher Culy, Ann Donovan, Susan Nash Fekety, Joe and Gay Haldeman, Marie Louise Hannan, Brian Harvey, Sparkle Hayter, Marilyn K. Hiscock, Paul Ingram, Suzanne McCune, Linda McIntyre, Christopher McKee, Barry Popik, Mary Beth Protomastro, Edward Roberts, Michael Seidman, Marion Severynse, Wallace Sizemore, L. Jay Stein, Joan Thompson, William Welburn, Bruce Wheaton, and members of the Dorothy-L LISTSERV e-mail group.

A great debt of a different sort is owed to three people for their forbearance: to Robert E. Sanders, who expected a promised article for his scholarly journal long before now, and to Mary Anne Madden, who expected more writing from me on our joint novel.

Above all, to my wife, Jane McCune, I am especially grateful. The time span of this project coincided precisely with that of the local real estate season. Knowing that, she nonetheless encouraged me to take on the project and uncomplainingly took over virtually all of my household tasks in addition to her job as CEO and broker of her own real estate firm, offering me constant encouragement and solace throughout.

ROBERT S. WACHAL
Iowa City, Iowa

A

a absent

A accusative; ace; across; adenine; alto; American Stock Exchange; ammeter; ampere; angstrom; area; Asian (as in personal ads)

a. acre; adjective; *Latin* anno (in the year); *Latin* annus (year); anode; answer; *Latin* ante (before); anterior; artery

aa author's alteration

AA Academy of Aphasia; Acts of the Apostles; administrative assistant; Alcoholics Anonymous; Alzheimer's Association; antiaircraft; Armed Forces Americas (except Canada)

aa. arteries

A.A. Associate in Arts

AAA American Arbitration Association; antiaircraft artillery

AAAA American Academy of Anesthesiologists Assistants

AAAAI American Academy of Allergy, Asthma, and Immunology

AAAC American Academy of Ambulatory Care

AAACN American Academy of Ambulatory Care Nursing

AAAD American Athletic Association of the Deaf (now **USADSF**: United States of America Deaf Sports Federation)

AAAE American Association of Engineers

AAAH American Association of Alternative Healers

AAAHC Accreditation Association for Ambulatory Health Care

AAAI American Association for Artificial Intelligence

AAAL American Academy of Arts and Letters; American Association of Applied Linguistics

AAALAC Association for Assessment and Accreditation of Laboratory Animal Care International

AAANA American Academy of Ambulatory Nursing Administration

AAAOM American Association of Acupuncture and Oriental Medicine

AAAP Association of Administrators in Academic Pediatrics

AAARRO Association of Administrators in Academic Radiology and Radiation Oncology

AAAS American Association for the Advancement of Science

AABA American Anorexia/Bulimia Association

AABB American Association of Blood Banks

AABH Association of Ambulatory Behavior Healthcare

AABIC Association for the Advancement of Brain Injured Children

AABP American Association of Bovine Practitioners

AABT Association for the Advancement of Behavior Therapy

AAC AIDS Action Council

A.A.C. *Latin* anno ante Christum (the year before Christ)

AACA Antique Automobile Club of America

AACAP American Academy of Child and Adolescent Psychiatry

AACC American Association for Clinical Chemistry

AACCR American Association of Central Cancer Registries

AACD American Academy of Cosmetic Dentistry

AACDP American Association of Chairs of Departments of Psychiatry

AACE American Association for Cancer Education; American Association of Clinical Endocrinologists

AACMHP American Association of Community Mental Health Center Psychiatrists

AACN American Association of Colleges of Nursing; American Association of Critical-Care Nurses

A.A.C.N. *Latin* anno ante Christum natum (the year before the birth of Christ)

AACOM American Association of Colleges of Osteopathic Medicine

AACOMAS American Association of Colleges of Osteopathic Medicine Applications Service

AACP American Academy for Child Psychoanalysts; American Academy of Clinical Psychiatrists; American Association of Colleges of Pharmacy; American Association of Community Psychiatrists

AACPDM American Academy for Cerebral Palsy and Developmental Medicine

AACPM American Association of Colleges of Podiatric Medicine

AACPMAS American Association of Colleges of Podiatric Medicine Application Service

AACPR American Association of Cardiovascular and Pulmonary Rehabilitation

AACR American Association for Cancer Research

AACS American Academy of Cosmetic Surgery

AACT American Academy of Clinical Toxicology

AACVPR American Association of Cardiovascular and Pulmonary Rehabilitation

Aad α-aminoadipic acid

AAD American Academy of Dermatology; Attitude Anomaly Detector

AADB American Association of the Deaf-Blind

AADE American Association of Dental Editors; American Association of Diabetes Educators

AADEP American Academy of Disability Evaluating Physicians

AADGP American Academy of Dental Group Practice

AADPRT American Association of Directors of Psychiatric Residency Training

AADS American Association of Dental Schools

AAED American Academy of Esthetic Dentistry

AAEE American Association of Electrical Engineers

AAEM American Academy of Emergency Medicine; American Academy of Environmental Medicine

AAEP American Association of Equine Practitioners

AAES American Association of Engineering Societies

AAETS American Academy of Experts in Traumatic Stress

AAF Army Air Forces

AAFA Alliance Against Fraud in Advertising; Asthma and Allergy Foundation of America

AAFP American Academy of Family Physicians; American Association of Feline Practitioners

AAFPRS American Academy of Facial Plastic and Reconstructive Surgery

AAFS Academy of Ambulatory Foot Surgery; American Academy of Forensic Sciences

AAFT Alliance Against Fraud in Telemarketing

AAGHP American Association of General Hospital Psychiatrists

AAGL American Association of Gynecologic Laparoscopists

AAGP American Association of Geriatric Psychiatry

AAGT Association for the Advancement of Gestalt Therapy

AAH Academy on Architecture for Health; Alliance for Alternatives in Healthcare

AAHA American Animal Hospital Association; American Association of Homes for the Aging

AAHC Alliance for Alternative Health Care; American Association of Healthcare Consultants

AAHE American Association for Health Education

AAHFP American Academy of Health and Fitness Professionals

AAHKS American Association of Hip and Knee Surgeons

AAHM American Association for the History of Medicine

AAHN American Association for the History of Nursing

AAHP American Association of Health Plans

AAHPERD American Alliance for Health, Physical Education, Recreation, and Dance

AAHPM American Academy of Hospice and Palliative Medicine

AAHS American Association for Hand Surgery

AAHSA American Association of Homes and Services for the Aging

AAHSL Association of Academic Health Sciences Libraries

AAHSLD Association of Academic Health Sciences Library Directors

AAI American Association of Immunologists

AAID American Academy of Implant Dentistry

AAIHDS American Association of Integrated Healthcare Delivery Systems

AAIM Association for Applied Interactive Multimedia

AAIP Association of American Indian Physicians

AAIR Asthma and Allergy Information and Research

AAKP American Association of Kidney Patients

AALA American Association for Laboratory Accreditation

AALAS American Association for Laboratory Animal Science

AALNC American Association of Legal Nurse Consultants

AALS Association of American Law Schools

AAM air-to-air missile; American Academy of Microbiology

AAMA American Academy of Medical Acupuncture; American Apparel Manufacturers Association

AAMC Association of American Medical Colleges

AAMCN American Association of Managed Care Nurses

AAMD American Academy of Medical Directors

AAMFT American Association for Marriage and Family Therapy

AAMI Association for the Advancement of Medical Instrumentation

AAMN American Assembly for Men in Nursing

AAMOF as a matter of fact

AAMR American Association on Mental Retardation

AAMRO American Association of Medical Review Officers

AAMS Association of Air Medical Services

AAMSG Asian American Medical Student Group

AAMSI American Association for Medical Systems and Informatics

AAMT American Association for Medical Transcription

AAN American Academy of Neurology; American Academy of Nursing

AANA American Association of Nurse Anesthetists

A & A astronomy and astrophysics

A & E Arts and Entertainment

a & h accident and health

A & M agricultural and mechanical

A & P anterior and posterior; [Great] Atlantic and Pacific Tea Company; avant-pop

A and R artists and repertory

AANE American Association of Nurse Executives

AAN/MA Allergy and Asthma Network/Mothers of Asthmatics

AANN American Association of Neuroscience Nurses

AANNT American Association of Nephrology Nurses and Technicians

AANP American Academy of Nurse Practitioners; American Association of Naturopathic Physicians; American Association of Neuropathologists

AANS American Association of Neurological Surgeons

AAO American Academy of Ophthalmology; American Academy of Optometry; American Academy of Osteopathy; American Association of Orthodontists

A-A-O awake-alert-oriented

AAoA American Alliance of Aromatherapy

AAOA Association of Academic Orthopedic Administrators

AAOB American Association for Oral Biologists

AAOHN American Association of Occupational Health Nurses

AAO-HNS American Academy of Otolaryngology-Head and Neck Surgery

AAOM American Association of Oriental Medicine

AAOMS American Association of Oral and Maxillofacial Surgeons

AAON American Association of Office Nurses

AAOP American Academy of Orthotists and Prosthetists

AAOS American Academy of Orthopaedic Surgeons

AAP affirmative action plan; American Academy of Pediatrics; American Academy of Periodontology; American Academy of Psychoanalysis; American Academy of Psychotherapists; Association for Academic Psychiatry; Association for the Advancement of Psychoanalysis; Association for the Advancement of Psychotherapy; Association of Academic Physiatrists; Association of American Physicians; Association of American Publishers

AAPA American Academy of Physician Assistants

AAPAA American Association of Psychiatrists in Alcoholism and Addictions

AAPB Association for Applied Psychophysiology and Biofeedback

AAPC American Association of Pastoral Counselors

AAPCC American Association of Poison Control Centers

AAPD American Academy of Pediatric Dentistry; American Association of People with Disabilities

AAPH Asian-Americans in Public Health; Association for the Advancement of Private Health

AAPHO American Association of Physician Hospital Organizations

AAPHR American Association of Physicians for Human Rights

AAPL American Academy of Psychiatry and the Law

AAPM American Academy of Pain Management

AAPMR American Academy of Physical Medicine and Rehabilitation

AAPOS American Association for Pediatric Ophthalmology and Strabismus

AAPPO American Association of Preferred Provider Organizations

AAPS American Association of Pharmaceutical Scientists; American Association of Plastic Surgeons; Association of American Physicians and Surgeons

AAPSA American Academy of Psychoanalysis

AAPSC American Association of Psychiatric Services for Children

AAPSS American Academy of Political and Social Sciences

AAPT Association for the Advancement of Psychotherapy

AAR against all risks; Alliance for Aging Research

a.a.r. against all risks

AARC American Association for Respiratory Care

AARDA American Autoimmune Related Diseases Association

AARP American Association of Retired Persons

AARS automated aircraft reporting system

AART American Association for Respiratory Therapy

AAS American Association of Suicidology; American Astronautical Society; American Astronomical Society

A.A.S. Associate in Applied Sciences

AASA American Association of Surgical Administrators

AASCIN American Association of Spinal Cord Injury Nurses

AASCU American Association of State Colleges and Universities

AASH adrenal androgen-stimulating hormone; American Association for the Study of Headache

AASK Adopt A Special Kid

AASLD American Association for the Study of Liver Diseases

AASP American Association for Social Psychiatry; American Association of Swine Practitioners

AAST American Association for the Surgery of Trauma

AAT Animal-Assisted-Therapy Teams

AATA American Art Therapy Association; American Association of Thoracic Surgeons

AATBS Association for Advanced Training in Behavioral Sciences

AAU Amateur Athletic Union

AAUI Apple Attachment Unit Interface

AAUP American Association of University Professors

AAUW American Association of University Women

AAV adeno-associated virus; Association of Avian Veterinarians

AAVA American Association of Veterinary Anatomists

AAVC American Association of Veterinary Clinicians

AAVE African American Vernacular English

AAVI American Association of Veterinary Immunologists

AAVMC American Association of Veterinary Medical Colleges

AAVSO American Association of Variable Star Observers

AAWP American Association of Working People

AAWR American Association for Women Radiologists

AAWV American Association of Wildlife Veterinarians

Ab antibody

AB about (shortwave transmission); airbase; airman basic; Alberta

ab. about; abbreviation

A.B. able-bodied [seaman]; *Latin* Artium Baccalaureus (Bachelor of Arts)

ABA abscisic acid; American Badminton Association; American Bankers Association; American Bar Association; American Basketball Association; American Booksellers Association

ABAA Antiquarian Booksellers Association of America

A.B.A.J. *American Bar Association Journal*

ABB American Brotherhood for the Blind

Abb. abbess; abbot

abbr. abbreviate; abbreviated; abbreviation

abbrev. abbreviate; abbreviated; abbreviation

ABC American Broadcasting Company; American-born Chinese

ABCC American Board of Clinical Chemistry

ABC's the alphabet; the basics

ABD all but dissertation

abd. abdicated; abdomen; abdominal

ABDC Association of Birth Defect Children

abdom. abdomen; abdominal

ABDR aircraft battle damage repair

ABEDA Arab Bank for Economic Development in Africa

ABEM American Board of Emergency Medicine

ABEND abnormal end of task

ABFP American Board of Forensic Psychiatry

ABG arterial blood gas

ABHES Accrediting Bureau of Health Education Schools

ABI acquired brain injury

ABIH American Board of Industrial Hygiene

ABIM American Board of Internal Medicine

ab init. *Latin* ab initio (from the beginning)

ABJS Association of Bone and Joint Surgeons

ABL airborne laser; atmospheric boundary layer

abl. ablative

abl. absol. ablative absolute

ABLE Association for Biology Laboratory Education

ABM antiballistic missile

ABMC American Battle Monuments Commission

ABMCM American Board of Managed Care Medicine

ABMM American Board of Medical Management

ABMR Academy of Behavioral Medicine Research

ABMS American Board of Medical Specialties

ABMT autologous bone marrow transplantation

ABMTR Autologus Blood and Marrow Transplant Registry

abn airborne

ABN abnormal

ABNF Association of Black Nursing Faculty [in Higher Education]

ABNS American Board of Nursing Specialties

ABO annular beam oscillator

A-bomb atomic bomb

ABOMBI American Board of Minor Brain Injury

Aborig. Aboriginal

ABP American Board of Pediatrics; androgen binding protein

Abp. archbishop

ABPA allergic bronchopulmonary aspergillosis

ABPN American Board of Psychiatry and Neurology

ABPP American Board of Professional Psychology

ABPS American Board of Plastic Surgery

ABR aeroballistic rocket; American Bankruptcy Reports

abr. abridged; abridgment

abs abdominal muscles; absolute temperature

ABS American Board of Surgery; Animal Behavior Society; antilock braking system

abs. absent; absolute; absolutely; abstract

ABSA American Biological Safety Association

abs. feb. *Latin* absente febre (when fever is absent)

absol. absolute; absolutely

abstr. abstract

ABT about (shortwave transmission); American Ballet Theatre

abt. about

ABTA American Brain Tumor Association

ABTP American Board of Transcultural Psychiatry

ABV above (shortwave transmission)

abv. above

ABVD adriamycin, bleomycin, vinblastine, and dacarbazine

Ac actinium; Acts of the Apostles

AC air conditioning; alternating current

ac. acre; air-cool

a.c. *Latin* ante cibum (before meals)

A.C. *Latin* anno Christi (the year of Christ); appellate court; Army Corps; Athletic Club

a/c account; account current; air conditioning

A/C aircraft

ACA American Camping Association; American Canoe Association; American Casting Association; American Chiropractic Association; American Collectors Association; American Counseling Association; Amputee Coalition of America

AC/A accommodative convergence/accommodation [ratio]

ACAAI American College of Allergy, Asthma, and Immunology

acad. academic; academy

ACAI American College of Allergy and Immunology

ACAM American College for Advancement in Medicine

ACAPN Association for Child and Adolescent Psychiatric Nurses

ACAT/H Academy of Clinical and Applied Thrombosis/Hemostasis

ACATS airborne chromatograph for atmospheric trace species

ACB American Council of the Blind; Association of Clinical Biochemists

ACC Air Combat Command; ambulatory care center; American College of Cardiology; anthropogenic climate change; Atlantic Coast Conference; Arab Cooperation Council

acc. accelerate; acceleration; accept; accompanied; according; account; accusative

ACCC Association of Community Cancer Centers

ACCD American Coalition of Citizens with Disabilities

ACCEL American College of Cardiology Extended Learning

ACCESS Architectural and Transportation Barriers Compliance Board

ACCH Association for the Care of Children's Health

ACCI American Council on Consumer Interests

ACCINTNET Air Combat Command Intelligence Network

ACCME Accreditation Council for Continuing Medical Education

accomp. accompaniment

ACCP American College of Chest Physicians; American College of Clinical Pharmacy

accrd. accrued

ACCRI Wright's Anaesthesia and Critical Care Resources on the Internet

ACCT *French* Agence de Coopération Culturelle et Technique (Agency for Cultural and Technical Cooperation)

acct. account; accountant

accum. accumulate

accus. accusative

ACD acid-citrate-dextrose; American College of Dentists

ACDA Arms Control and Disarmament Agency

AC/DC alternating current/direct current; bisexual

ACDS Association for Children with Down Syndrome

ACE American Council on Education; angiotensin-converting enzyme; Army Corps of Engineers

ACEC Area of Critical Environmental Concern

ACEDB A Caenorhabditis Elegans Database

ACEHSA Accrediting Commission on Education for Health Services Administration

ACEI angiotensin-converting enzyme inhibitor

ACEP American College of Emergency Physicians

ACES adaptation controlled environment system

acet. acetone

ACF Administration for Children and Families; Albedo Correction Factor; Asian Christian female

ACFE American College of Forensic Examiners

acft aircraft

ACG American College of Gastroenterolgy

ac-g accelerator globulin

ACGE Accreditation Council for Gynecologic Endoscopy

ACGIH American Conference of Governmental Industrial Hygienists

ACGME Accreditation Council for Graduate Medical Education

ACGP American College of General Practitioners in Osteopathic Medicine and Surgery

ACh acetylcholine

ACH Association for Computers and the Humanities; automated clearing house

ACHA American College Health Association; American College of Hospital Administrators

ACHE American College of Healthcare Executives; American Council for Headache Education

achiev. achievement

ACHIS Association of Consumer Health Information Specialists

ACHNE Association of Community Health Nursing Educators

ACHR Advisory Committee on Health Research

AC/HR aircraft per hour

ACHRE Advisory Committee on Human Radiation Experiments

ACHSA American Correctional Health Services Association

ACIC Aeronautical Charting and Information Center

ACICS Accrediting Council for Independent Colleges and Schools

ACID aircraft identification

ACIDS American College of Integrated Delivery Systems

ACIP Advisory Committee for Immunization Practices

ack. acknowledge; acknowledgment

ack emma A.M. (*Latin ante meridiem*—before noon)

ACL anterior cruciate ligament

ACLAD American Committee on Laboratory Animal Diseases

ACLAM American College of Laboratory Animal Medicine

ACLI American Council of Life Insurance

ACLM American College of Legal Medicine

ACLs Alternate Concentration Limits

ACLS advanced cardiology life support; American Council of Learned Societies

ACLT actual calculated landing time

ACLU American Civil Liberties Union

ACM asbestos-containing material; Asian Christian male; Association for Computing Machinery

ACMCM American College of Managed Care Medicine

ACME Advisory Committee on the Marine Environment

ACMHA American College of Mental Health Administration

ACMHS Asian Community Mental Health Services

ACMP Advisory Committee on Marine Pollution; American College of Medical Physics

ACMPD American Council on Marijuana and other Psychoactive Drugs

ACMPE American College of Medical Practice Executives

ACMQ American College of Medical Quality

ACMS advanced cost management systems

ACN Association for Comprehensive Neurotherapy

ACNM American College of Nuclear Medicine; American College of Nurse-Midwives

ACNP American College of Neuropsychiatrists; American College of Nuclear Physicians; American College of Nurse Practitioners

ACNPP American College of Neuropsychopharmacology

ACO Association of Commissioned Officers

ACOEM American College of Occupational and Environmental Medicine

ACOFP American College of Osteopathic Family Physicians

ACOG American College of Obstetricians and Gynecologists

ACOM American College of Occupational Medicine

ACOOG American College of Osteopathic Obstetricians and Gynecologists

ACOPS Advisory Committee on Protection of the Sea

ACOR Association of Cancer Online Resources

ACP African, Caribbean, and Pacific Countries; American College of Physicians; American

College of Psychiatrists; Association for Child Psychoanalysis

ACPA American Chronic Pain Association; American College of Psychoanalysts

ACPE American College of Physician Executives; American Council on Pharmaceutical Education

ACPM American College of Prehospital Medicine; American College of Preventive Medicine

ACPOC Association of Children's Prosthetic-Orthotic Clinics

ACPPD average cost per patient day

ACPS acrocephalosyndactyly

acpt. acceptance

acq. acquire

ACQIP Ambulatory Care Quality Improvement Program

ACR American College of Radiology; American College of Rheumatology

ACRM American Congress of Rehabilitation Medicine

ACRO American College of Radiation Oncology

ACRP Association of Clinical Research Professionals

ACRR American Council on Race Relations

ACRS accelerated cost recovery system

ACS American Cancer Society; American Chemical Society; American College of Surgeons

ACSA American Center for Social Awareness

ACSH American Council on Science and Health

ACSM American College of Sports Medicine

ACSMA American Canine Sports Medicine Association

ACSN Aspartame Consumer Safety Network

A/cs pay. accounts payable

ACSR *Annual Cancer Statistics Review*

A/cs rec. accounts receivable

acst. acoustic

ACSUS AIDS Cost and Services Utilization Survey

ACSW Academy of Certified Social Workers

ACT a trademark for a standardized college entrance examination (originally American College Test)

act. acting; action; active; actively; actor; actual; actuary

A.C.T. Australian Capital Territory

ACTe anodal closure tetanus

actg. acting

ACTH adrenocorticotropic hormone

ACTION American Council to Improve Our Neighborhoods

ACTIS AIDS Clinical Trials Information Service

ACTIVE advanced controls technology for integrated vehicles

ACT-UP AIDS Coalition to Unleash Power

ACU Association of Clinicians for the Underserved; Attitude Control Unit

ACURP American College of Utilization Review Physicians

ACUS Administrative Conference of the United States

acv actual cash value

ACV air-cushion vehicle

ACVA American College of Veterinary Anesthesiologists

ACVD arteriosclerotic cardiovascular disease

ACVIM American College of Veterinary Internal Medicine

ACVM American College of Veterinary Microbiologists

ACVP American College of Veterinary Pathologists; American College of Veterinary Radiology

ACVRD arteriosclerotic cardiovascular renal disease

ACVS American College of Veterinary Surgeons

ACW alternating continuous waves

ACYF Administration for Children, Youth, and Families

ad advertisement

AD active duty; air-dried; Alzheimer's disease; athletic director

ad. adapter; adverb

.ad Andorra

a.d. after date; *Latin* ante diem (before the day); autograph document

A.D. *Latin* anno Domini (in the year of our Lord); *Latin* auris

dexter (right ear); average deviation

A/D arrival/departure

A-D analog to digital

ADA American Dental Association; American Diabetes Association; American Dietetic Association; Americans for Democratic Action; Americans with Disabilities Act; assistant district attorney

ADAA Anxiety Disorders Association of America

ADACS Attitude Determination and Control Subsystem

ADAD *Alzheimer Disease and Associated Disorders*

ADAM Animated Dissection of Anatomy for Medicine

ADAMHA Alcohol, Drug Abuse and Mental Health Administration

Adapt American Disabled for Attendant Programs Today

adapt. adaptation; adapted by

ADARA American Deafness and Rehabilitation Association

ADAS airborne data acquisition system

adb accidental death benefit

ADB Asian Development Bank

ADC advanced developing country; aide-de-camp; Aid to Dependent Children; Air Defense Command; Alzheimer's Disease Center; analog to digital converter

ADCC antibody-dependent cell-mediated cytotoxicity

ADCP acoustic Doppler current profiler

ADD Administration on Developmental Disabilities; attention deficit disorder

add. addendum; addition

ADDA [National] Attention Deficit Disorder Association

addn. addition

addnl. additional

ADDS American Digestive Disease Society

Ade adenine

ADE Array Drive Electronics

ADEAR Alzheimer's Disease Education and Referral [Center]

ADEC Association of Death Education and Counseling

ADF automatic direction finder

ADFS Alternative Delivery and Financing System

ADH antidiuretic hormone

ADHA American Dental Hygienists Association

ADHD attention deficit hyperactivity disorder

ADHF American Digestive Health Foundation

adhib. *Latin* adhibendus (to be administered)

ad inf. *Latin* ad infinitum (to infinity)

ad init. *Latin* ad initium (at the beginning)

ad int. *Latin* ad interim (in the meantime)

ADIOS Asian Dust Input to the Oceanic System

ADIZ air defense identification zone

adj. adjectival; adjective; adjunct; adjutant

Adjt. adjutant

ADL activities of daily living; Anti-Defamation League

ad lib *Latin* ad libitum (at pleasure, speak without notes or script—that is, an unscripted comment)

ad loc. *Latin* ad locum (to, or at, the place)

ADM admiral

adm. administration; administrative; administrator; admission

admin. administration; administrator

admov. *Latin* admove (apply)

ADMSEP Association of Directors of Medical Student Education in Psychiatry

adn adenoid

ADN any day now

A.D.N. Associate Degree in Nursing

ADOL Adolescence Directory Online

AdoMet S-adenosyl-L-methionine

ADP adenosine diphosphate; automatic data processing

ADPANA Alcohol and Drug Problems Association of North America

ADPE automated data processing equipment

ADR address (shortwave transmission); adverse drug reaction; alternative dispute resolution; American depositary receipt; asset depreciation range

ADRC Alzheimer's Disease Research Center

ADRDA Alzheimer's Disease and Related Disorders Association

ADS alternative delivery systems; American Dialect Society

ads. *Latin* ad sectam (at the suit of)

a.d.s. autograph document, signed

ad sat *Latin* ad saturatum (to saturation)

ADSL asymmetric digital subscriber line

ADSS Alcohol and Drug Services Study

ADT Alaska Daylight Time; Atlantic Daylight Time

ADTA American Dance Therapy Association

ADTe anodal duration tetanus

adv. advance; adverb; *Latin* adversus (against); advertisement; advisory

Adv. Advent; advocate

ad val. *Latin* ad valorem (in proportion to the value)

advb. adverbial; adverbially

advs. adverbs; *Latin* adversus (against)

advt. advertisement

ADWAS Abused Deaf Women's Advocacy Services

ADZ advise (shortwave transmission)

AE account executive; adult education; American English; Armed Forces Europe; atomic energy

ae. *Latin* aetatis (at the age of)

.ae United Arab Emirates

A.E. aeronautical engineer; aeronautical engineering; astronautical engineer; astronautical engineering

AEA Actors Equity Association

AEC Atomic Energy Commission

AECOPD acute exacerbations of COPD

AECT Association for Educational Communications and Technology

AED Automatic External Defibrillator

AEDC Arnold Engineering Development Center

AEDS Atomic Energy Detection System

Ae.E aeronautical engineer; aeronautical engineering

AEF American Enuresis Foundation; American Expeditionary Force

aeg. *Latin* aequalis (equal, equals)

AEGIS AIDS Education Global Information System

AEHF American Environmental Health Foundation

AEIDC Arctic Environmental Information and Data Center

AEK all electric kitchen

AELDS Advanced Earth Location Data System

AEOS advanced electro-optical system

AEP Association of Emergency Physicians

aeq. *Latin* aequalis (equal)

AERA American Educational Research Association

AERC Association of Ecosystem Research Centers

aero. aeronautical; aeronautics

AEROCE Atmosphere/Ocean Chemistry Experiment

aerodyn. aerodynamics

aeron. aeronautics

aeronaut. aeronautics

AERS Association of Educators in Radiological Sciences

AES Adlai E. Stevenson

AESOP Airborne Experiment to Study Ozone Production

aet. *Latin* aetatis (at the age of, aged)

aetat. *Latin* aetatis (at the age of, aged)

AEW airborne early warning

AEWC Alaska Eskimo Whaling System

AF acre-feet; after (shortwave transmission); air force; Anglo-French; Arthritis Foundation; Asian female; audio frequency

af. affix

Af. Afghani; Afghanistan; Africa; African; Afrikaans

.af Afghanistan

AFA Adoptive Families of America

A.F.A. Associate in Fine Arts

AFAA Air Force Audit Agency

AFAICR as far as I can recall

AFAICT as far as I can tell

AFAIK as far as I know

AFAIR as far as I recall

A.F.A.M. Ancient Free and Accepted Masons

AFAR American Federation for Aging Research

AFB air force base; American Foundation for the Blind

AFBCMR Air Force Review Board for Correction of Military Records

AFBF American Farm Bureau Federation

AFC American Football Conference; automatic flight control; automatic frequency control

AFCARA Air Force Civilian Appellate Review Agency

AFCEE Air Force Center for Environmental Excellence

AFCR American Federation for Clinical Research (now **AFMR**: American Federation for Medical Research)

AFCS automatic flight control system

AfDB African Development Bank

AFDBA Armed Forces Dental Benefit Association

AFDC Aid to Families with Dependent Children

AfDF African Development Fund

AFED Alliance to Fight Eating Disorders

AFESD Arab Fund for Economic and Social Development

AFEWES Air Force Electronic Warfare Effectiveness Simulator

aff. affairs; affectionate; affirmative; affix

affd. affirmed

affg. affirming

afft. affidavit

Afg. Afghanistan

AFGE American Federation of Government Employees

Afgh. Afghanistan

AFGIHS Air Force Geographic Information Handling System

AFGWC Air Force Global Weather Center

AFH anterior facial height

AFI American Film Institute

A-fib atrial fibrillation

AFICC Academy of Forensic and Industrial Chiropractic Consultants

AFIP Armed Forces Institute of Pathology

AFIPS American Federation of Information Processing Societies

AFIS American Forces Information Service

AFIT Air Force Institute of Technology

AFK away from keyboard

Afk. Afrikaans

AFL American Federation of Labor; American Football League

AFL-CIO American Federation of Labor and Congress of Industrial Organizations

AFM American Federation of Musicians; audio frequency modulation

AFMA American Film Marketing Association

AFMC Air Force Material Command

AFMR American Federation for Medical Research

AFN American Forensic Nurses

AFOS [National Weather Service] Automation of Field Operations and Services

AFOSI Air Force Office of Special Investigations

AFOSR Air Force Office of Scientific Research

AFP acute flaccid paralysis; alpha-fetoprotein

AFPA Association of Family Practice Administrators

AFPC Armed Forces Policy Council

AFPEO Air Force Program Executive Office

AFPPS American Forces Press and Publications Service

AFQT Armed Forces Qualification Test

Afr. Africa; African

AFRES Air Force Reserves

Afrik. Afrikaans

AFRRI Armed Forces Radiobiology Research Institute

AFRTS Armed Forces Radio and Television Service

AFS American Field Service; American Folklore Society

AFSAA Air Force Studies and Analysis Agency

AFSC Armed Forces Staff College

AFSCF Air Force Satellite Control Facility

AFSCME American Federation of State, County, and Municipal Employees

AFSCN Air Force Satellite Control Network

AFSFC Air Force Space Forecasting Center

AFSOC Air Force Special Operations Command

AFSPC Air Force Space Command

AFT American Federation of Teachers

aft. afternoon

AFTA American Family Therapy Association

AFTAD Analysis-Forecast Transport and Diffusion

AFTN Aeronautical Fixed Telecommunications Network

AFTRA American Federation of Television and Radio Artists

AFUD American Foundation for Urologic Disease

AFV alternate fuel vehicle

AFY acre-feet per year

ag agricultural; agriculture

Ag silver

AG adjutant general; again (shortwave transmission); attorney general

Ag. August

.ag Antigua and Barbuda

a.g. above ground (for example, as applied to an outdoor pool)

A.G. *German* Aktiengesellschaft (joint-stock company, that is, incorporated)

AGA Amateur Gymnastics Association; American Gastroenterological Association

AGAC American Guild of Authors and Composers

AGARD [NATO] Advisory Group for Aerospace Research and Development

AGBAD Alexander Graham Bell Association for the Deaf

AGC advanced graduate certificate; automatic gain control

AGCA automatic ground-controlled approach

AGCM atmospheric general circulation model

agcy. agency

AGD Academy of General Dentistry

A.G.Dec. Attorney General's Decisions

AGE acute gastroenteritis

Ag.E. agricultural engineer; agricultural engineering

agent-n agent-noun

AGFS Aviation Gridded Forecast System

AGGG [World Climate Program] Advisory Group on Greenhouse Gases

AGHE Association for Gerontology in Higher Education

AGI adjusted gross income

AGL above ground level

AGLP Association of Gay and Lesbian Psychiatrists

AGM air-to-ground missile

AGN active galactic nucleus; again (shortwave transmission)

AGO American Gastroenterological Organization

AGP accelerated graphics port

AGPA American Group Practice Association; American Group Psychotherapy Association

AGPAM American Guild of Patient Account Management

AGpO Academy of Gp Orthodontics

agr. agreement; agricultural; agriculture

A/G ratio albumin-globulin ratio

agri. agricultural; agriculture

agric. agricultural; agriculture

AGRICOLA Agricultural Online Access

agron. agronomy

AGS American Geriatrics Society

AGSD Association for Glycogen Storage Disease

AGSG Alliance of Genetic Support Groups

AGSN Ambiguous Genitalia Support Network

AGSS attitude ground support system

agst. against

agt. agent; agreement

AGU American Geophysical Union

AH *American Health*; assisted hatching

A.h. ampere-hour

A.H. *Latin* Anno Hebraico (in the Hebrew year); *Latin* Anno Hegirae (in the year of the Hegira)

A-h ampere-hour

AHA American Heart Association; American Historical Association; American Hospital Association; American Hyperlexia Association

AHAF American Health Assistance Foundation

AHC Association of Academic Health Centers

AHCA American Health Care Association

AHCPR Agency for Healthcare Policy and Research

AHD arteriosclerotic heart disease

AHDL analog hardware descriptive language

AHEAD Association on Higher Education and Disability

AHEC Area Health Education Center

AHF antihemophilic factor

AHFS American Hospital Formulary Service

AHFS DI American Hospital Formulary Service Drug Information

AHG antihemophilic globulin

AHI American Health Institute; Animal Health Institute; at-home insemination

AHILA Association for Health Information and Libraries in Africa

AHIMA American Health Information Management Association

AHIP Academy of Health Information Professionals

AHL American Hockey League

AHM Academy for Healthcare Management

AHMA American Holistic Medical Association

AHME Association for Hospital Medical Education

AHNA American Holistic Nurses' Association

AHP Academy of Hospice Physicians; Accountable Health Plan; Association for Humanistic Psychology

AHQ Air Headquarters; Army Headquarters

AHR Association for Health Records

AHRA American Healthcare Radiology Administrators

AHRC Association for the Help of Retarded Children

AHRIS Automated Health Research Information System

AHS Academy of Health Sciences; American Humane Society

AHSR Association for Health Services Research

AHTA American Horticultural Therapy Association

AHVMA American Holistic Veterinary Medical Association

ai airborne intercept

AI adapter interface; Amnesty International; artificial insemination; artificial intelligence; Associate Investigator

.ai Anguilla

a.i. *Latin* ad interim (in the meantime)

AIA American Iatrogenic Association

A.I.A. American Institute of Architects

AIAA American Institute of Aeronautics and Astronautics

AIBD Association of International Bond Dealers (now **ISMA**: International Securities Market Association)

AIBS American Institute of Biological Sciences

A.I.C. American Institute of Chemists

AICPA American Institute of Certified Public Accountants

AICR American Institute for Cancer Research

AID Agency for International Development

AIDS acquired immune deficiency syndrome

AIDSLINE AIDS Information Online

AIDSTRIALS AIDS clinical trials

AIFF audio interchange file format

AIH homologous artificial insemination

AIHA American Industrial Hygiene Association; American International Health Alliance

AIHC American Industrial Health Council

AIHCE American Industrial Hygiene Conference and Exposition

AIHS Academy for International Health Studies

AILC adult independent living center

AILD angioimmunoblastic lymphadenopathy with dysproteinemia

aIle alloisoleucine

AIM American Indian Movement

AIN American Institute of Nutrition

AIO Advances in Osteoporosis

AIP American Institute of Physics

Aipac American Israel Public Affairs Committee

AIPP American Institute for Psychotherapy and Psychoanalysis

AIR American Institutes for Research

AIRMoN Atmospheric Integrated Research Monitoring Network

AIRST advanced infrared search and track

AIS American Institute of Stress; automated information security

AISC [National Environmental Satellite, Data, and Information Service] Assessment and Information Services Center

AISI American Iron and Steel Institute; as I see it

AIT assembly, integration, and test; atomic international time

AIUM American Institute of Ultrasound in Medicine

AIV assembly-integration-verification; aviation impact variable

AJ adjust (shortwave transmission); anti-jam

AK Alaska

a.k. ass kisser

aka also known as

AKC American Kennel Club

AK-47 *Russian* avtomat Kalashnikova 1947 (Kalashnikoff automatic [rifle] 1947)

AKNF Adair-Koshland-Némethy-Filmer [model]

AJAO American Juvenile Arthritis Organization

AJCC American Joint Committee on Cancer

Al aluminum

AL Alabama; American League; Anglo-Latin; artificial life

al. alcohol; alcoholic

.al Albania

a.l. autograph letter

A.L. American Legion

ALA alpha-linolenic acid; American Library Association; American Lung Association; Association for Laboratory Automation

Ala. Alabama; alanine

ALAD Academic Librarians Assisting the Disabled

ALADI *Spanish* Asociación Latinoamericana de Integración

(American Integration Association)

Al-Anon Alcoholics Anonymous [Family Group]

ALARA as late as reasonably achievable; as low as reasonably achievable

ALARM air-launched antiradiation missile

Alas. Alaska

Alb. Albania; Albanian; Albany; Alberta

alb. albumen

Alba. Alberta

ALBM air-launched ballistic missile

alc. alcohol; alcoholic

ALCA American Lock Collectors Association

Alcan Alaska-Canada

alch. alchemy

ALCI appliance leakage circuit interrupter

ALCM air-launched cruise missile

ALD adrenoleukodystrophy

Ald. alderman; alderwoman

ALE additional living expense

A.L.E.R.T. Allergy to Latex Education and Resource Team

ALEXIS array of low energy x-ray imaging sensors

ALF American Liver Foundation

ALFA Association for Low Flow Anaesthesia

ALG antilymphocyte globulin

alg. algebra

Alg. Algeria; Algerian

ALGOL Algorithmic-Oriented Language

ALH advanced liquid hydrogen

A.L.I. American Law Institute

A-life artificial life

ALJ administrative law judge

alk. alkali; alkaline

alky. alkalinity

ALL acute lymphocytic leukemia

allo allegro

ALLSA Allergy Society of South Africa

allus. allusion; allusively

alm. alarm

ALOS average length of stay

ALP American Labor Party

alp. alpine

ALPA Air Line Pilots Association

ALPCA Auto License Plate Collectors Association

alpha alphabetical

alphanumeric alphabetical and numerical

ALPO Association of Lunar and Planetary Observers

ALR American Law Reports

ALS advanced life support; amyotrophic lateral sclerosis

A.L.S. autograph letters, signed

ALSA Amyotrophic Lateral Sclerosis Association

ALSC Association of Literary Scholars and Critics

ALSP atmosphere and land surface processes

Alt alternate

ALT alanine aminotransferase

alt. alteration; altered; alternate; altitude; alto

Alta. Alberta

A.L.T.A. American Land Title Association

alter. alteration

alt. hor. *Latin* alternis horis (every other hour)

altm. altimeter

ALU arithmetic logic unit

alum alumna; alumnae; alumni; alumnus

alum. aluminum

alw. allowance

A.L.W. arch-loop-whorl system

Am americium; Amos

AM amplitude modulation; Asian male

am. ammeter

Am. America; American

.am Armenia

a.m. *Latin* ante meridiem (before noon)

A.M. airmail; *Latin* anno mundi (in the year of the world); *Latin* ante meridiem (before noon); *Latin* Artium Magister (Master of Arts)

AMA American Management Association; American Medical Association; American Motorcycle Association

AMA EIB American Medical Association Enterprise Information Base

AMAHC Accreditation Manual for Ambulatory Health Care

AMAP American Medical Accreditation Program

amb. ambassador; ambiguous; ambulance

AMC American Maritime Cases; American Movie Classics; antecedent moisture condition; Atlantic Marine Center

AMCHAM American Chamber of Commerce

AMCHP Association of Maternal and Child Health Programs

AMCP Association of Managed Care Providers

AMCRA American Managed Care and Review Association

AMD acid mine drainage

amd. amended

AMDA American Medical Directors Association

AMDRFM advanced monolithic digital radio frequency memory

Ame America; American

AmE American English

A.M.E. African Methodist Episcopal

AMED Allied and Alternative Medicine

AMEDS Army Medical Service

Amer. America; American

AmerF. American French

AmerInd American Indian

AMERSA Association for Medical Education and Research in Substance Abuse

AmerSp. American Spanish

Ameslan American Sign Language

Amex American Stock Exchange

AmEx American Express

AMF Arab Monetary Fund

AmFAR American Foundation for AIDS Research

AMGA American Medical Group Association

AMGO Association of Manager of Gynecology and Obstetrics

AMHA Association of Mental Health Administrators

AMHC Association of Mental Health Clergy

AMHCA American Mental Health Counselors Association

AMHF American Mental Health Foundation

AMHL Association of Mental Health Librarians

AMHPA Assembly of Mental Healthcare Practice Administrators

AMI acute myocardial infarction

AMIA American Medical Informatics Association

AMIA-IWG American Medical Informatics Association-Internet Working Group

AMLCD active matrix liquid crystal display

AMM antimissile missile

ammo ammunition

Amn airman

AMN American Mobile Nurses

AMNH American Museum of Natural History

Amoco American Oil Company

A.M.O.R.C. Ancient Mystical Order Rosae Crucis

amort. amortization

AMOS Automated Meteorological Observing System

amp ampere; amplifier

AMP adenosine monophosphate; Association for Molecular Pathology

AMPAS Academy of Motion Picture Arts and Sciences

amp hr ampere-hour

ampl. *Latin* amplus (large)

AMPRO American Medical Peer Review Organization

AMRA American Medical Record Association

AMRAAM advanced medium-range air-to-air missile

AMRC Association of Medical Research Charities

AMRTA Alchemical Medicine Research and Teaching Association

AMS Agricultural Marketing Service; American Mathematical Society; American Meteorological Society; auditory memory span

AMSA American Medical Society on Alcoholism [and Other Drug Dependencies]; American Medical Student Association

AMSAODD American Medical Society on Alcoholism and Other Drug Dependencies

AMSAT [Radio] Amateur Satellite [Corporation]

AmSECT American Society of Extra-Corporeal Technology

AMSN Academy of Medical-Surgical Nursing

AMSO American Medical Specialty Organization

AMSSM American Medical Society for Sports Medicine

AMSU Advanced Microwave Sounding Unit

AMT alternative minimum tax

amt. amount

AMTA American Massage Therapy Association

AMTEC Association for Media and Technology in Education

Amtrak National Railroad Passenger Corporation (from "American track")

amu atomic mass unit

AMU Arab Maghreb Union

AMVETS American Veterans

AMWA American Medical Women's Association; American Medical Writers Association

AN airman, Navy; Anglo-Norman

an. above named; *Latin* anno (in the year); annual; annotated; *Latin* ante (before)

.an Netherlands Antilles

A.N. Associate in Nursing

ANA Administration for Native Americans; American Newspaper Association; American Nurses Association; Association of National Advertisers

ANAC Association of Nurses in AIDS Care

anal. analogous; analogy; analysis; analytic

analyt analytical

ANAP anionic neutrophil activating peptide

anat. anatomical; anatomist; anatomy

ANC African National Congress; Army Nurse Corps

anc. ancient

AnCC anodal closure contraction

ANCC American Nurses Credentialing Center

ANCS Automated Nautical Charting System

and. andante

And. Andorra; Andorran

ANDA abbreviated new drug application

ANDP Association of Neuroscience Departments and Programs

AnDTe anodal duration tetanus

anes. anesthesia

ANF American Nurses Foundation; atrial natriuretic factor

ANG Air National Guard

ang. angiogram; angle; angular

Ang. Angola; Angolan

Angl. Anglican; Anglicized

Anglo *Spanish* angloamericano (Anglo-American) [that is, White North American of non-Hispanic descent]

Anglo-Ind. Anglo-Indian

Anglo-Ir. Anglo-Irish

angst angstrom

ANHS American Natural Hygiene Society

anhyd. anhydrous

anhydr. anhydrous

ANICA Atmospheric Nutrient Input to Coastal Areas [Project]

anim. animato

ANL Argonne National Laboratory; automatic noise limiter

ANMA American Naturopathic Medical Association

ann. annals; annual; annotated; annuity

ANNA American Nephrology Nurses' Association

anniv. anniversary

annot. annotated; annotation; annotator

AnOC anodal opening contraction

anon. anonymous

ANOVA analysis of variance

ANP atrial natriuretic peptide

ANPA American Newspaper Publishers Association

ANPACC Advanced Nursing Practice in Acute and Critical Care

ANR American Negligence Reports; Americans for Nonsmokers' Rights; another (shortwave transmission)

ANRC American National Red Cross

ANRED Anorexia Nervosa and Related Eating Disorders

ANRF Americans for Nonsmokers' Rights Foundation

ANS American Name Society; aquatic nuisance species; autonomic nervous system

ans. answer

ANSI American National Standards Institute

ANT antenna (shortwave transmission)

ant. antenna; anterior; antiquarian; antiquity; antonym

Ant. Antarctica

ANTA American National Theatre and Academy

anthol. anthology

anthro anthropology

anthrop. anthropological; anthropology

anthropol. anthropological; anthropology

antiq. antiquarian; antiquary; antiquities; antiquity

ANTS Antenna Subsystem

ANTU alpha-naphthylthiourea

ANUG acute necrotizing ulcerative gingivitis

Anzac Australia and New Zealand Army Corps

ANZUS Australia–New Zealand–United States [Security Treaty]

AO aorta

.ao Angola

a/o account of; and others

AOA Administration on Aging; American Optometric Association; analysis of alternatives; angle of attack

AOARD Asian Office of Aerospace Research and Development

AOASM American Osteopathic Academy of Sports Medicine

AOBGP American Osteopathic Board of General Practice

AOC anodal opening contraction

A.O.C. *Latin* anno orbis conditi (the year of the creation of the world)

AOCA American Osteopathic College of Anesthesiologists

AOCE attitude and orbit control electronics

AOCMS attitude and orbit control measurement system

AOCOOHNS American Osteopathic Colleges of Ophthalmology and Otolaryngology, Head and Neck Surgery

AOCPM American Osteopathic College of Preventive Medicine

AOCR American Osteopathic College of Radiology

AOCS attitude and orbit control system

AOD aerosol optical depth

AODM adult onset diabetes mellitus

AODME Association of Osteopathic Directors and Medical Educators

AOEC Association of Occupational and Environmental Clinics

AOFAS American Orthopaedic Foot and Ankle Society

AOFLA Atlantic Offshore Fish and Lobster Association

AOH Ancient Order of Hibernians

AOHA Administrators in Oncology/Hematology Assembly; American Osteopathic Hospital Association

AOHP Association of Occupational Health Professionals

AOIPS Atmospheric and Oceanographic Information Processing System

A-OK in perfect condition or order

AOL America Online

AOML Atlantic Oceanographic and Meteorological Laboratory

AON all or none

AONE American Organization of Nurse Executives

A-1 first class

A-one first class

A1C airman first class

A1NA Alpha1 National Association

AOO American Oceanic Organization

AOPA American Orthotic and Prosthetic Association

AOPR Americans for Open Planetary Research

AOR advice of rights; album-oriented radio; album-oriented rock; at own risk

aor. aorist

AORN Association of Operating Room Nurses

AOS Academic Orthopaedic Society; acquisition of signal; American Otological Society

AOSB Arctic Ocean Science Board

AOSP Atmospheric and Ocean Sciences Program

AOSSM American Orthopaedic Society for Sports Medicine

AOSW Association of Oncology Social Work

AOT astronomical observation template

AOTA American Occupational Therapy Association

AOTF American Occupational Therapy Foundation

AOU American Ornithologists Union

AP adjective phrase; advanced placement; airplane; air police; American plan; antipersonnel; aorticopulmonary; Armed Forces Pacific; Associated Press

ap. apothecary

Ap. Apostle; April

a.p. additional premium; author's proof

A/P account paid; accounts payable; authority to pay; authority to purchase

APA also printed as; American Paralysis Association; American Philological Association; American Philosophical Association; American Podiatry Association; American Psychiatric Association; American Psychological Association

A.P.A. Administrative Procedure Act

APACHE acute physiology and chronic health evaluation

APAMSA Asian Pacific Medical Student Association

APAOG Association of Physician Assistants in Obstetrics and Gynecology

APAP Association of Physician Assistant Programs

A-part alpha particle

APB all points bulletin

APC armored personnel carrier; aspirin, phenacetin, and caffeine

A.P.C. alien property custodian

A-P-C adenoidal-pharyngeal-conjunctival

A.P.C.N. *Latin* anno post Christum natum (the year after the birth of Christ)

APDA American Parkinson's Disease Association

APDIM Association of Program Directors in Internal Medicine

APDR Association of Program Directors in Radiology

APE acute pulmonary edema

APEC Asia Pacific Economic Co-operation

aper. aperture

APEX Arctic Polynya Experiment

APF animal protein factor; Asian professional female

APG Aberdeen Proving Grounds; ambulatory patient group

aph. aphetic

APhA American Pharmaceutical Association

APHA American Public Health Association

aphet. aphetic; aphetized

APHIS [United States Department of Agriculture] Animal

and Plant Health Inspection Service

APHS American Pseudo-obstruction and Hirschsprung's Disease Society

API antecedent precipitation index; application program interface; Asian and Pacific Islander

APIC American Political Items Collectors; Association for Professionals in Infection Control and Epidemiology

APID Application Identification

APL American Poetry and Literacy [Project]; Applied Physics Laboratory; A Programming Language

Apl. April

APLS Antiphospholipid Syndrome

APM Academy of Psychosomatic Medicine; antenna pointing mechanism; Asian professional male; Association of Professors of Medicine

APMA American Podiatric Medical Association; American Preventive Medical Association

APME Attitude Pointing Mechanism Electronics

APMR Association for Physical and Mental Rehabilitation

APNA American Psychiatric Nurses Association

apo apoenzyme; apolipoprotein

APO Army Post Office

Apoc. Apocalypse; Apocrypha

apo-E apolipoprotein-E

APON Association of Pediatric Oncology Nurses

app [software] application

APP approved

app. apparatus; apparently; appendix; applied; appoint; appointed; apprentice

APPA American Professional Practice Association; American Psychopathological Association

APPAP Association of Postgraduate Physician Assistant Programs

appar. apparent; apparently

App. Ct. appellate court

appd. approved

appl. appliances; applied

applicand. *Latin* applicandus (to be applied)

APPM Association for Psychoanalytic and Psychosomatic Medicine

appmt. appointment

appr. approximate; approximately

appro. approval

approx. approximate; approximately

appt. appoint; appointment

apptd. appointed

appx. appendix

appy. appendectomy

APR annual percentage rate

Apr. April

A.P.R.C. *Latin* anno post Roman conditam (year after the foundation of Rome)

APS American Pain Society; American Peace Society; American Philatelic Society; American Philosophical Society; American Physical Society; American Physiological Society; American Protestant Society; American Psychosomatic Society

APSA American Political Science Association; American Psychoanalytic Association

APSF Anesthesia Patient Safety Foundation

APT admissions per thousand; advanced personnel testing; apartment

apt. apartment

APTA American Physical Therapy Association

aPTT activated partial thromboplastin time

apu auxiliary power unit

APWA American Public Welfare Association; American Public Works Association

apx. appendix; approximate; approximately

APY annual percentage yield

AQ as quoted

aq. aqua; *Latin* aqua (water); aqueous

.aq Antarctica

aq. bull. *Latin* aqua bulliens (boiling water)

aq. dest. *Latin* aqua destillata (distilled water)

aq. ferv. *Latin* aqua fervens (hot water)

aq. frig. *Latin* aqua frigida (cold water)

AQL acceptable quality level

AQR Aquarius

AQU Aquarius

Ar argon

AR account receivable; accounts receivable; anal retentive; answer (shortwave transmission); Arkansas

ar. arrival; arrive

Ar. Arabia; Arabic; Aramaic

.ar Argentina

a.r. all risks

A.R. *Latin* anno Regni (in the year of the reign); annual return; army regulation

A/R account receivable; accounts receivable

ARA American Railway Society; Academy of Rehabilitative Audiology; American Rheumatism Association

Arab. Arabia; Arabian; Arabic

Arabsat Arab Satellite Communications Organization

AraC cytosine arabinoside

Aram. Aramaic

ARAMIS American Rheumatism Association Medical Information System

ARARs applicable, relevant, or appropriate requirements

ARAT atmospheric research and remote sensing plane

arb arbitrageur

ARB *Accounting Research Bulletin*

ARBIAS Alcohol Related Brain Injury Association

arc archive

ARC Addiction Research Center; advance readers copy; AIDS-related complex; American Red Cross; [National Aeronautics and Space Administration] Ames Research Center

Arc. Arcade; Arctic

arc cos arc cosine

arc cot arc cotangent

arc csc arc cosecant

arch. archaic; archaism; archery; archipelago; architect; architectural; architecture; archives

Arch. archbishop

archaeol. archeological; archeology

Archbp. archbishop

Archd. archdeacon

Arch.E. architectural engineer

archit. architecture

archt. architect

ARCS assessment and remediation of contaminated sediments

arc sec arc secant

arc sin arc sine

ARCSS Arctic System Science [Program]

arc tan arc tangent

ARD acute respiratory disease

ARDMS American Registry of Diagnostic Medical Sonographers

ARDS adult respiratory distress syndrome

AREP [United Nations] Atmospheric Research and Environment Program

ARF acute renal failure; Addiction Research Foundation

arg. argent; *Latin* arguendo (for the sake of the argument, in the course of the argument)

Arg. Argentina; Argentine; Argentinean

ARGOS advanced research and global observation satellite

ARHP Association of Reproductive Health Professionals

ARI Aries; Arthritis and Rheumatism International

ARIA advanced range instrumented aircraft

aristo aristocrat

arith. arithmetic

Ariz. Arizona

Ark. Arkansas

ARL [National Oceanic and Atmospheric Administration] Air Resources Laboratory; Arctic Research Laboratory; Association of Research Libraries

ARM adjustable rate mortgage; Alien Resistance Movement; antiradiation missile

Arm. Armenia; Armenian

ARMA Association of Records Managers and Administrators International; autoregressive moving average

ARN Association of Rehabilitation Nurses

ARNA American Radiological Nurses Association

ARNMD Association for Research in Nervous and Mental Disease

ARO after receipt of order; Army Research Office; Association for Research in Otolaryngology

ARP Address Resolution Protocol; air-raid precautions

ARPA Advanced Research Projects Agency

ARPS Advanced Regional Prediction System

ARq authentication request

arr. arranged; arrangement; arranger; arrival; arrived

arrgt. arrangement

ARRS American Roentgen Ray Society

ARRT American Registry of Radiologic Technologists

ARs authentication response

ARS Agricultural Research Service; Agricultural Restructuring Scenario; Archive Retrieval System

ART airborne radiation thermometer; assisted reproductive technology

art. article; artificial; artillery; artist

ARTCC air route traffic control center

ARTEMIS Advanced Research Testbed for Medical Informatics

ARTS automated radar terminal system

arty. artillery

ARU audio response unit

ARV AIDS-related virus; American Revised Version

ARVIN Army of the Republic of Vietnam

ARVO Association for Research in Vision and Ophthalmology

A.R.V.R. *Latin* anno Regni Victoriae Reginae (in the year of the reign of Queen Victoria)

As arsenic

AS air speed; American Samoa; Anglo-Saxon; antisubmarine; Associate in Science

As. Asia; Asian

.as American Samoa

A.S. *Latin* auris sinister (left ear)

A/S account sales; after sight; at sight

A's [Oakland] Athletics

ASA Acoustical Society of America; American Schizophrenia Association; American Society of Andrology; American Society of Anesthesiologists; American Society on Aging; American Standards Association; Autism Society of America

ASAA American Sleep Apnea Association

ASAE American Society of Association Executives

ASAIO American Society for Artificial Internal Organs

ASAM American Society of Addiction Medicine

ASAM PPC American Society of Addiction Medicine Patient Placement Criteria

ASAP American Society for Adolescent Psychiatry; American Society of Adults with Pseudo-Obstruction; as soon as possible

ASAPS American Society for Aesthetic Plastic Surgery

ASAR advanced synthetic aperture radar

ASAT American Society of Alternative Therapists; antisatellite

ASATT American Society of Anesthesia Technologists and Technicians

ASB American Society of Biomechanics; Associated Services for the Blind

asb. asbestos

ASBCD American Society of Bookplate Collectors and Designers

ASBM air-to-surface ballistic missile

ASBMB American Society for Biochemistry and Molecular Biology

ASBS American Society for Bariatric Surgery

asc. ascending

ASC American Society of Cinematographers

ASCAD atherosclerotic coronary artery disease

ASCAP American Society of Composers, Authors, and Publishers

ASCB American Society for Cell Biology

ASCE American Society of Civil Engineers

ASCI Accelerated Strategic Computing Initiative; American Society of Clinical Investigation

ASCII American Standard Code for Information Interchange

ASCLD American Society of Crime Lab Directors

ASCLS American Society for Clinical Laboratory Science

ASCN American Society for Clinical Nutrition

ASCO American Society of Clinical Oncology

ASCOT American Share Coalition on Transplantation

ASCP American Society of Clinical Pathologists

ASCPT American Society for Clinical Pharmacology and Therapeutics

ASCRS American Society of Cataract and Refractive Surgery

ASCS Agricultural Stabilization and Conservation Service

ASCU Association of State Colleges and Universities

ASCVD arteriosclerotic cardiovascular disease

ASCVRD arteriosclerotic cardiovascular renal disease

ASD American Society for the Deaf; atrial septal defect

ASDA American Sleep Disorders Association

ASDAR aircraft-to-satellite data relay system

AsDB Asian Development Bank

ASDC American Society for Deaf Children

ASDS American Society of Dermatologic Surgery

ASDVS American Society of Directors of Volunteer Services

ASE airborne support equipment; American Stock Exchange; available solar energy

ASEAMS Association of South-East Asian Marine Scientists

ASEAN Association of Southeast Asian Nations

ASEP American Society of Exercise Physiologists

ASER American Society of Emergency Radiology

ASES American Shoulder and Elbow Surgeons

ASF African swine fever; American Schizophrenia Foundation

ASFIS Aquatic Sciences and Fisheries Information System

asg. assigned; assignment

asgd. assigned

ASGE American Society for Gastrointestinal Endoscopy

asgmt. assignment

ASGPA Assembly of Surgical Group Practice Administrators

ASGPI Association of Sea Grant Program Institutes

ASGPP American Society of Group Psychotherapy and Psychodrama

ASH Action on Smoking and Health; American Society of Hematology; American Society of Hypertension; asymmetric septal hypertrophy

ASHA American School Health Association; American Social Health Association; American Speech-Language and Hearing Association

ASHCMPR American Society for Health Care Marketing and Public Relations

ASHCRM American Society of Health Care Risk Managers

ASHCSP American Society for Healthcare Central Service Personnel

ASHD arteriosclerotic heart disease

ASHE American Society for Healthcare Engineering

ASHES American Society for Healthcare Environmental Services

ASHET American Society for Healthcare Education and Training

ASHFSA American Society for Hospital Food Service Administrators

ASHG American Society of Human Genetics

ASHHRA American Society for Healthcare Human Resources Administration

ASHI American Society for Histocompatibility and Immunogenetics

ASHMM American Society for Hospital Materials Management

ASHNR American Society of Head and Neck Radiology

ASHNS American Society for Head and Neck Surgery

ASHOE Airborne Southern Hemisphere Ozone Expedition

ASHP American Society of Health-System Pharmacists

ASHRM American Society for Healthcare Risk Management

ASI air speed indicator

ASIA American Spinal Injury Association

ASIC application-specific integrated chip; application-specific integrated circuit

ASIDIC Association of Information and Dissemination Centers

ASIG American Special Interest Group

ASIM American Society of Internal Medicine

ASIP American Society of Investigative Pathology

ASITN American Society of Interventional and Therapeutic Neuroradiology

ASL American Sign Language; American Soccer League; atmospheric surface layer

ASLA American Society of Landscape Architects

ASLME American Society of Law, Medicine, and Ethics

ASLO American Society of Limnology and Oceanography

ASM air-to-surface missile; American Society for Microbiology

asm. assembly

AsMA Aerospace Medical Association

ASME American Society of Mechanical Engineers

ASMI American Sports Medicine Institute

ASMIC American Society of Military Insignia Collectors

ASMP American Society of Media Photographers

ASMS Ambulatory Surgery Management Society; American Society for Mohs Surgery

ASMT American Society of Medical Technologists

Asn asparagine

ASN American Society of Nephrology; American Society of Neuroradiology; Army service number

ASNC American Society of Nuclear Cardiology

ASNE American Society of Newspaper Editors

ASNR American Society of Neuroradiology

ASNS American Society for Nutritional Sciences

ASNT American Society for Neural Transplantation

ASO administrative services only

ASORN American Society of Ophthalmic Registered Nurses

ASOS American Society of Outpatient Surgeons; Automated Seismological Observation System; [National Oceanic and Atmospheric Administration] Automated Surface Observing Systems

Asp aspartic acid

ASP American selling price; American Society for Photogrammetry [and Remote Sensing]; American Society of Parasitologists; Association of Subspecialty Professors

ASPAN American Society of PeriAnesthesia Nurses

ASPCA American Society for the Prevention of Cruelty to Animals

ASPCC American Society for the Prevention of Cruelty to Children

ASPEN American Society for Parenteral and Enteral Nutrition

ASPET American Society for Pharmacology and Experimental Therapeutics

ASPH Association of Schools of Public Health

ASPI advanced small computer systems interface

ASPNR American Society of Pediatric Neuroradiology

ASPP American Society of Psychoanalytic Physicians

ASPR Armed Services Procurement Regulations

ASPRS American Society of Plastic and Reconstructive Surgery

ASPRSN American Society of Plastic and Reconstructive Surgical Nurses

ASPS advanced sleep phase syndrome

ASR airport surveillance radar; air-sea rescue; available solar radiation

ASRAAM advanced short-range air-to-air missile

ASRM advanced solid rocket motor; American Society for Reproductive Medicine

ASRS Association of Students of the Radiologic Sciences

ASRT American Society of Radiologic Technologists

ass. assistant; association

assem. assembly

ASSH American Society for Surgery of the Hand

assim. assimilated; assimilation

assn. association

assoc. associate; associated; association

ASSP aerosol scattering spectrometer probe; approved species-specific protocol

ASSR Autonomous Soviet Socialist Republic

asst. assistant

asstd. assisted; assorted

assy. assembly

Assyr. Assyrian

AST Alaska Standard Time; Atlantic Standard Time

ASTA American Society of Travel Agents

ASTC Association of Science and Technology Centers

ASTDN Association of State and Territorial Directors of Nursing

ASTE Association of State and Territorial Epidemiologists

ASTHO Association of State and Territorial Health Officials

ASTM American Society for Testing and Materials

ASTMH American Society of Tropical Medicine and Hygiene

ASTP American Society of Transplant Physicians; Army Specialized Training Program

ASTREX Advanced Space Structures Technology Research Experiment

ASTRO American Society for Therapeutic Radiology and Oncology

astrol. astrologer; astrological; astrology

astron. astronomer; astronomical; astronomy

astronaut. astronautics

ASTS American Society of Transplant Surgeons

ASV American Standard Version

ASW antisubmarine warfare

asym. asymmetric; asymmetrical

aT attotesla

At ampere-turn; astatine

AT achievement test; advanced technology; air temperature; antitank; Atlantic Time; automatic transmission

at. airtight; atmosphere; atomic; attorney

.at Austria

ata atmosphere absolute

ATA advanced technology attachment; Air Transport Association; American Telemedicine Association; American Tinnitus Association; American Tunaboat Association

ATAD atmospheric transport and dispersion [model]

ATAF Allied Tactical Air Forces

ATAGS advanced technology anti-G suit

AT&T American Telephone and Telegraph Company

ATB antibiotic

ATC air traffic control; Air Transport Command

ATCC American Type Culture Collection

atch. attach

ATCP Antarctic Treaty Consultative Parties

ATCSCC air traffic control system command center

ATCT airport traffic control tower

ATDRS advanced tracking and data relay satellite

ATE automatic test equipment

ATEGG Advanced Turbine Engine Gas Generator

ATF automatic transmission fluid; [Bureau of] Alcohol, Tobacco, and Firearms

ath athletic; athletic; athletics

athl. athlete; athletic; athletics

aThr allothreonine

ATIRCM advanced threat infrared countermeasures

ATL adult T-cell leukemia; adult T-cell lymphoma; Atlanta airport code

Atl. Atlantic

ATLA American Trial Lawyers Association

ATLAS [National Aeronautics and Space Administration] Atmospheric Laboratory for Applications and Science

atm atmosphere

ATM Adobe Type Manager; asynchronous transfer mode; at the moment; automated teller machine; automatic teller machine

ATMCH Association of Teachers of Maternal and Child Health

ATMI American Textile Manufacturers Institute

atmos. atmosphere; atmospheric

ATMS Advanced Traffic Management System

ATN Aeronautical Telecommunications Network

at. no. atomic number

ATOC Acoustic Thermography of Ocean Climate

ATP adenosine triphosphate; Association for Transpersonal Psychology

ATPase adenosine triphosphatase

ATPM Association of Teachers of Preventive Medicine

ATR air turbo rocket; automatic target recognition

ATRA Assistive Technology Resource Alliance

ATS American Temperance Society; American Thoracic Society; American Tract Society; American Transport Service

ATSDR Agency for Toxic Substances and Disease Registry

ATSL along the same line

ATSR along-track scanning radiometer

att. attached; attachment; attention; attorney

Att. Gen. attorney general

attn. attention

attr attractive

attrib. attribute; attributed to; attributive; attributively

Atty. attorney

att'y. attorney

Atty. Gen. Attorney General

ATV all-terrain vehicle

ATWC Alaska Tsunami Warning Center

A2 Ann Arbor [Michigan]

A2LA American Association for Laboratory Accreditation

at. wt. atomic weight

Au gold

AU astronomical unit

au. author

.au Australia

a.u. angstrom unit

A.U. *Latin* auris uterque (each ear, both ears)

AUA American Urological Association

A.U.A. American Unitarian Association

AUAA American Urologic Association Allied

AUC area under curve

A.U.C. *Latin* ab urbe condita (from the founding of the city [of Rome in 753? B.C.]); anno urbis conditae (in the year from the founding of the city [of Rome in 753? B.C.])

aud audience

aud. audit; auditor; audition

augm. augmentative

aug. augmentative; augmented

Aug. August

AUI attachment unit interface

AUM air-to-underwater missile

AUP acceptable use policy

AUPHA Association of University Programs in Health Administration

AUQ *French* Association des urologues du Québec (Quebec Urological Association)

AUR ambulatory utilization review; Association of University Radiologists

AURP AppleTalk Update-based Routing Protocol

AUS Army of the United States

Aus. Australia; Australian; Austria; Austrian

Aust. Australia; Australian; Austria; Austrian

Austl. Australia; Australian

Austral. Australasia; Australasian; Australia; Australian

auth. authentic; author; authority; authorized

Auth. Ver. Authorized Version

auto automobile

auto. automatic; automotive

AUTOCAP Automotive Consumer Action Program

Autodin Automatic Digital Network

AUV autonomous underwater vehicle

AUX auxiliary; auxiliary verb

aux. auxiliary; auxiliary verb

aux. v. auxiliary verb

AV arteriovenous; atrioventricular; audiovisual; Authorized Version; average variability

av. avenue; average; avoirdupois

Av. Avestan

a.v. *Latin* ad valorem (in proportion to the value)

A/V *Latin* ad valorem (in proportion to the value); audiovisual

A-V arteriovenous; atrioventricular; audiovisual

AVA antiovarian antibody

AVACI Academy of Veterinary Allergy and Clinical Immunology

avail. available

AVC AIDS Volunteer Clearinghouse; American Veterans Committee; automatic volume control

AVCA American Veterinary Chiropratic Association

AVD alternate voice/data; atrioventricular dissociation

AVDA American Venereal Disease Association

avdp. avoirdupois

AVE atrioventricular extrasystole

Ave. avenue

Avest. Avestan

AVF all-volunteer force

AVFI Action on Violence and Family Intervention

AVG ambulatory visit group

avg. average

avgas aviation gasoline

AVH Academy of Veterinary Homeopathy

AVHRR advanced very high-resolution radiometer

AVI audio-video interleave

AVIR Association of Vascular and Interventional Radiographers

AVIRIS airborne visible and infrared imaging spectrometer

AVL available

avlbl. available

AVLINE AudioVisuals Online

AVM arteriovenous malformation

AVMA American Veterinary Medical Association

AVMF American Veterinary Medical Foundation

avn. aviation

A-V node [cardiac] atrioventricular node

AVP antiviral protein; arginine vasopressin

AVR aortic valve replacement

AVSC Access to Voluntary and Safe Contraception

A-V shunt arteriovenous shunt

AVSL Association of Vision Science Librarians

A-V valves [cardiac] atrioventricular valves

AW aircraft warning; Articles of War; automatic weapon

.aw Aruba

a.w. actual weight; all water

AWACS airborne warning and control system

A.W.A.K.E. Alert, Well, and Keeping Energetic [Network]

AWARDS Automated Weather Acquisition and Retrieval Data System

AWD all-wheel drive

AWG American wire gauge

AWHONN Association of Women's Health, Obstetric, and Neonatal Nurses

AWHP Association for Worksite Health Promotion

AWIPS Advanced Weather Interactive Processing System

AWIPS-90 Advanced Weather Interactive Processing System for the 1990s

awk. awkward

AWL absent with leave

AWOL absent without leave

AWP any will provider; average wholesale price

AWT advanced wastewater treatment

A.W.W. average weekly wage

AWWA American Water Works Association

AX ask (shortwave transmission)

ax. axiom; axis

AXAF Advanced X-ray Astrophysics Facility

AXBT airborne expendable bathythermograph

AXCP airborne expendable current profiler

AY any (shortwave transmission)

AYC American Youth Congress

AYG anything (shortwave transmission)

AYH American Youth Hostels

AYM any more (shortwave transmission)

AZ Arizona

az. azimuth; azure

.az Azerbaijan

AZE Azerbaijan

AZT azidothymidine

B

b bit; barn

B baryon number; bass; be (shortwave transmission); billion; bishop; Black (as in personal ads); boron; byte; magnetic flux density

b. base; book; born; breadth; brother

B. bacillus; Baumé scale; bay; Bible

Ba barium; Baruch

BA batting average; budget authority

ba. bathroom

.ba Bosnia-Herzegovina

B.A. Bachelor of Arts; bare ass; British Academy

B.A.A. Bachelor of Applied Arts

B.A.A.E. Bachelor of Aeronautical and Astronautical Engineering

Bab. Babylonian

BAC blood alcohol concentration; born again Christian; by any chance

back-form back-formation

bact. bacteria; bacterial; bacteriology

bacteriol. bacteriology

BAD French Banque africaine de développement (African Development Bank)

BADEA French Banque Arabe pour le Développement Économique en Afrique (Arab Bank for Economic Development in Africa)

BADT best available demonstrated technology

BAE Bureau of Agricultural Economics; Bureau of Ethnology

B.A.E. Bachelor of Aeronautical Engineering; Bachelor of Agricultural Engineering; Bachelor of Architectural Engineering; Bachelor of Art Education; Bachelor of Arts in Education

B.A.Ed. Bachelor of Arts in Education

B.Ae.E. Bachelor of Aeronautical Engineering

B.A.E.E. Bachelor of Arts in Elementary Education

BAER brainstem auditory evoked response

BAFO best and final offer

BAG busting a gut [laughing]

B.Ag. Bachelor of Agriculture

B.Ag.E. Bachelor of Agricultural Engineering

B.Ag.Eco. Bachelor of Agricultural Economics

B.Agr. Bachelor of Agriculture

B.Ag.Sc Bachelor of Agricultural Science

Ba. Is. Bahama Islands

B.A.Jour. Bachelor of Arts in Journalism

.bak backup file

BAL blood alcohol level; British Anti-Lewisite

bal. balance; balancing; balcony

balc balcony

Balt. Baltic; Baltimore

Balto-Slav. Balto-Slavic; Balto-Slavonic

BAM Brooklyn Academy of Music

B.A.M. Bachelor of Applied Mathematics; Bachelor of Arts in Music

B.A.Mus.Ed. Bachelor of Arts in Music Education

Banana Build Absolutely Nothing Anywhere Near Anybody

B & B bed-and-breakfast; benedictine and brandy

B & D bondage and discipline; bondage and domination

B and E breaking and entering

B and L building and loan

B & O Baltimore and Ohio

B & P bid and proposal

B and S bourbon and soda; brandy and soda

b & w black and white

BAO Boulder Atmospheric Observatory

BaP benzo(a)pyrene

Bap. Baptist

BAPMoN [United Nations] Background Air Pollution Monitoring Network

bapt. baptized

Bapt. Baptist

BAR Browning Automatic Rifle

bar. barometer; barometric; barrel

Bar. Baruch

B.Ar. Bachelor of Architecture

Barb. Barbados

bar-b-q barbecue

B.Arch. Bachelor of Architecture

barit. baritone

BARM block acceptance reporting mechanism

BART Bay Area Rapid Transit

Bart. baronet

BAS block acquisition sequence

bas. basal

B.A.S. Bachelor of Agricultural Science; Bachelor of Applied Science

B.A.Sc. Bachelor of Agricultural Science; Bachelor of Applied Science

BASIC Beginner's All-Purpose Symbolic Instruction Code

BAT best available technology

bat. battalion; battery

B.A.T. Bachelor of Arts in Teaching

BATF Bureau of Alcohol, Tobacco, and Firearms

batt. battalion; battery

Bav. Bavaria; Bavarian

bb ball bearing; base on balls

BB B'nai B'rith; small shot pellet (from "ball bearing")

bb. books

.bb Barbados

b.b. bail bond

B.B.A. Bachelor of Business Administration

BBB Better Business Bureau

BBC British Broadcasting Corporation

B.B.E. Bachelor of Business Education

BBFN bye-bye for now

BBL be back later

bbl. barrel

BBQ barbecue

BBS bulletin board service; bulletin board system

BBT basal body temperature

bc blind copy

BC because (shortwave transmission); board certified

B.C. Bachelor of Chemistry; before Christ; Breeders Cup; British Columbia

B/C bill for collection

BCA Boys' Clubs of America

BCAOCS Bureau of Consular Affairs Overseas Citizens Services

BC/BS Blue Cross and Blue Shield

BCBSA Blue Cross and Blue Shield Association

bcc blind carbon copy

BCCA Beer Can Collectors Association

BCD binary coded decimal

BCE book club edition

B.C.E. Bachelor of Chemical Engineering; Bachelor of Civil Engineering; Before the Common Era

B cell bone-marrow-derived cell

BCF bioconcentration factor; Black Christian female; [The] Breast Cancer Fund

bcf. billion cubic feet

BCG bacillus Calmette-Guérin vaccine

B.Ch. Bachelor of Chemistry

B.Ch.E. Bachelor of Chemical Engineering

BCHSM Board of Certified Healthcare Safety Management

bci binary-coded information

BCI *Biotechnology Citation Index*; broadcast interference (shortwave transmission); Bureau of Criminal Investigation

BCIC Breast Cancer Information Clearinghouse

BCIE *Spanish* Banco Centroamericano de Integración Económico (Central American Bank for Economic Integration)

BCIS Breast Cancer Information Service

BCL broadcast listener (shortwave transmission)

B.C.L. Bachelor of Canon Law; Bachelor of Civil Law

BCM Black Christian male

BCMD *Blood Cells, Molecules, and Diseases*

bcn beacon

BCNU be seeing you

B.Com.Sc. Bachelor of Commercial Science

BCP bioconcentration potential; birth control pill; Book of Common Prayer

B.C.S. Bachelor of Chemical Science; Bachelor of Commercial Science

BCT breast-conserving therapy

bd bundle

BD bank draft; bomb disposal

bd. baud; board; bond; bound

.bd Bangladesh

B.D. Bachelor of Divinity

b/d barrels per day

B/D bank draft; bills discounted; brought down

BDA bomb damage assessment

B.D.A. Bachelor of Domestic Arts; Bachelor of Dramatic Art

BDB big dumb booster

BDC bottom dead center

BDDD [Division of] Birth Defects and Developmental Disabilities

bde. brigade

BDEAC *French* Banque de Développement des États de l'Afrique Centrale (Central African States Development Bank)

bd. ft. board foot

bdg. binding

bdl. bundle

bdle. bundle

BDMP Birth Defects Monitoring Program

BDR battery discharge regulator

bdrm. bedroom

bdry boundary

Bds Barbados

BDS bomb disposal squad

bds. bound in boards

B.D.S. Bachelor of Dental Surgery

BDSA Business and Defense Services Administration

B.D.Sc. Bachelor of Dental Science

BDSRA Batten Disease Support and Research Association

Bdx. Bordeaux

bdy. boundary

Bdy. Burgundy

Be beryllium

BE barium enema; board eligible

.be Belgium

B.E. Bachelor of Education; Bachelor of Engineering; Board of Education

B/E bill of entry; bill of exchange

Bé Baumé scale

BEA Bureau of Economic Analysis

BEAM biology, electronics, aesthetics, and mechanics (robotics)

BEC Bureau of Employees' Compensation

bec. because

BECO booster engine cutoff

B.Ed. Bachelor of Education

B.E.E. Bachelor of Electrical Engineering

beemer BMW car

beep borough president

bef. before

beg. begin; beginning

BEH benign essential hypertension; Bureau of Education for the Handicapped

BEI butanol-extractable iodine

Bel. Belgian; Belgium

Belg. Belgian; Belgium

BEM bug-eyed monster

B.E.M. Bachelor of Engineering of Mines

BEMT Bureau of Health Professions Education and Manpower Training

ben *Latin* bene (well)

Benelux Belgium, the Netherlands, and Luxembourg

Beng. Bengal; Bengali

B.Eng. Bachelor of Engineering

B.Engr. Bachelor of Engineering

B.Eng.Sci. Bachelor of Engineering Science

BEP Bureau of Engraving and Printing

B.E.P. Bachelor of Engineering Physics

BER basic electrical rhythm; bit error rate

Ber. Is. Bermuda Islands

B.E.S. Bachelor of Engineering Science

bet. between

BET Black Entertainment Television

betw. between

BeV billion electron volts

BEV Black English Vernacular

BEZS bandwidth efficient zero suppression

bf boldface

BF before (shortwave transmission); Black female

.bf Burkina Faso (formerly Upper Volta)

b.f. board-foot; boy friend; brought forward

B/F brought forward

B.F.A. Bachelor of Fine Arts

BFD big fucking deal

BFN bye for now

bfo beat frequency oscillator

BFOQ bona fide occupational qualification

bft biofeedback training

BG brigadier general

bg. background; bag

.bg Bulgaria

<bg> big grin

B. Gen. brigadier general

BGH bovine growth hormone

BGI *French* Bureau Gravimétrique International (International Gravimetric Bureau)

B-girl bar girl

b.g.l. below ground level

BGP bone Gla protein

BGS balanced groundwater scenario

B.G.S. Bachelor of General Studies

bgt. bought

Bh bohrium

BH bill of health; black hole; both (shortwave transmission)

.bh Bahrain

B/H bill of health

BHA Bankcard Holders of America; butylated hydroxyanisole

BHC benzene hexachloride

BHCDA Bureau of Health Care Delivery and Assistance

bhd. bulkhead

BHI Better Hearing Institute

B.H.L. Bachelor of Hebrew Letters; Bachelor of Hebrew Literature

Bhn. Brinell hardness number

BHNM bowels have not moved

bhp brake horsepower

BHPr Bureau of Health Professions

BHRD Bureau of Health Resources Development

BHT butylated hydroxytoluene

Bhu. Bhutan

Bi bisexual; bismuth

BI bodily injury; built-in

.bi Burundi

BIA Brain Injury Association; Bureau of Indian Affairs

BIAC Business and Industry Advisory Committee

BiAF bisexual Asian female

BiAM bisexual Asian male

BIB Board for International Broadcasting

bib. biblical

Bib. Bible; biblical

BiBF bisexual Black female

bibl. biblical

bibliog. bibliographer; bibliography

bibliogr. bibliography

BiBM bisexual Black male

BICBW but I could be wrong

BID *Spanish* Banco Interamericano de Desarrollo (Inter-American Development Bank)

b.i.d. *Latin* bis in die (twice a day)

B.I.D. Bachelor of Industrial Design

B.I.E. Bachelor of Industrial Engineering

BiFET bipolar field effect transistor

Big A AIDS; Atlanta; Atlas ICBM; Big Apple (New York City)

Big B Baltimore

Big BX Big Base Exchange (United States of America)

Big C cancer; Chicago; cocaine

Big D death; defense; Denver; Detroit; Dallas; LSD

Big H heart attack; heroin

Big M marriage; Memphis; morphine

Big Mo [political campaign] momentum

Big O opium; orgasm

Big P Pentagon building

Big PX Big Post Exchange (United States of America)

Big Q San Quentin prison

Big T Tampa; Tucson

Big V Las Vegas; Vietnam

BiHF bisexual Hispanic female

BiHM bisexual Hispanic male

BiJF bisexual Jewish female

BiJM bisexual Jewish male

BIL brother-in-law

bil. bilateral

bilat. bilateral

bin binary

binocs binoculars

bio biographical summary; biology

BIO Biotechnology Industry Organization

bio. biology

biochem. biochemistry

biog. biographer; biographical; biography

biol. biological; biologist; biology

BIOMASS Biological Investigations of Marine Antarctic Systems and Stocks

BIOS Basic Input/Output System

biotech biotechnology

BIOYA blow it out your ass

BIOYIOP blow it out your input output port

BIP band interleaved by pixel

BIPS billion instruction per second

BIS Bank for International Settlements; Brain Injury Society

Bish. Bishop

BIST built-in self-test

bit binary digit

BIT built in test

BitBlt bit-block transfer

BITE built-in test equipment

BITNET Because It's Time Network

BITNIC BITNET Network Information Center

BIU bus interface unit

BiWF bisexual White female

BiWM bisexual White male

biz business

BJ biceps jerk (reflex); blowjob

.bj Benin

B.J. Bachelor of Journalism

BJA Bureau of Justice Assistance

BJM bones, joints, muscles

BJS Bureau of Justice Statistics

bk black

Bk berkelium

BK because

Bk. bank; book

bkbndr. bookbinder

bkcy. bankruptcy

bkfst. breakfast

bkg. banking; bookkeeping

bkgd. background

bklr. black letter

bkpg. bookkeeping

bkpr. bookkeeper

bkpt. bankrupt

bks. barracks

bkt. basket; bracket

bl. bale; barrel; black; block; blue

B.L. Bachelor of Laws; Bachelor of Letters; Bachelor of Literature

B/L bill of lading

B.L.A. Bachelor of Landscape Architecture; Bachelor of Liberal Arts

BLAB Biomedical Library Acquisitions Bulletin

BLB Blind Leading the Blind Foundation

bld. blood; boldface

bldg. building

BLDG building

bldr. builder

BLE Brotherhood of Locomotive Engineers

BLIPS Benthic Layer Interactive Profiling System

B-list bozo list

B.Lit. *Latin* Baccalaureus Litterarum (Bachelor of Letters, Bachelor of Literature)

B.Litt. *Latin* Baccalaureus Litterarum (Bachelor of Letters, Bachelor of Literature)

blk. black; block; bulk

BLLRS Blood Lead Laboratory Reference System

BLM Bureau of Land Management

BLMRCP Bureau of Labor Management Relations and Cooperative Programs

Blnd blond

BLOB very large binary file (from "binary large object")

BLS basic life support; Berkeley Linguistics Society; Bureau of Labor Statistics

B.L.S. Bachelor of Library Science

BLT bilateral lung transplantation; bacon, lettuce, and tomato [sandwich]

blt. built

Blu blue

BLV bovine leukemia virus

Blvd. boulevard

B lymphocyte bone marrow–derived lymphocyte

BLZ Belize

BM basal metabolism; Black male

bm. beam

.bm Bermuda

b.m. board measure; bowel movement

B.M. Bachelor of Medicine; Bachelor of Music; British Museum

BMDO Ballistic Missile Defense Organization

B.M.E. Bachelor of Mechanical Engineering; Bachelor of Mining Engineering; Bachelor of Music Education

B.M.Ed. Bachelor of Music Education

BME/RAPD Biomedical Engineering and the Research to Aid Persons with Disabilities

BMES Biomedical Engineering Society

B.Met. Bachelor of Metallurgy

BMEWS Ballistic Missile Early Warning System

BMI body mass index; Broadcast Music Incorporated

BMJ *British Medical Journal*

BMOC big man on campus

BMR basal metabolic rate

BMRC Bureau of Meteorology Research Center

BMS baby-making sex

B.M.S. Bachelor of Marine Science

BMT ballistic missile technology

B.M.T. Bachelor of Medical Technology

B.Mus. Bachelor of Music

BMW *German* Bayerische Motoren Werke (Bavarian Motor Works)

BMX bicycle motocross

BN bank note; Bureau of Narcotics

Bn. baron; battalion

.bn Brunei Darussalam

B.N. Bachelor of Nursing

BNA British North America

bnd. bound

BNDD Bureau of Narcotics and Dangerous Drugs

BNF big name fan

BNNRC Behavioral Neurogenetics and Neuroimaging Research Center

B.N.S. Bachelor of Naval Science

.bo Bolivia

b.o. back order; best offer; box office; branch office; broker's order; buyer's option

B.O. body odor; box office

B/O best offer

BOA basic ordering agreement; beginning of activity

BOAD *French* Banque Ouest Africaine de Développement (West African Development Bank)

boatel hotel in a marina

BOB best of breed; Bureau of the Budget

BOBW best of both worlds

Boc t-butoxycarbonyl

BOD biochemical oxygen demand; biological oxygen demand

BOD5 biological oxygen demand–5 days

BOHICA bend over, here it comes again

BOJ Bank of Japan

bol bolus

BOL beginning of life

Bol. Bolivia; Bolivian

BOM business office must

BOMC Book-of-the-Month Club

BOOP bronchiolitis obliterans with organizing pneumonia

BOP blatant other promotion (that is, blatant promotion of work of others)

BOQ Bachelor Officers' Quarters

Bor. borough

BOREAS Boreal Ecosystem-Atmosphere Study

BOS Boston airport code

bot small computer program (from "robot")

BOT back on topic; Board of Trade

bot. botanical; botanist; botany; bottle; bottom

Boul. boulevard

BOW bag of waters (the amniotic sac in pregnancy)

bp boiling point

BP barometric pressure; basis point; bills payable; blood pressure; borough president

bp. baptized; birthplace

Bp. bishop

B.P. Bachelor of Pharmacy; Bachelor of Philosophy

BPA Black Psychiatrists of America; Bonneville Power Administration

BPC biomass production chamber

bpd barrels per day

BPD bronchopulmonary dysplasia

B.Pd. Bachelor of Pedagogy

B.P.E. Bachelor of Physical Education

BPF Black professional female

BPH benign prostatic hypertrophy

B.Ph. Bachelor of Philosophy

B.Pharm. Bachelor of Pharmacy

BPHC Bureau of Primary Health Care

B.Phil. Bachelor of Philosophy

bpi bits per inch; bytes per inch

bpl birthplace

bpm beats per minute

BPM Black professional male

BPO bargain purchase option; blanket purchase order

BPOE Benevolent and Protective Order of Elks

BPR bypass ratio

bps bits per second; bytes per second

BPT best practicable control technology

BPW Business and Professional Women

Bq becquerel

br bedroom

Br bromine; brown

BR bedroom; bills receivable

br. branch; brief

Br. Britain; British; brother

.br Brazil

B.R. *Latin* Bancus Regis (King's Bench); *Latin* Bancus Reginae (Queen's Bench)

B/R bills receivable

bra brassiere

brat bratwurst

Braz. Brazil; Brazilian

BrazPg. Brazilian Portuguese

BRB be right back

BRC Biennial Report on Carcinogens

BRCA Brotherhood of Railway Carmen of America

BRCA1 breast cancer 1 (gene)

brd board

BRDF bidirectional reflectance distribution function

BrDu bromodeoxyuridine

BRE business reply envelope

B.R.E. Bachelor of Religious Education

Bret. Breton

brev. brevet

BRF Brain Research Foundation

BRFSS Behavioral Risk Factor Surveilllance System

brg. bearing; bridge

BRHR Basic Research and Human Resources

BRI basic rate interface

brig brigade

Brig. brigadier

Brig. Gen. brigadier general

Brit person from Great Britain

Brit. Britain; British

Britcom British sitcom

brkfst breakfast

brl barrel

brlp. burlap

Brn brown

bro [soul] brother

Bro. brother

bronc bronco

bros. brothers

BRP bathroom privileges

brt. bright; brought

B.R.T. Brotherhood of Railroad Trainmen

BRU battery reconditioning unit; battery regulation unit

BRV Bravo (cable TV)

brwnstn brownstone (that is, townhouse)

BS Bar Sirach; bowel sounds

.bs Bahamas

b.s. balance sheet; bill of sale

b/s bill of sale

B.S. Bachelor of Science; bullshit

BSA body surface area; Boy Scouts of America

B.S.A. Bachelor of Science in Agriculture

B.S.A.A. Bachelor of Science in Applied Arts

B.S.A.E. Bachelor of Science in Aeronautical Engineering

B.S.Arch. Bachelor of Science in Architecture

B.S.B.A. Bachelor of Science in Business Administration

BSC Biological Sciences Center

B.Sc. Bachelor of Science

B.S.C. Bachelor of Science in Commerce

B.S.C.E. Bachelor of Science in Civil Engineering

B.S.Ch. Bachelor of Science in Chemistry

B.Sc.N. Bachelor of Science in Nursing

BSCs Business Service Centers

B.S.D. Bachelor of Science in Design

BSE bovine spongiform encephalopathy

B.S.E. Bachelor of Science in Education; Bachelor of Science in Engineering

BSEC Black Sea Economic Cooperation [Zone]

B.S.Ec. Bachelor of Science in Economics

B.S.Econ. Bachelor of Science in Economics

B.S.Ed. Bachelor of Science in Education

B.S.E.E. Bachelor of Science in Electrical Engineering; Bachelor of Science in Elementary Education

B.S.Eng. Bachelor of Science in Engineering

BSER brainstem evoked response

B.S.For. Bachelor of Science in Forestry

B.S.F.S. Bachelor of Science in Foreign Service

bsh. bushel

B.S.H.A. Bachelor of Science in Health Administration

B.S.H.E. Bachelor of Science in Home Economics

B.S.H.Ec. Bachelor of Science in Home Economics

BSI British Standards Institution

B.S.I.E. Bachelor of Science in Industrial Engineering

B.S.J. Bachelor of Science in Journalism

bsk. basket

bskt. basket

B.S.L. Bachelor of Sacred Literature; Bachelor of Science in Law; Bachelor of Science in Linguistics

Bs/L bills of lading

B.S.L.S. Bachelor of Science in Library Science

B.S.M. Bachelor of Sacred Music

B.S.M.E. Bachelor of Science in Mechanical Engineering

bsmt. basement

BSMT basement

B.S.M.T. Bachelor of Science in Medical Technology

B.S.N. Bachelor of Science in Nursing

B.S.N.A. Bachelor of Science in Nursing Administration

BSO Boston Symphony Orchestra

B.S.O.T. Bachelor of Science in Occupational Therapy

BSP blatant self-promotion

B.S.P. Bachelor of Science in Pharmacy

B.S.P.A. Bachelor of Science in Public Administration

B.S.P.E. Bachelor of Science in Physical Education

B.S.P.H. Bachelor of Science in Public Health

B.S.Phar. Bachelor of Science in Pharmacy

B.S.Pharm. Bachelor of Science in Pharmacy

B.S.P.H.N. Bachelor of Science in Public Health Nursing

B.S.P.T. Bachelor of Science in Physical Therapy

BSR Back Surface Reflection

BSRF Borderlands Science Research Foundation

BSRN [United Nations] Baseline Surface Radiation Network

BSS balanced salt solution

B.S.S. Bachelor of Social Science

B.S.S.E. Bachelor of Science in Secondary Education

B.S.S.S. Bachelor of Science in Social Science

BST bovine somatotropin

B.S.T. Bachelor of Sacred Theology

B.S.W. Bachelor of Social Work

BT bacillus thuringiensis; bathythermograph; brightness temperature

bt. boat; bought

Bt. baronet

.bt Bhutan

B.t. Bacillus thuringiensis

B.T. Bachelor of Theology

BTA but then again

B.T.A. Board of Tax Appeals

BTDT been there, done that

BTDTGTS been there, done that, got the T-shirt

B.T.E. Bachelor of Textile Engineering

bth bathroom

B.Th. Bachelor of Theology

BTL bilateral tubal ligation

btl. bottle

BTN between (shortwave transmission)

btn. button

BTO big-time operator

BTR better (shortwave transmission)

BTRS Behavior Therapy and Research Society

btry. battery

BTS Bureau of Transportation Statistics

BTSOOM beats the shit out of me

Btss. baronetess

btty battery

Btu British thermal unit

BTW by the way

btwn. between

BTX beacon transmitter; brevotoxins

bu. bureau; bushel

Bucks. Buckinghamshire

Bud Budweiser [beer]

BUFR Binary Universal Form for Representation

bul. bulletin

Bulg. Bulgaria; Bulgarian

bull. bulletin

BUMED United States Navy Bureau of Medicine and Surgery

BUN blood urea nitrogen

bur. bureau; buried

Bur. Burma; Burmese

burb suburb

Burm. Burmese

bus. business

bush. bushel

bute butethol

.bv Bouvet Island

b.v. book value

B.V. Blessed Virgin

BVA Board of Veterans Appeals

BVD Bradley, Voorhees & Day (A trademark used for undershirts and underpants. This trademark sometimes occurs in print with a final 's.)

BVE Black Vernacular English

BVI Better Vision Institute

B.V.I. British Virgin Islands

B.V.M. Blessed Virgin Mary

BVP blood volume pulse

BVR beyond visual range

bvt. brevet

bw bandwidth; birth weight

BW bacteriological warfare; biological warfare; black and white

.bw Botswana

B/W black and white

B'way Broadway

bwd. backward

BWG big wide grin; Birmingham Wire Gauge

B.W.I. British West Indies

BWR boiling water reactor

Bx biopsy

BX Base Exchange

bx. box

bxd. boxed

.by Belarus

b.y. billion years

BYKT but you knew that

BYKTA but you knew that already

BYO bring your own [food and drink]

BYOB bring your own booze; bring your own bottle

byp. bypass

BYU bayou; Brigham Young University

Byz. Byzantine

Bz benzene; benzoyl

BZ busy

.bz Belize

BZD benzodiazepine

C

c candle; carat; charm quark; circumference; constant; cubic

C capacitance; carbon; Celsius; center; centigrade; charge; charm; Christian (as in personal ads); cloudy; cocaine; complement; conjugation; consonant; coulomb; couple(s) (as in personal ads); cytosine; 100; see (shortwave transmission); yes (shortwave transmission)

c. capacity; cent; centavo; centime; centimo; chapter; *Latin* circa (in approximately, about); *Latin* congius (gallon); copy; copyright; *Latin* cum (with); cup

C. cape; Celtic; century; Chancellor

ca carcinoma; *Latin* circa (in approximately, about)

Ca calcium

CA California; chronological age; Cocaine Anonymous

.ca Canada

C.A. Central America; chartered accountant

c/a capital account; credit account; current account

C/A central air [conditioning]

CAA Civil Aeronautics Administration; Clean Air Act

CAADE Commission on Accreditation/Approval for Dietetics Education

CAAP Children's AIDS Awareness Project

cab cabernet

CAB Civil Aeronautics Board; coronary artery bypass

cab. cabin; cabinet; cable

CABG coronary artery bypass graft

CABS Current Awareness in Biological Sciences

cab sav cabernet sauvignon

CAC central air conditioning; [National Oceanic and Atmospheric Administration] Climate Analysis Center; Coalition for America's Children

CAC&F Coalition for Asian-American Children and Families

CaCC cathodal closure contraction

CACGP Committee on Atmospheric Chemistry and Global Pollution

CACM Central American Common Market

CAD carbohydrate addict's diet; computer-aided design; coronary artery disease

CADA Chinese American Dietetic Association

CAD/CAM computer-aided design/computer-aided manufacturing

CADD computer-aided design and drafting

CADS Clinical Administrative Data Service

CaDTe cathodal duration tetanus

CAE computer-aided engineering

CAEC Center for Analysis of Environmental Change

CAEHR Center for the Advancement of Electronic Health Records

CAeM [United Nations] Commission for Aeronautical Meteorology

CAEN computer-aided engineering network

CAEU Council of Arab Economic Unity

CAF Cooley's Anemia Foundation; cost and freight

C.A.F. Canadian Armed Forces; cost and freight

CAFE corporate average fuel economy

CAgM [United Nations] Commission for Agricultural Meteorology

CAGS Certificate of Advanced Graduate Study

CAH congenital adrenal hyperplasia

CAHD coronary artery heart disease

CAHSA Congenital Adrenal Hyperplasia Support Association

CAI computer-aided instruction

cal calibration; calorie (large calorie); calorie (mean calorie); calorie (small calorie)

cal. calendar; caliber

Cal. California

calc. calculate; calculus

CALGB Cancer and Leukemia Group B

Calif. California

CALM Children Affected with Lymphatic Malformations

CALResCo Complexity and Artificial Life Research Concept [for Self-Organizing Systems]

CALS/CE Computer-aided Acquisition and Logistic Support/Concurrent Engineering [Program]

CAM computer-aided manufacturing

cam. camouflage

Cam. Cambridge

Camb. Cambridge

camcorder video camera recorder

CAMEO computer-aided management of emergency operations

CAMH Comprehensive Accreditation Manual for Hospitals

CAMI Civil Aeromedical Institute

CAMIS Center for Advanced Medical Informatics at Stanford; computer-assisted minimally invasive surgery

cAMP cyclic adenosine monophosphate

CAMP cyclophosphamide doxorubicin methotrexate procarbazine

campanol. campanology

CAMS Chinese American Medical Society

CAN cancer (constellation)

can. canceled; cancellation; canon; canto

Can. Canada; Canadian

Canad. Canadian

canc. canceled; cancellation

CANCERLIT Cancer Literature

CanCom Women's Cancer Information Project

C&DH command and data handling

C & F cost and freight

C&GC [National Oceanic and Atmospheric Administration] Climate and Global Change Program

C&GS [National Oceanic and Atmospheric Administration Office of] Charting and Geodetic Services

C & I cost and insurance

c & lc capitals and lower case

C & S culture and sensitivity

c & sc capitals and small capitals

C & SS card and socket services

C & W country and western

Can. F. Canadian French

Can. Fr. Canadian French

Cant. Canterbury; Canticle of Canticles; Cantonese

Cantab. *Latin* Cantabrigiensis (of Cambridge)

CAO chief accounting officer; chief administrative officer; chronic airflow obstruction

CaOC cathodal opening contraction

CaOCl cathodal opening clonus

CA-125 cancer antigen 125 test

cap capsule

CAP Capricorn; Civil Air Patrol; carcinoma of prostate; community-acquired pneumonia

cap. capacity; capital; capitalize; foolscap

CAPA Critical Aquifer Protection Area

CAPCO Custom Academic Publishing Company

CAPD continuous ambulatory peritoneal dialysis

CAPHIS Consumer and Patient Health Information Section

caps capital letters

CAPS Center for AIDS Prevention Studies; Center for Analysis and Prediction of Storms; Chinese American Physicians Society

caps. capsule

caps & lc capitals and lower case

caps & sc capitals and small capitals

Caps Lock capital letter lock key

Capt. captain

CAR computer-assisted retrieval

car. carat; cargo

carb carburetor; carbohydrate

carb. carbohydrate; carbon; carburetor

carbo carbohydrate

Card player on St. Louis Cardinals baseball team

Card. cardinal

CARE Cooperative for American Relief Everywhere; Cooperative for American Relief to Europe; [Ryan White] Comprehensive AIDS Resources Emergency [Act]

ca. resp. *Latin* capias ad respondendum (take the body to answer, that is, hold a defendant for court appearance)

CARF Commission on Accreditation of Rehabilitation Facilities

Caricom Caribbean Community

carp. carpenter; carpentry

carr. carrier

CART Championship Auto Racing Team; cocaine- and amphetamine-regulated transcript

CAS Certificate of Advanced Study; collision-avoidance system; cost accounting standards

cas. castle; casualty

CASA computer-assisted sperm [motion] analysis

ca. sa. *Latin* capias ad satisfaciendum (jail the defendant)

CASE computer-aided software engineering

cass. cassette

cast broadcast

CAST Center for Applied Special Technology

cat cataract

CAT clear air turbulence; computerized axial tomography

cat. catalog; catapult; catechism

Catal. Catalan

cath catheter

cath. cathode

Cath. cathedral; Catholic

CATLINE Catalog Online

CATS cheap access to [outer] space

CATT Computer Assisted Technology Transfer

CATV community antenna television

Cauc. American of European origin; Caucasian

CAUS Citizens Against UFO Secrecy

caus. causative

CAUSES Child Abuse Unit for Studies, Education, and Services

CAV cyclophosphamide doxorubicin vincristine

cav. cavalry; caveat; cavity

c.a.v. *Latin* curia advisari vult (the court will be advised, will consider, will deliberate)

C.A.V. the court will consider (curia advisare vult)

CA virus croup-associated virus

CAV PE cisplatin etoposide alternating with CAV

CAVU ceiling and visibility unlimited

caz OK (from "casual")

cb centibar

Cb columbium (no longer in scientific use)

CB chronic bronchitis; citizens band; construction battalion; cornerback

C.B. common bench

c/b carry back

CBA cost-benefit analysis

CBBB Council of Better Business Bureaus

CBC Canadian Broadcasting Corporation; complete blood count

CBD central business district; common bile duct

C.B.D. cash before delivery

C.B.E. Commander of the Order of the British Empire

CBEL *Cambridge Bibliography of English Literature*

CBF cerebral blood flow; coronary blood flow

CBG corticosteroid-binding globulin

CBH catalyst bed heater

CBHP Community Breast Health Project

CBI China, Burma, India; computer-based instruction; cumulative book index

Cbl cobalamin

CBL computer-based learning; convective boundary layer

CBM *Current Bibliographies in Medicine*

CBMT *Clinical Bulletin of Myofascial Therapy*

CBMTS Chemical and Biological Medical Treatment Symposia

CBN *Cancer Biotherapeutics Newsletter*; Christian Broadcasting Network

cbn. carbine

CBO collateralized bond obligation; Community-based Organization; Congressional Budget Office

CBOE Chicago Board of Options Exchange

CBOS Chesapeake Bay Observing System

CBOT Chicago Board of Trade

CBPP contagious bovine pleuropneumonia

CBR chemical, bacteriological, and radiological; chemical, biological, and radiological; cost-benefit ratio

CBS Columbia Broadcasting System

CBSO City of Birmingham Symphony Orchestra

CBSS Council of the Baltic Sea States

CBT Chicago Board of Trade; computer-based training

CBW chemical and biological warfare

Cbz carbobenzoxy

cc carbon copy; contributor's copy; cubic centimeter

Cc cirrocumulus

CC Canadian Club; chief complaint; closed-captioned; credit cards [accepted]

cc. centuries; chapters; copies

.cc Cocos (Keeling) Islands

C.C. circuit court; civil code; criminal case

CCA Career College Association; Children's Craniofacial Association

C.C.A. Circuit Court of Appeals

CCAD Center for Computer Aided Design

CCAFS Cape Canaveral Air Force Station

CCAM collision and contamination avoidance maneuver

CCAMLR Convention of the Conservation of Antarctic Marine Living Resources

CCB configuration control board

CCC Civilian Conservation Corps; Commodity Credit Corporation

CCCC Conference on College Composition and Communication

CCCF Candlelighters Childhood Cancer Foundation

CCCID Center for Children with Chronic Illness and Disability

CCCO Committee on Climate Changes and the Oceans

CCCT clomiphene citrate challenge test

CCD charge-coupled device; Confraternity of Christian Doctrine

CCDM *Control of Communicable Diseases in Man*

CCE carbon-chloroform extract; Council on Chiropractic Education

CCEA Cabinet Council on Economic Affairs

CCF Cooperative Commonwealth Federation of Canada

CCFA Crohn's and Colitis Foundation of America

CCGP Commission for Certification in Geriatric Pharmacy

CCHS congenital central hypoventilation syndrome

CCI chronic coronary insufficiency

CCID Community Colleges for International Development

CCIP continuously computed impact point

CCITT *French* Comité Consultatif International Télégraphique et Téléphonique (International Consultative Committee on Telecommunications and Telegraphy), now **ITU-T**

CCK cholecystokinin

cckw. counterclockwise

CCl [United Nations] Commission for Climatology

CCL close circuit loop; Couple to Couple League [for Natural Family Planning]

C.Cls. Court of Claims

CCM community climate model; counter-countermeasure

CCN conclusion (shortwave transmission); Cooperative Caring Network

CCNY City College of New York

CCO complete/coordinated care organization

CCOL [United Nations] Coordinating Committee on the Ozone Layer

CCOM control center operations manager

CCP Campus Custom Publishing

C.C.P. Code of Civil Procedure

CCR cloud cover radiometer; Commission on Civil Rights

CCRF Children's Cancer Research Fund

CCRIS Chemical Carcinogenesis Research Information System

CCS command and control subsystems; combined chiefs of staff

CCSC Cemetery Consumer Service Council

CCSDS Consultive Committee for Space Data Systems

CCSM control center systems manager

CCSR Center for Climate System Research

CCT clomiphene challenge test; closed cranial trauma

CCTe cathodal closure tetanus

CCTR Cochrane Controlled Trials Register

CCTV closed-circuit television

CCU coronary care unit

CCW command and control warfare; counter clockwise

ccw. counterclockwise

CCWCP Coordinating Committee for the World Climate Program

cd candela

Cd cadmium

CD cash discount; certificate of deposit; cesarean delivery; civil defense; cluster of differentiation; compact disk; cycle day

cd. cord

.cd Democratic Republic of the Congo

C/D carried down; certificate of deposit

CDA Certified Dental Assistant; command and data acquisition; confidential data agreement

CDB Caribbean Development Bank

CDBG Community Development Block Grant

CDC Centers for Disease Control [and Prevention]; [National Oceanic and Atmospheric Administration] Climate Diagnostics Center

CDC NAC Centers for Disease Control [and Prevention] National AIDS Clearinghouse

CDC WONDER Centers for Disease Control [and Prevention] Wide-ranging Online Data for Epidemiologic Research

CDD certificate of disability for discharge

CDDI copper distributed data interface

CDE cyclophosphamide doxorubicin etoposide

CD-E compact disk-erasable

CDEM Continuous Dynode Electron Multiplier

CDER Center for Drug Evaluation and Research

CDEV [Macintosh] control panel device

CDF Celiac Disease Foundation; channel definition format; Children's Defense Fund; Children's Dream Foundation; common data format

CDFC Cloud Depiction and Forecast System

cdg commanding

CDGS carbohydrate deficient glycoprotein syndrome

CDGSFN Carbohydrate-Deficient Glycoprotein Syndrome Family Network

CDHF central data handling facility

CDI capacitive deionization

CD-I compact disk–interactive

CDIAC [United States] Carbon Dioxide Information Analysis Center

CDIM Clerkship Directors in Internal Medicine

CdLS Cornelia de Lange Syndrome [Foundation]

CDMA code division multiple access

CDMU central data management unit

Cdn. Canadian

cDNA complementary deoxyribonucleic acid

CDP certificate in data processing; cytidine 5c-diphosphate

CDPC Communicable Disease Prevention and Control

CDP-choline cytidine diphosphocholine

CDPD cellular digital packet data

CDP-glyceride cytidine diphosphoglyceride

CDP-sugar cytidine diphosphosugar

CDR collateralized depository receipt; Commander; critical design review

CD-R compact disk–recordable

CDRD Cutaneous Drug Reaction Database

CDRH Center for Devices and Radiological Health

CDRL contract data requirements list

CD-ROM compact disk–read-only memory; consumer device, rendered obsolete in months

CDRR Coalition for the Medical Rights of Women

CD-RW compact disk–read-write

CDS coronal diagnostic spectrometer

CDT Central Daylight Time

CDVIK Computerized Disease Vector Identification Keys

Ce cerium

CE communications engineer; Council of Europe

c.e. *Latin* caveat emptor (let the buyer beware); compass error

C.E. chemical engineer; Church of England; civil engineer; Common Era; [United States Army] Corps of Engineers; counterespionage

CEA carcinoembryonic antigen; cost-effectiveness analysis; Council of Economic Advisers

CEAM Center for Exposure Assessment Modeling

CEAO *French* Communauté Économique de l'Afrique de l'Ouest (West African Economic Community)

CEBBI Center for Enhancement of the Biology/Biomaterial Interfaces

CEC cation exchange capacity

CED Committee for Economic Development; Council on Education of the Deaf

CEDDA [National Oceanic and Atmospheric Administration] Center for Experiment Design and Data Analysis

CEDR Comprehensive Epidemiologic Data Resource

CEEAC *French* Communauté économique des états de l'Afrique centrale (Economic Community of Central African States)

CEEB College Entry Examination Board

CEES Committee on Earth and Environmental Sciences

CEG continuous edge graphics

CEHN Children's Environmental Health Network

CEI Central European Initiative

cel celluloid

Cel. Celsius

celeb celebrity

CELIAS Charge, Element, and Isotope Analysis System

cell cellular; celluloid

cell phone cellular telephone

Cels. Celsius

CELSS closed ecological life support system; controlled environment life support system

Celt. Celtic

cem. cement; cemetery

CEMA Council for Mutual Economic Assistance

CEMF counterelectromotive force

CEMSCS Central Environmental Satellite Computer System

cen. center; central; century

Cen. Cenozoic

CENR Committee on Environment and Natural Resources

cent. centigrade; central; *Latin* centum (hundred); century

Cent. central

CENTO Central Treaty Organization

CEO chief executive officer

CEOS Committee on Earth Observation Satellites

CEP Committee on Environmental Protection

CEPGL *French* Communauté Économique des Pays des Grands Lacs (Economic Community of the Great Lakes Countries)

CEPN Certification Examination for Practical and Vocational Nurses

CEPN-LTC Certification Examination for Practical and Vocational Nurses in Long-Term Care

CEQ Council on Environmental Quality

CER coordinated ecosystem research

CERCLA Comprehensive Environmental Response, Compensation, and Liability Act (also called "Superfund")

CERCLIS Comprehensive Environmental Response, Compensation, and Liability Information System

CERI Center for Environmental Research Information

CERN *French* Conseil Européen pour la Recherche Nucléaire (European Organization for Nuclear Research, now known as the European Laboratory for Particle Physics)

cert certain; certainly

cert. certificate; certified; certiorari

cert. den. certiorari [writ] denied

certif. certificate; certificated

cerv. cervical

CES Center for Epidemiologic Studies; Consumer Electronics Show

CES-D Center for Epidemiologic Studies Depression [Scale]

CET Central European Time

CETA Comprehensive Employment and Training Act

cet. par. *Latin* ceteris paribus (other things being equal)

CEU continuing education unit

Cf californium

CF center field; center fielder; conversion factor; cystic fibrosis

cf. calfskin; *Latin* confer (compare)

.cf Central African Republic

C.F. cost and freight

C/F carried forward

CfA [Harvard-Smithsonian] Center for Astrophysics

CFA Campus Freethought Association; Cat Fanciers' Association; Chartered Financial Analyst; Commission of Fine Arts; Consumer Federation of America; Craniofacial Foundation of America

CFC chlorofluorocarbon

cfd cubic feet per day

CFD computational fluid dynamics

CFDA Catalog of Federal Domestic Assistance

CFE contractor-furnished equipment

CFF critical fusion frequency; Cystic Fibrosis Foundation

CFG Camp Fire Girls

cfh cubic feet per hour

CFH Council on Family Health

CFHI Child Family Health International

C.F.I. cost, freight, and insurance

CFIDS chronic fatigue immune dysfunction syndrome

CFIDSAA Chronic Fatigue and Immune Dysfunction Syndrome Association of America

CFIT controlled flight into terrain

CFL Canadian Football League

cfm cubic feet per minute

CFM chlorofluoromethane; confirm (shortwave transmission)

CFO cancel former order; chief financial officer

C4 Command, Control, Communication, and Computer Systems

C4I Command, Control, Communication, Computers, and Intelligence

CFP call for proposals; Certified Financial Planner

CFR *Code of Federal Regulations*

CFRBCS Cooperative Family Registry for Breast Cancer Studies

cfs cubic feet per second

CFS chronic fatigue syndrome

CFSAN Center for Food Safety and Applied Nutrition

cfsm cubic feet per second per square mile

CFSS certified fragrance sales specialist

CFT complement fixation test

c. ft. cubic feet

CFTC Commodity Futures Trading Commission

CFV call for voting

cg centigram

CG cloud to ground; computer graphics; Contadora Group

.cg Republic of the Congo

c.g. center of gravity

C.G. coast guard; commanding general; consul general

CGA color graphics adapter; color graphics array

CGAP Cancer Genome Anatomy Project

CGCP [National Oceanic and Atmospheric Administration] Climate and Global Change Program

CGEAN Council on Graduate Education for Administration in Nursing

CGI common gateway interface; computer-generated imaging; computer graphics interface

cgm. centigram

cGMP cyclic guanosine 3c,5c-monophosphate

CGMS Coordination Group for Meteorological Satellites

CGMW Commission for the Geological Map of the World

CGRP calcitonin gene-related peptide

cgs centimeter-gram-second [system]

CGS Committee on Geological Sciences

ch chain; check

Ch Christian (as in personal ads); Chronicles

CH central heating; compass heading; conference host

ch. champion; chapter; check; child; children; church

Ch. Champion; channel; chaplain; chief; China; Chinese; church

.ch Switzerland

C.H. clearing-house; courthouse; customhouse

CHAANGE Center for Help for Anxiety/Agoraphobia through New Growth Experience

CHAART Center for Health Applications of Aerospace Related Technologies

CHADD Children and Adults with Attention Deficit Disorder

Chal. Chaldean

Chald. Chaldean

CHAMP Comprehensive Healthcare Analysis and Management Program

Champ. champion

CHAMPUS Civilian Health and Medical Program of the Uniformed Services

CHAMPVA Civilian Health and Medical Program of the Veterans Administration

Chan. Channel

Chanc. Chancellor

CHAP Community Health Accreditation Program

chap. chapter

Chap. chaplain

char. character; characteristic; charity; charter

chard chardonnay

CHARM Coupled Hydrosphere–Atmosphere Research Model

CHART continuous hyperfractionated accelerated radiotherapy

CHAS Center for Health Administration Studies

Chas. Charles

CHASER Congenital Heart Anomalies–Support, Education, and Resources

CHASP Community Health Accreditation and Standards Program

Ch.B. Chirurgiae Baccalaureus, Bachelor of Surgery

CHC choke coil; community health center

CHCC Coalition for Healthier Cities and Communities

CHCE Center for Healthcare Ethics

CHD coronary heart disease

Ch.D. Chirurgiae Doctor, Doctor of Surgery

CHDCT Coalition for Heritable Disorders of Connective Tissue

CHDF Children's Health Development Foundation

Ch.E. chemical engineer; chemical engineering

CHEC Children's Health Environmental Coalition

CHEL *Cambridge History of English Literature*

chem chemistry (academic course)

chem. chemical; chemist; chemistry

Chem.E. chemical engineer; chemical engineering

CHEMID chemical identification

CHEMLINE Chemical Dictionary Online

chemo chemotherapy

CHES certified health education specialist

Ches. Cheshire

CHF congestive heart failure

ChFC Chartered Financial Consultant

C-HFET complementary heterostructure field effect transistor

chg. change; charge

chgd. changed; charged

Chgo. Chicago

Chi Chicago

CHI Consumer Health Information

CHID Combined Health Information Database

CHIM Center for Healthcare Information Management

CHIME College of Healthcare Information Management Executives

CHIN Children's Health Information Network; Community Health Information Network

Chin. Chinese

CHIP Community Health Information Partnerships

CHIPS Clearing House Interbank Payments Systems

chirurg. *Latin* chirurgicalis (surgical)

CHITA Community Health Information Technology Alliance

Chi Town Chicago

Ch.J. chief justice

chk. check

CHL crown–heel length

chl. chloroform

CHLC Cooperative Human Linkage Center

chm. chairman; checkmate

CHMIS Community Health Management Information Systems

chmn. chairman

CHMR Center for Health Management Research

CHO carbohydrate

choc. chocolate

CHOICE Center for Humanitarian Outreach and Intercultural Exchange

CHOICES Children's Healthcare Options Improved through Collaborative Efforts and Services

chol. cholesterol

chor. choreographed by; choreographer

chp. chairperson

CHPA community health purchasing alliances

chpn. chairperson

CHQ Corps Headquarters

chr chrome

CHR [National] Center for Human Reproduction

Chr. Christ; Christian; Chronicles

Chr. Ch. Christian Church

CHRIS Chemical Hazards Response Information System

christie christiania (skiing)

christy christiania (skiing)

Chr.L Christian Latin

chron. chronicle; chronological; chronology

Chron. Chronicles

chronol. chronological; chronology

CHRP common hardware reference platform

chug chug-a-lug

Chunnel [English] Channel Tunnel

chutist parachutist

Ci cirrus; curie

CI certificate of insurance; confidence interval

.ci Côte d'Ivoire

C.I. Cayman Islands; Channel Islands; cost and insurance; counterintelligence

CIA Central Intelligence Agency; Culinary Institute of America

CIAA Central Intercollegiate Athletic Association

cib. *Latin* cibus (food)

CIC commander in chief; completely in the canal; Consumer Information Center

CICA Competition in Contracting Act

CICS Cooperative Institute for Climate Studies

CID Choice in Dying; Criminal Investigation Department

CIDEM Center for Inherited Disorders of Energy Metabolism

CIDI Composite International Diagnostic Interview

CIDP chronic inflammatory demyelinating polyneuropathy

CIDR Center for Inherited Disease Research

CIDS Computer Information Delivery Service

Cie *French* Compagnie (Company)

CIEA Committee on International Ocean Affairs

CIEP Coastal Energy Impact Program

CIESIN Consortium for International Earth Science Information Network

C.I.F. cost, insurance, and freight

CIFAR Cooperative Institute for Arctic Research

CIHI Center for International Health Information

CIIT Chemical Industry Institute of Toxicology

CILER Cooperative Institute for Limnology and Ecosystems Research

CIM computer input microfilm; computer-integrated manufacturing

CIMAS Cooperative Institute for Marine and Atmospheric Studies

CIMMS Cooperative Institute for Mesoscale Meteorological Studies

cIMP cyclic inosine 3,5-monophosphate

CIMRS Cooperative Institute for Marine Resources Studies

CIMS chemical ionization mass spectrometer

CIMSS Cooperative Institute of Meteorology Satellite Studies

CIN Circumcision Information Network

Cin. Cincinnati

CIN-BAD Chiropractic Information Network–Board Action Databank

C in C commander in chief

CINC commander in chief

cinemat. cinematography

CIO chief information officer; Congress of Industrial Organizations

CIOMS Council for International Organizations of Medical Sciences

CIP cataloging in publication

CIPR Center for Imaging and Pharmaceutical Research

CIR Consumptive Irrigation Requirement; Crop Irrigation Requirement

cir. circle; circuit; circular; circumference

CIRA Cooperative Institute for Research in the Atmosphere

circ circumcised

circ. circle; circuit; circular; circulation; circumference

circum. circumference

CIRES Cooperative Institute for Research in Environmental Sciences

CIS Cancer Information System; Commonwealth of Independent States; CompuServe Information Service

CISC complex instruction set computer

CISS Community Integrated Service Systems

CIT California Institute of Technology; Carnegie Institute of Technology; circumstellar imaging telescope

cit. citation; cited; citizen; citrate

cite citation

CITES Convention on International Trade in Endangered Species [of Wild Fauna and Flora]

cito disp. *Latin* cito dispensetur (let it be dispensed quickly)

CIU computer interface unit; control interface unit

civ. civil; civilian

civie civilian

civvy civilian

civvies civilian clothes

CIWS close-in weapons system

C.J. chief justice

CJD Creutzfeldt-Jakob disease

CJE Council for Jewish Elderly

C.J.S. *Corpus Juris Secundum* (Principles of American Law)

CK Calvin Klein; check (shortwave transmission); Christ the King; creatine kinase

ck. cask; check; cook; creek

.ck Cook Islands

CKT circuit (shortwave transmission)

ckt. circuit

ckw. clockwise

cl centiliter

Cl chlorine

CL call (shortwave transmission); common law

cl. class; classification; clause; clearance; closet; cloth

.cl Chile

c.l. carload; common law

C.L. civil law

C/L cash letter

CLA Children's Liver Alliance

CLAS Clinical Ligand Assay Society

class classic; classical; classification; classified

CLASS cross-chain LORAN atmospheric sounding system

CLCW command link control word

cld. called; cleared; cooled

cldy cloudy

CLEK Collaborative Longitudinal Evaluation of Keratoconus [Study]

CLEP College Level Examination Program

clg. ceiling

Cl. Gk Classical Greek

CLI command line interface; cost of living index

CLIA Clinical Laboratory Improvement Act

CLIBCON Chiropractic Library Consortium

CLICOM climate computing

clin. clinical

CLIP corticotropin-like intermediate-lobe peptide

clk. clerk; clock

clkg. caulking

CLL chronic lymphocytic leukemia

Cl. L Classical Latin

cl liq clear liquid (diet)

CLM career-limiting maneuver

clm. column

CLMA Clinical Laboratory Management Association

cln. clean

CLO close (shortwave transmission)

clo. closet; clothing

clos. closet; closets

C. L. P. common law procedure

CLQ cognitive laterality quotient

CLR classical linear regression (model); clear (shortwave transmission)

clr. clear; color; cooler

CLS Chicago Linguistics Society; Commission on Life Sciences

CLSF Coffin-Lowry Syndrome Foundation

CLST closet

CLU chartered life underwriter

CLV constant linear velocity

cm centimeter

cM centimorgan

Cm curium

CM common market; countermeasure

.cm Cameroon

c.m. center of mass; circular mil; court-martial

C.M. *Latin* Chirurgiae Magister (Master in Surgery)

c/m call of more

CMA certified medical assistant

C-MAN Coastal Marine Automated Network (National Weather Service)

CMAWS common missile approach warning system

CMB combine (shortwave transmission)

CMBR cosmic microwave background radiation

cmc critical micelle concentration

CMC certified management consultant; Commandant of the Marine Corps

cmd. command; commander

CMDF Children's Motility Disorder Foundation

cmdg. commanding

CMDL [National Oceanic and Atmospheric Administration] Climate Monitoring and Diagnostics Laboratory

Cmdr. commander

Cmdre. commodore

CME Chicago Mercantile Exchange; continuing medical education

CMEA Council for Mutual Economic Assistance

CMEIS Continuing Medical Education Information Services

CMF Christian Medical Fellowship; Compressed Mortality File

CMG cystometrogram

C.M.G. Companion of the Order of St. Michael and St. George

CMHC Community Mental Health Center

CMHS Center for Mental Health Services

CMI computer-managed instruction; Council for Media Integrity

CMIIW correct me if I'm wrong

CMIS Computerized Medical Imaging Society

CMIST Configuration Management Integrated Support Tool

CML current mode logic

cml. commercial

CMLB ceramic multilayer board

CMM [United Nations] Commission for Marine Meteorology

CMMD VER command verification

CMO calculated mean organism; collateralized mortgage obligation

CMOS complementary metal oxide semiconductor

CMP Coastal Management Programs; competitive medical plan; cytidine monophosphate

cmpd. compound

CMPE Certified Medical Practice Executive

CMPH Clinical Microbiology Procedures Handbook

cmpt compute

CMR common mode rejection

CMRS Clinical Magnetic Resonance Society

CMS *The Chicago Manual of Style*; command management system

CMSA Consolidated Metropolitan Statistical Area

CMSC Consortium of Multiple Sclerosis Centers

CMSE command management systems engineer

CMSGT chief master sergeant

CMSS Council of Medical Specialty Societies

CMT Certified Medical Transcriptionist

CMTA Charcot-Marie-Tooth Association

CMU Carnegie-Mellon University

CMV cytomegalovirus

CMWS common missile warning system

CM-XMP cloud model with explicit microphysics

CMY cyan-magenta-yellow

CMYK cyan-magenta-yellow-black

CN Certified Nutritionist; cranial nerve

.cn China

C/N circular note; credit note

CNA Center for Naval Analysis

CNBC Consumer News and Business Channel

CNC Cancer (constellation); computer numerical control

CNCB Clinical Nutrition Certification Board

CND Commission on Narcotic Drugs

CNE Continuing Nursing Education

CNFN Cable News Financial Network

CNG compressed natural gas

CNI Community Nutrition Institute

CNM certified nurse midwife

CNN Cable News Network

CNO carbon-nitrogen-oxygen; chief of naval operations

CNR [United Nations] Committee on Natural Resources

CNS Catholic News Service; central nervous system; clinical nurse specialist

cnvt convert

CNVRT convertible

CNVRTBL convertible

Co cobalt; Corinthians

CO carbon monoxide; cardiac output; Colorado; commanding officer; common orders; conscientious objector; cutoff; cut out

co. company; county

Co. company; county

.co Colombia

c.o. carried over; cash order

c/o care of; carry over; complains of

C/O cash order; certificate of origin

CoA coenzyme A

COA certificate of authenticity; certificate of authority

COADS Comprehensive Ocean–Atmosphere Data Set

coag. coagulation

COAP [National Oceanic and Atmospheric Administration] Center for Ocean Analysis and Prediction; Clinical Outcomes Assessment Program

coax coaxial cable

COB coordination of benefits

COBOL Common Business-Oriented Language

cobot cooperative robot

COBRA Consolidated Omnibus Budget Reconciliation Act

COBS central on board software

COC cathodal opening contraction; certificate of competency; certificate of coverage

coch. *Latin* cochleare (spoonful)

coch. amp. *Latin* cochleare amplum (tablespoonful)

coch. parv. *Latin* cochleare parvum (teaspoonful)

COCl cathodal opening clonus

COCOM Coordinating Committee [on Export Controls]

COD *Concise Oxford Dictionary*

cod. *Latin* codex (manuscript volume); codicil

C.O.D. cash on delivery; collect on delivery

CoDA Co-Dependents Anonymous

CODA Children of Deaf Adults

CODAR Coastal Ocean Dynamics Applications Radar

CODATA Committee on Data for Science and Technology

CoDE coherent digital exciter

CODE Confederation of Dental Employers

COE Corps of Engineers

COEA cost and operational effectiveness analysis

coef. coefficient

coeff. coefficient

COEs Centers of Excellence

C. of C. chamber of commerce

C. of E. Church of England

COFI Committee on Fisheries

C. of S. chief of staff

cog. cognate

COGA Collaborative Study on the Genetics of Alcoholism

cogn. cognate

C.O.G.S.A. Carriage of Goods by Sea Act

COH carbohydrate

c.o.h. cash on hand

COHIS Community Outreach Health Information System

COI cone of influence

Co-I co-investigator

COIL chemical oxygen-iodine laser

COIN counterinsurgency

coin-op coin-operated

coke cocaine

Col colonial

COL computer-oriented language; cost of living; Council on Ocean Law

col. collect; college; colony; colophon; color; column

Col. Colombia; Colombian; colonel; Colorado; Colossians

COLA cost-of-living adjustment; cost-of-living allowance

COLD chronic obstructive lung disease

colet. *Latin* coletur (let it be strained)

coll. collateral; collect; collection; college; colloquial

collab. collaboration; collaborator

collat. collateral

collect. collective; collectively

colloq. colloquial; colloquialism; colloquially

collut. *Latin* collutorium (mouth wash)

collyr. *Latin* collyrium (eye wash)

Colo. Colorado

colog cologarithm

COM Comedy Central; computer-output microfilm; computer-output microfilmer

com. combining; combustion; comedy; comic; comma; commentary; commerce; commission; commissioner; committee; common; commune; communication; community

Com. commander; commissioner; commodore; commonwealth; communist

.com commercial organization

COMB Center of Marine Biotechnology

comb. combination; combining; combustion

comb. form combining form

comd. command; commander

Comdex Communications and Data Processing Exhibition

comdg. commanding

Comdr. commander

Comdt. commandant

COMECON Council for Mutual Economic [Assistance]

COMET Cooperative Program for Operational Meteorology, Education, and Training (National Center for Atmospheric Research)

COMEX [New York] Commodity Exchange

Comintern *Russian* Kommunisticheskij Internatsional (Communist International)

commie communist

coml. commercial

comm. commentary; commerce; commercial; commission; committee; communication

Comm. commander; commonwealth; community

commo commodore

comp complimentary; composition (academic course)

comp. comparative; compensation; compiled; complete; composer; compound; comprehensive

compander compressor-expander

compar. comparative

compd. compound

Comp. Gen. Comptroller General

compl. complement; complete

compo composition material

COM port communications port

compt. compartment; comptroller

Comr. commissioner

Comsat Communications Satellite [Corporation]

COMSS Council of Musculoskeletal Specialty Societies

con confidence game; convict

CON certificate of need

con. concerto; conclusion; *Latin* conjunx (wife); connection; consolidate; consul; continued; *Latin* contra (against); convention

Con. Congo

con A concanavalin A

CONAD Continental Air Defense [Command]

conc. concentrate; concentrated; concentration; concerning; concrete

concl. conclusion

concn. concentration

concr. concrete

cond. condenser; condition; conductivity; conductor

condo condominium

conf. conference; confidential

confab confabulation

confed. confederation

Confed. confederate

config. configuration

cong. *Latin* congius (gallon)

Cong. Congregational; Congress

con game confidence game

Cong. Rec. *Congressional Record*

conj. conjugation; conjunction; conjunctive

con man confidence man

conn. connected; connotation

Conn. Connecticut

CONQUEST Computerized Needs-Oriented Quality Measurement Evaluation System

CONRAD Contraceptive Research and Development [Program]

Conrail Consolidated Rail [Corporation]

cons. consigned; consignment; consonant; constable; constitution; construction; consul

Cons. Constitution; conservative; consul

consec. consecutive

consol. consolidated

const. constable; constant; constitution; construction

Const. Constitution

constr. construction

cont. contents; continent; continued; contract; contraction; control

contd. continued

contemp. contemporary

contempt. contemptuous; contemptuously

contg. containing

contn. continuation

contr. contract; contracted; contraction; contractor; contralto; contrary; control

Contr. controller

contrail condensation trail

cont. rem. *Latin* continuentur remedia (continue the medicines)

contrib. contributor; contributing; contribution

conv. convention; conversation; convertible; convocation

Conv. Conventual

CONVINCE Consortium of North American Veterinary Interactive New Concept Education

COO chief operating officer

coon raccoon

coop cooperative

co-op cooperative

coord. coordinate

COP coefficient of performance

cop. copper; copula; copy; copyright

Cop. Coptic

COPD chronic obstructive pulmonary disease

copr. copyright

COPS Coastal Ocean Prediction Systems Program

Copt. Coptic

CoQ coenzyme Q

COR Center for Orthopaedic Research; College of Radiographers

cor. corner; cornet; coroner; corpus; correction; correlative; correspondence; corrupt

Cor. Corinthians

CORBA common object request broker architecture

CORD Council of Emergency Medicine Residency Directors

CORE Congress of Racial Equality

CORF comprehensive outpatient rehabilitation facility

Corn. Cornish; Cornwall

corol. corollary

coroll. corollary

Corp. corporal; corporation

Corpl. corporal

corpocrat corporate bureaucrat

CORR *Clinical Orthopaedics and Related Research*

corr. correction; correspondent; correspondence; corrugated; corrupt

correl. correlative

corresp. correspondence; corresponding

corrupt. corruption

cos cosine

cos. companies; consul; counties

C.O.S. cash on shipment

cosec cosecant

cosh hyperbolic cosine

COSHH control of substances hazardous to health

Cosmo *Cosmopolitan*

COSNA Composite Observing System for the North Atlantic

COSPAR Committee on Space Research

COSTED Committee on Science and Technology in Developing Countries

COSTEP comprehensive supra thermal and energetic particle [analyzer]

COSTR Collaborative Solar-Terrestrial Research

cot cotangent

COTA certified occupational therapy assistant; Children's Organ Transplant Association

COTe cathodal opening tetanus

coth hyperbolic cotangent

COTH Council of Teaching Hospitals

COTR contracting officer's technical representative

COTS commercial off-the-shelf

COTT Committee of Ten Thousand

coun. council; counsel

covers versed cosine

COW cellsite on wheels

COWPS Council on Wage and Price Stability

COWRR Committee on Water Resources Research

coz cousin

cp candlepower

cP centipoise

CP cerebral palsy; chemically pure; command post; Communist Party; creatine phosphate; cultural practices

cp. compare; coupon

c.p. chemically pure

C.P. Cape Province; Common Prayer

C/P custom of the port

CPA certified public accountant

CPAF cost-plus-award-fee

CPAP continuous positive airway pressure

CPB Corporation for Public Broadcasting

CPC cheap personal computer; Climate Prediction Center; condensation particle counter

CPCA Cigarette Pack Collectors Association

CPCU Chartered Property and Casualty Underwriter

cpd. compound

CPDB Clinical Pathway Database

CPDS Commerce Procurement Data System

CPF Cleft Palate Foundation

CPFF cost plus fixed fee

CPFS computer program functional specification

cpi characters per inch

CPI consumer price index

CPIF cost-plus-incentive-fee

CPK creatine phosphokinase

cpl complete; complin; compline

Cpl. corporal

cpm cost per thousand; cycles per minute

CPM continuous passive motion

CPO chief petty officer

CPOM master chief petty officer

CPOS senior chief petty officer

CPPB continuous positive pressure breathing

CPPD calcium pyrophosphate deposition disease

CPPV continuous positive pressure ventilation

CPR cardiopulmonary resuscitation; customary, prevailing and reasonable reimbursement

CPRI Computer-based Patient Record Institute

cps characters per second; cycles per second

CPS certified professional secretary; Coalition for Positive Sexuality

CPSC Consumer Product Safety Commission

CPS I [American Cancer Society] Cancer Prevention Study I

CPS II [American Cancer Society] Cancer Prevention Study II

cpt carpet

CPT captain; current procedural terminology

cpt. carport; counterpoint

cptd. carpeted

CPU central processing unit

CPUE catch per unit of effort

CPV canine parvo virus

CQ call to quarters

CQI continuous quality improvement

Cr chromium

CR carriage return; complete remission; complete response; conditioned reflex; conditioned response; consciousness raising; *Consumer Reports*; critical ratio

cr. credit; creditor; creek; crescendo; crown

.cr Costa Rica

c.r. *Latin* curia regis (the king's court); chancery reports

C.R. Costa Rica

CRAFT can't remember a fucking thing

CRAHCA Center for Research in Ambulatory Health Care Administration

C ration canned ration

CRB Commodity Research Bureau

CRC camera-ready copy; Civil Rights Commission; cyclic redundancy check

CRD chronic respiratory disease

CRDC Climate Research Data Center

CREBBI [Center for] Cell Regulation and Enhancement of Biology/Biomaterial Interfaces

CREEP Committee to Reelect the President

CREF College Retirement Equities Fund

CREN Corporation for Research and Educational Networking

crep crepitation

Cres. crescent

cresc. crescendo

CRF chronic renal failure; corticotropin releasing factor

CRFA Cancer Research Foundation of America

CRH corticotropin releasing hormone

CRI Carpet and Rug Institute

crim. criminal

crim. con. criminal conversation (adultery)

criminol. criminologist; criminology

CRIR Caitlin Raymond International Registry

CRISD computer resources integrated support document

CRISP Computer Retrieval of Information on Scientific Projects; Consortium Research on Indicators of System Performance

crit. critic; critical; criticism; criticized

CRL crown-rump length

cr/lf carriage return/line feed

CRM cross-reacting material

cRNA complementary ribonucleic acid

CRNA Certified Registered Nurse Anesthetist

crnr. corner

CRO cathode ray oscilloscope

Croat. Croatia; Croatian

croc crocodile

cross-refs. cross-references

CRP C-reactive protein; Crop Reserve Program

crpt. carpet; carport

CRQ Chronic Respiratory Questionnaire

CRRB Change Request Review Board

CRREL Cold Regions Research and Engineering Laboratory

CRRES combined release and radiation effects satellite

CRS can't remember shit; can't remember stuff; Community Relations Service; Congressional Research Service

crt court; crate

CRT cathode-ray tube

CRTT certified respiratory therapy technician

CRUFAD Clinical Research Unit for Anxiety Disorders

crypto. cryptographer; cryptographic; cryptography

cryst. crystalline; crystallized; crystallography

cs cesarean section

Cs cesium

CS capital stock; chief of staff; Christian Science; civil service; conditioned stimulus

cs. case

CSA Community Services Administration; Confederate States of America

CSAP Center for Substance Abuse Prevention

CSAR combat search and rescue

CSAT Center for Substance Abuse Treatment

CSA/USA Celiac Sprue Association/United States of America

csc cosecant

CSC Civil Service Commission

CSCA Cardiovascular/Thoracic Surgery and Cardiology Assembly

C-SCAT C-band scatterometer

CSCE Coffee, Sugar, and Cocoa Exchange; Conference on Security and Cooperation in Europe

csch hyperbolic cosecant

CSCI computer software configuration item

CSCS consolidated scientific computing system

CSE Center for Social Epidemiology

CSEEE Center for the Study of Environmental Endocrine Effects

CSES Center for the Study of Earth from Space

CSETI Center for the Study of Extraterrestrial Intelligence

C-section cesarean section

CSF cerebrospinal fluid

csg. casing

CSHCN children with special health care needs

CSHS Cancer and Steroid Hormonal Study

CSI calculus surface index; conditional symmetric instability

CSICOP Committee for the Scientific Investigation of Claims of the Paranormal

csk. cask; countersink

CSM climate system monitoring

C.S.M. command sergeant major

CSN Children's Safety Network

CSO Chicago Symphony Orchestra; combined sewer overflow; computer security officials

CSOM computer systems operators manual

CSP casual sex partner; C-SPAN

CSPAAD Coarse Sun Pointing Attitude Anomaly Detection

C-SPAN Cable Satellite Public Affairs Network

CSPI Center for Science in the Public Interest

C-spine cervical spine

CSR certified shorthand reporter; customer service representative

CSRA Civil Service Reform Act

CSRS Cooperative State Research Service

CSS cascading style sheets; combined sewer system

CSSA [Stanford] Center for Space Science and Astrophysics

CST Central Standard Time; convulsive shock treatment

CSTA computer-supported telephony applications

CSTC Consolidated Satellite Test Center

CSTD [United Nations] Center for Science and Technology for Development

CSTE Council of State and Territorial Epidemiologists

CSU computer software unit

CSW Certificate in Social Work

CT Central Time; computerized tomography; Connecticut

ct. cent; certificate

Ct. carat; Connecticut; count; county; court

CTA Chicago Transit Authority; controlled thrust assembly

c.t.a. *Latin* cum testamento annexo (with the will annexed)

CTBT Comprehensive Test Ban Treaty

CTC centralized traffic control; Citizens' Training Corps

CTD cheapest to deliver; cumulative trauma disorder

CTDMPLUS improved complex terrain dispersion model

CTEP Cancer Therapy Evaluation Program

CTF capture the flag

ctf. certificate; certified

ctg. cartage; cartridge

ctge. cartage

C3I Command, Control, Communications, and Intelligence

CTIA capacitive feedback transimpedance amplifier

CTL cytotoxic T lymphocytes

ctl. cental

CTMBL cloud-topped marine boundary layer

ctmo. centesimo; centimo

ctn cotangent

ctn. carton

cto. concerto

c. to c. center to center

CTOF charge time-of-flight

CTOL conventional takeoff and landing

CTP cytidine 5c-triphosphate
CTR cash transaction report; currency transaction report
ctr. center; counter
ctrl control
CTS carpal tunnel syndrome; clear to send
CTU centigrade thermal unit
ctvo. centavo
Ctx contractions
Cty. city; county
Cu copper; cumulus
CU Consumers Union; see you
cu. cubic
.cu Cuba
CUA commonly used acronym; commonly used acronyms; common user access; cost-utility analysis
cube cubicle
CUC chronic ulcerative colitis
cu. cm. cubic centimeter
CUD could (shortwave transmission)
CUFOS [J. Allen Hynek] Center for UFO Studies
CUFT Center for the Utilization of Federal Technology
cu. ft. cubic foot
cu. in. cubic inch
cuke cucumber
CUL catch you later; see you later
cul. culinary
CU L8R see you later
cult. culture
cum. cumulative
cu. m. cubic meter
Cumb. Cumbria

cu. mm. cubic millimeter
cUMP cyclic uridine 3c,5c-monophosphate
CUNA Credit Union National Association
CUNY City University of New York
CUP Cambridge University Press
cur. currency; current
curr. currency
curric. curriculum
cust. custodian; custody; customer
cu. yd. cubic yard
CUZ because (shortwave transmission)
'cuz because
cv convertible (bonds)
CV cardiovascular; code violations; coefficient of variation; *Latin* curriculum vitae (resumé)
cv. cultivar
.cv Cape Verde
c.v. chief value
C.V. Cape Verde
CVA cardiovascular accident; cerebrovascular accident
CVD cardiovascular disease
CVI cerebrovascular insufficiency
CVIC Center for Violence and Injury Control
CVM [Food and Drug Administration] Center for Veterinary Medicine
CVO Credentials Verification Organization
CVP central venous pressure
cvr cover

CVS cardiovascular system; chorionic villus sampling; computer vision syndrome

CVSA Cyclic Vomiting Syndrome Association

cvt. convertible

CW call waiting; chemical warfare; carrier wave; continuous wave

cw. clockwise

c/w consistent with

C/W country western

CWA Civil Works Administration; Clean Water Act; Communications Workers of America

CWAS contractor weighted average share [in cost risk]

CWHC Community Wholistic Health Center

CWO chief warrant officer

C.W.O. cash with order

CWSU [Federal Aviation Administration] Central Weather Service Unit

cwt hundredweight

CWT Consumers for World Trade

CWW clinic without walls

cx cervix

cx. convex

.cx Christmas Island

CXBR cosmic x-ray background radiation

CXR chest x-ray

Cy cyanide

CY calendar year; copy (shortwave transmission)

cy. capacity; currency; cycle

Cy. county

.cy Cyprus

CYA cover your ass

cyber cybernetic; cybernetics

cyborg cybernetic organism

cyc. cyclopedia

cycl. cyclopedia

CYL see you later

cyl. cylinder; cylindrical

Cym. Cymric

CYO Catholic Youth Organization

cytol. cytological; cytology

CZ Canal Zone; colorized version

.cz Czech Republic

CZCS Coastal Zone Color Scanner

CZE capillary zone electrophoresis

Czech. (former) Czechoslovakia

CZM [National Oceanic and Atmospheric Administration] Coastal Zone Management

CZMA Coastal Zone Management Act

D

d deuteron; diameter; differential; down quark

D dative; day; Democrat; determiner; deuterium; [suggestive] dialogue (television rating); diction; divorced; down; Dutch; 500

d. date; daughter; deputy; died; dose; drachma; pence

D. department; Deus; diopter; Don; duchess; duke

DA delayed action; Department of the Army; deposit account; dining area; didn't answer; *Dissertation Abstracts*; doesn't answer; don't answer

Da. Danish

D.A. district attorney; Doctor of Arts; duck's ass (hair style)

D/A digital/analog

DAA data availability acknowledgment

DAAC Distributed Active Archive Center

DAAPPP Data Archive on Adolescent Pregnancy and Pregnancy Prevention

DAB *Dictionary of American Biography*

DACS Data Acquisition and Control Subsystems

D.A.D. Dogs Against Drugs

dAdo deoxyadenosine

DAE *Dictionary of American English*

DAF divorced Asian female

dag decagram

DAG diacylglycerol

DAGC delayed automatic gain control

DAH *Dictionary of American History*; disordered action of heart

DAI *Dissertation Abstracts International*

dal decaliter

dam decameter

DAM diacetylmonoxime; divorced Asian male

dAMP deoxyadenylic acid

DAN Divers Alert Network

Dan. Daniel; Danish

DANA Drug and Alcohol Nursing Association

D & C dilation and curettage; drugs and cosmetics

D & D drug and disease free

D & E dilation and evacuation; dilation and extraction

D & O directors and officers

D & S domination and submission

D & X dilation and extraction

Danl Daniel

DANS 1-dimethylaminonaphthalene-5-sulfonic acid

DAO departmental administrative order

DAP Diagnostic Accreditation Program

DAPI 4c6-diamidino-2-phenylindole•2HCl

DAR damage assessment routine; Daughters of the American Revolution

DARC Device for Automatic Remote Data Collection

DARE *Dictionary of American Regional English*; Drug Abuse Resistance Education

DARFC ducking and running for cover

DARPA Defense Advanced Research Projects Agency

DART Developmental and Reproductive Toxicology

DAS days at sea

DASA Defense Atomic Support Agency

DASD direct access storage device

DASH Dietary Approaches to Stop Hypertension

DAT digital audiotape

dat. dative

dATP deoxyadenosinetriphosphate

dau daughter

DAU decryption authentication unit

DAV digital audio-video; Disabled American Veterans

DAWN Drug Abuse Warning Network

DAWS defense automated warning system

DAX *German* Deutsche Aktienindex (German stock index)

dB decibel

Db dubnium

DB damp basement; data base; daybook; defensive back

d.b. day book

D.B. *Domesday Book*

d.b.a. doing business as

D.B.A. Doctor of Business Administration

d/b/a doing business as

DBCP Data Buoy Cooperation Council

DBDDD [National Center for Environmental Health] Division of Birth Defects and Developmental Disabilities

d.b.e. *Latin* de bene esse (to be decided later)

D.B.E. Dame Commander of the British Empire

DBF divorced Black female

d.b.h. diameter at breast height

dBI decibels referenced to isotropic gain

D.Bib. Douay Bible

DBIR Directory of Biotechnology Resources

dbl. double

dble. double

dBm decibels per milliwatt; decibels referenced to one milliwatt

DBM divorced Black male

DBMS data base management system

d.b.n. *Latin* de bonis non [administratis] (of the goods not administered)

DBP vitamin D-binding protein

DBPs disinfection by-products

DBS direct broadcast satellite

dBW decibels referenced to one watt

dc discontinue; discounted

DC developed country; direct command; direct current; District of Columbia; dual choice

D.C. da capo; district court; Doctor of Chiropractic

d/c discharge

DCA [IBM's] Document Content Architecture; Ronald Reagan Washington National airport code

DCAA Defense Contract Audit Agency

DCASR Defense Contract Administration Services Region

DCC Dependent Care Connection

DCCPS Division of Cancer Control and Population Sciences

DCE distributed computing environment

DCEG Division of Cancer Epidemiology and Genetics

DCF data capture facility

D.Ch.E. Doctor of Chemical Engineering

DCHP *Dictionary of Canadianisms on Historical Principles*

DCI duplicate coverage inquiry

DCIS ductal carcinoma in situ

DCL declare

D.C.L. Doctor of Canon Law; Doctor of Civil Law

DCM Distinguished Conduct Medal

dCMP deoxycytidylic acid

DCN document change notice

DCP Division of Cancer Prevention

DCPC Division of Cancer Prevention and Control

DCS Defense Communications System; Direct Credits Society

DCS/2 Data Collection System/2

dCTP deoxycytidine triphosphate

DD days after date; double density; dry-dock; due date

dd. delivered

D.D. demand draft; dishonorable discharge; *Latin* Divinitatis Doctor (Doctor of Divinity)

DDA data delivery acknowledgment; dideoxyadenosine

DDB double-declining balance [depreciation]

DDBMS distributed database management system

D/DBP disinfectant and disinfection byproduct

ddC dideoxycytidine

DDC Dewey Decimal Classification

DDD direct distance dialing

DDE Dwight David Eisenhower; dynamic data exchange

DDF data distribution facility

D/DF drug and disease free

DDI dideoxyinosine

DDIM dry deposition inferential method

DDN data delivery notice

DDNA Developmental Disabilities Nurses Association

DDP distributed data processing

D.D.S. Doctor of Dental Science; Doctor of Dental Surgery

DDT dichlorodiphenyl-trichloroethane

DDTE design, development, test, and evaluation

DDVP dimethyl dichlor vinyl phosphate

DDW Digestive Disease Week

DE defensive end; Delaware; donor eggs

.de Germany

D.E. Doctor of Engineering

DEA Drug Enforcement Administration

DEAL-MCH Data Enhancement for Accountability and Leadership in Maternal and Child Health

deb debutante

deb. debenture

DEBRA Dystrophic Epidermolysis Bullosa Research Association

dec decoration

DEC Digital Equipment Corporation

dec. deceased; declaration; declension; declination; decorated; decorative; decrease; decrescendo

Dec. December

DEC decorated; Digital Equipment Corporation

decaf decaffeinated coffee

decal decalcomania

DecCen decadal-to-centennial

decd. deceased

decl. declension

decn. decision

decomp. decomposition

ded. dedication; deduct

D.Ed. Doctor of Education

de d. in d. *Latin* de die in diem (from day to day)

DEECS digital electronic engine control system

DEET diethyl toluamide; n-diethyltoluamide; N,N-diethyl-m-toluamine

def definite; definitely

def. defective; defendant; defense; deferred; definite; definition

DEFCON defense readiness condition

deg. degree

deglut. *Latin* deglutiatur (swallow)

D.E.I. Dutch East Indies (now, Indonesia)

DEIS draft environmental impact statement

Del delete

DEL data evaluation laboratory

del. delegate; delegation; delete; delivered; delivery

Del. Delaware

dele delete

deli delicatessen

delts deltoid muscles

dely delivery

dem demodulator

dem. demonstrative; demurrage

Dem. Democrat; Democratic

demo demonstration

demob demobilize

demon. demonstrative

demonstr. demonstrative

den. denotation

Den. Denmark

D.Eng. Doctor of Engineering

denom. denomination

dens. density

dent. dental, dentist; dentistry

DEP dedicated experiment processor

dep. department; departure; dependency; deponent; deposed; deposit; depot; deputy

depr. depreciation; depression

dept. department; deputy

DEPT department

der. derivation; derivative

d.e.r.i.c. *Latin* de ea re ita censuere (concerning that matter have so decreed)

deriv. derivation; derivative

derm. dermatitis; dermatology

derog. derogatory

DERWeb Dental Education Resources on the Web

DES data encryption standard; diethylstilbestrol

des. designation; dessert

Des. desert

desc. descendant; descending; describe

destn. destination

DET diethyltryptamine

det. detachment; detail

DETLA double extended three-letter abbreviation

detn. determination

DEU dead-end user

Deut. Deuteronomy

DEV duck embryo origin vaccine

dev. developed by; development; deviation

devel. development

DEW directed energy weapon; distant early warning

DF direction finder

d.f. degrees of freedom

D.F. Defender of the Faith; Doctor of Forestry

D.F.A. Doctor of Fine Arts

DFC Distinguished Flying Cross

DFCD data format control documents

DFD data flow diagram

dFdC difluorodeoxycytidine

DFI disease-free interval

DFM Distinguished Flying Medal

DFP diisopropyl fluorophosphate

dft. defendant; draft

DFW Dallas/Fort Worth airport code

dg decigram

D.G. *Latin* Dei gratia (by the grace of God); *Latin* Deo gratias (thanks to God); Director General

dgl dangling construction

dGlc 2-deoxyglucose

dGMP deoxyguanylic acid

DGPS differential global positioning system

dgt digit

dGTP deoxguanosine triphosphate

DH Darling Husband; Dear Husband; designated hitter

D.H. Doctor of Humanities

DHA docosahexaenoic acid

DHAC dihydro-5-azacytidine; doesn't have a clue; don't have a clue

DHAP dihydroxyacetone phosphate

DHEA dihydroepiandrosterone

DHEAS dihydroepiandrosterone sulfate

DHF dihydrofolic acid; divorced Hispanic female

DHFR dihydrofolate reductase

DHHS [United States] Department of Health and Human Services

DHJ doing his job

D.H.L. Doctor of Hebrew Letters; Doctor of Hebrew Literature

DHM divorced Hispanic male

DHP direct high power

DHS Demographic and Health Surveys; Division of HIV Services

DHSS data handling subsystem

DHT dihydrotestosterone

DHTML Dynamic Hypertext Markup Language

D.Hy. Doctor of Hygiene

Di didymium

DI donor insemination; drill instructor

DIA Defense Intelligence Agency; document interchange architecture

dia. diameter

diab diabetic

diag. diagonal; diagonally; diagram

DIAL differential absorption lidar

dial. dialect; dialectal; dialectally; dialogue

diam. diameter

DIARAD dual irradiance absolute radiometer

DIC dissolved inorganic carbon; Drug Information Center

DICE data integration and collection environment

dict. dictation; dictionary

DID data item description; direct inward dial

DIEB Department of the Interior Energy Board

dieb. alt. *Latin* diebus alternis (every other day)

dies non. *Latin* dies non juridicus (not a court day)

diet. dietary

Diet. dietitian

di. et fi. *Latin* dilecto et fideli (to one's beloved and faithful)

DIF data interchange format; device input format; Drug Information Fulltext

dif. difference

diff difference

diff. difference

dig. digest; digitalis

digiverse digital universe

DIIK damned if I know

dil. dilute

dim. dimension; diminished; diminuendo; diminutive

dimin. diminuendo; diminutive

DIMM dual in-line memory module

din dining room

Din dinar

DINFOS Defense Information School

DINK dual income, no kids

dioc. diocese; diocesan

DIP dual in-line package

dip. diploma

D.I.P. desquamative interstitial pneumonia

D.I. particle defective interfering particle

DIPEC Defense Industrial Plant

diph. diphtheria

DIPI direct intraperitoneal insemination

dipl. diploma; diplomat; diplomatic

dir. direct; direction; director

DIRCM directed infrared countermeasures

DIRLINE Directory of Information Resources Online

dir. prop. *Latin* directione propria (with proper direction)

dis disease; to be disrespectful toward

DIS Defense Investigative Service; Disney Channel

dis. discharge; discount; distance; distant

DISA Defense Information Services Activity; Defense Information Systems Agency

disab. disability

DISAM Defense Institute of Security Assistance Management

disc. discount; discovered

D.I.S.C. domestic international sales corporation

disch. discharge

disco discotheque

DISH diffuse idiopathic skeletal hyperostosis

DISIDA diisopropyl iminodiacetic acid

disp. dispensary

displ. displacement

diss to be disrespectful toward

diss. dissertation

dissd. dissolved

dist. distance; distant; district

Dist. Atty. district attorney

Dist. Ct. district court

distn distillation

distr. distribution; distributor

distrib. distributive

DIT diiodotyrosine

DITD down in the dumps

div. divergence; divergency; diversion; divided; dividend; division; divorced

div. in p. aeg. *Latin* divide in partes aequales (divide into equal parts)

divvy divide

divx digital video express

DIY do-it-yourself

dj dust jacket

DJ disc jockey

.dj Djibouti

D.J. district judge; *Latin* Doctor Juris (Doctor of Law)

DJD degenerative joint disease

DJF December-January-February

DJI Dow-Jones Index

DJIA Dow-Jones Industrial Average

D.J.S. Doctor of Juridical Science

dk. dark; deck; dock

.dk Denmark

dkg dekagram

dkl dekaliter

dkm dekameter

dkt. docket

dl deciliter

DL disturbance lines

d.l. quiet (from "down low")

D.L. Doctor of Law

D/L demand loan; downlink

DLA Defense Logistics Agency

DLC data link control

DLC/LLC data link control/logical link control

DLD delivered (shortwave transmission); Direct Link for the Disabled, Inc.

DLG devilish little grin

D.Lit. *Latin* Doctor Litterarum (Doctor of Letters, Doctor of Literature)

D.Litt. *Latin* Doctor Litterarum (Doctor of Letters, Doctor of Literature)

DLL dynamic-link library

DLO dead letter office

dlr. dealer

dls. dollars

D.L.S. Doctor of Library Science

DLSA Defense Legal Services Agency

DLT digital linear tape; dose-limiting toxicity

dlvy. delivery

dm decimeter

DM data management; deutsche mark; diabetes mellitus

.dm Dominica

DMA Defense Mapping Agency; Direct Marketing Association; direct memory access

D.M.A. Doctor of Musical Arts

DMAHTC Defense Mapping Agency Hydrographic/Topographic Center

D-mark deutsche mark

DMAT Disaster Medical Assistance Team

DMC p,p,c-dichlorodiphenyl methyl carbinol

DMD digital micromirror device

D.M.D. *Latin* Dentariae Medicinae Doctor (Doctor of Dental Medicine)

DME distance-measuring equipment; durable medical equipment

DMF decayed, missing, and filled teeth

DMFO Defense Medical Facilities Office

DMFS decayed, missing, and filled surfaces

DMH [United States] Department of Mental Health

DML direct memory load

D.M.L. Doctor of Modern Languages

DMPP dimethylphenylpiperazinium

DMR detailed mission requirements

DMRF Dystonia Medical Research Foundation

DMS Defense Mapping School; digital matrix switch; dimethylsulfide

DMSA Defense Medical Support Activity

DMSO dimethylsulfoxide

DMSP Defense Meteorological Satellite Program

DMSSC Defense Medical System Support Center

DMT N,N-dimethyltryptamine

DMV Department of Motor Vehicles

DMZ demilitarized zone

Dn Daniel

DN dibucaine number

dn. down

DNA Defense Nuclear Agency; deoxyribonucleic acid; Dermatology Nurses Association

DNAase deoxyribonuclease

DNase deoxyribonuclease

DNB *Dictionary of National Biography*

DNC Democratic National Committee

DNF did not finish

DNR Department of Natural Resources; do not resuscitate

DNS Domain Name Service; Domain Name System

DO defense order; dissolved oxygen

do. ditto

.do Dominican Republic

D.O. Doctor of Optometry; Doctor of Osteopathy

D/O delivery order

DOA dead on arrival; Department of Agriculture

DOALOS [United Nations] Division for Ocean Affairs and the Law of the Sea

DOB date of birth

dobe doberman pinscher

doc doctor

DOC Department of Commerce; dissolved organic carbon

doc. document

D.O.C. Doctors Opposing Circumcision

DOD Department of Defense

DODDS Department of Defense Dependent Schools

DoDIIS Department of Defense Intelligence Information System

DOE Department of Education; Department of Energy; dyspnea on exertion

DOF degree of freedom

DOI Department of the Interior; digital object identifier

DOJ Department of Justice

DOL Department of Labor

dol. dolce; dollar

DOM dirty old man; dissolved organic matter; 2,5-dimethoxy-4-methylamphetamine

dom. domestic; dominant; dominion

Dom. Dominica; Dominican

D.O.M. *Latin* Deo Optimo Maximo (to God, the best and the greatest)

Dom. Proc. *Latin* Domus Procerum (House of Lords)

Dom. Rep. Dominican Republic

DOMSAT domestic communications satellite; domestic satellite

DON dissolved organic nitrogen

Don. Donegal

DOO departmental organization order

dopa dihydroxyphenylalanine

DOPLIGHT Doppler-lighting

DOPLOON Doppler-balloon

Dor. Doric

DORA Directory of Rare Analyses

DORIS Doppler orbitography and radiopositioning integrated by satellite

dorm dormitory

Dors. Dorset

DOS denial of service; Department of State; disk operating system

DOST direct oocyte-sperm transfer

DOT death on [the operating] table; Department of Transportation

doublexing double-crossing

doz. dozen

dozer bulldozer

dp dot pitch

DP data processing; demolition proceding; development prototype; dew point; disabled person; displaced person; double play

D.P. Doctor of Podiatry

DPC Data Product Code; Domestic Policy Council

DPD Drug Product Database

DPDT double pole, double throw

DPE Data Processing Engineer

D.P.E. Doctor of Physical Education

DPF divorced professional female

DPH Department of Public Health

D.Ph. Doctor of Philosophy

D.P.H. Doctor of Public Health

D.Phil. Doctor of Philosophy

dpi dots per inch

DPI Data Processing Installation

DPL diode-pumped laser

DPLX duplex

DPM divorced professional male

D.P.M. Doctor of Podiatric Medicine

DPN diphosphopyridine nucleotide

DPNH reduced diphosphopyridine nucleotide

DPO days post-ovulation

DPN+ oxidized diphosphopyridine nucleotide

DPP [National Center for Environmental Health] Disabilities Prevention Program

DPST double pole single throw

DPT diphtheria, pertussis, tetanus

dpt. department; deponent

DPU data processing unit

DPW Department of Public Works

DQ disqualified; disqualify

DQDB distributed queue data bus

DQM data quality message

DQOTD dumb question of the day

DQT design qualification test

DR dead reckoning; dining room

dr. debtor; door; dram

Dr. Doctor; drive

DRA Deficit Reduction Act

DRADA Depression and Related Affective Disorders Association

DRAM dynamic random access memory

dram. dramatic; dramatist

dram. pers. *Latin* dramatis personae (the cast of the play)

DR&A data reduction and analysis

dr. ap. apothecaries' dram

dr. avdp. avoirdupois dram

DRFM digital radio frequency memory

DRG diagnosis-related group

DRH [Centers for Disease Control and Prevention] Division of Reproductive Health

DRI Diabetes Research Institute

DRK dark

drng drainage

DRO destructive readout

droid android

Dr.P.H. Doctor of Public Health

DRR deployment readiness review

DRS data receiving system; data relay satellite; direct receiving station

drsg dressing

dr. t. troy dram

DRTC Diabetes Research and Training Center

DRU data recovery unit

ds double stranded

DS data set; double sided; double strength

d.s. dal segno; days after sight; document signed

DSA digital subtraction angiography; Direct Selling Association

DSAA Defense Security Assistance Agency

DSB Defense Science Board

DSC Discovery Channel; Distinguished Service Cross

D.Sc. Doctor of Science

D.S.C. Doctor of Surgical Chiropody

DSCC Deep Space Communications Complex

DSCS defense satellite communication system

DSD direct stream digital

DSDD double sided, double density

DSDS data storage and distribution system

DSL digital subscriber line; document style language

DSM *Diagnostic and Statistical Manual [of Mental Disorders]*; Distinguished Service Medal

DSN deep space network; defense switched network

DSNA Dictionary Society of North America

DSO Distinguished Service Order

DSP digital signal processing; digital signal processor

d.s.p. *Latin* decessit sine prole (died without issue)

DSPS delayed sleep phase syndrome

DSR delivery status report

DSRS Drug Services Research Survey

DSS digital satellite system

DSSSL Document Style Semantics and Specification Language

DST daylight-saving time

DSTN Double-layer Supertwisted Nematic

DSU data servicing unit

DSUM data summary

DSVD digital simultaneous voice and data

D.S.W. Doctor of Social Welfare; Doctor of Social Work

dT diphtheria

Dt Deuteronomy

DT Daylight Time; defensive tackle

d.t. double time

D.T. Doctor of Theology

DTA disk transfer address

DT&E development test and evaluation

DTaP diphtheria, tetanus, and acellular pertussis

DTD document type definition

dTDP thymidine 5c-diphosphate

DTF diagnostic turbulent flux

DTH delayed-type hypersensitivity; direct-to-home

D.Th. Doctor of Theology

dThd thymidine

D.Theol. Doctor of Theology

DTIC dacarbazine; Defense Technical Information Center

DTM data transfer module

DTMF dual tone multifrequency

dTMP deoxythymidylic acid; thymidine 5c-monophosphate

DTP desktop publishing; diphtheria, tetanus, and pertussis

DTPA diethylenetriamine pentaacetic acid

DTPH diphtheria, tetanus, pertussis, and Hib

DTR data transfer rate; deep tendon reflex

DTRT do the right thing

DT's delirium tremens

DTSA Defense Technology Security Administration

dTTP thymidine 5c-triphosphate

DTW Detroit airport code

D2T2 dye diffusion thermal transfer

DU distribution uniformity; Dobson unit (for measuring ozone concentration); duodenal ulcer

Du. duke; Dutch

Dub. Dublin

Dubl. Dublin

DUI driving under the influence [of alcohol or drugs]

dup. duplicate

DUR drug utilization review

Dur. Durham

dur. dolor. *Latin* durante dolore (while pain lasts)

dUTP deoxyuridine 5-triphosphate

DUX duplex (shortwave transmission)

D.V. *Latin* Deo volente (God willing); Douay Version

DVD digital versatile disk; digital videodisk

DVD-R digital versatile disk–recordable

DVD-RAM digital versatile disk–random-access memory

DVD-ROM digital versatile disk–read-only memory

DVD-RW digital versatile disk–read-write

D.V.M. Doctor of Veterinary Medicine

DVP delivery versus payment

D.V.T. deep vein thrombosis

DW Darling Wife; dead weight; Dear Wife; distilled water

D/W dishwasher; dock warrant

DWA damaging winds algorithm

DWB Doctors Without Borders

DWBC deep western boundary current

DWD Dying with Dignity

DWEM dead White European male

DWF divorced White female

DWI died without issue; driving while intoxicated

DWM divorced White male

dwnstrs downstairs

DWR Doppler Weather Radar

DWSN Dandy-Walker Syndrome Network

DWT deadweight tonnage; deadweight tons

dwt. pennyweight

dx diagnosis

DX distance

DXF drawing interchange file

Dy dysprosium

dy. delivery; duty

dyn dyne

DYNMX dynamic mixing model

DYOH do your own homework

DYSIM dynamic simulator

DZ drop zone

dz. dozen

.dz Algeria

DZA Algeria

E

e electron; error

e. eastern; engineer; engineering

e- electronic

E east; eastern; electronic; English; error; especial; etiology; excellent; extra

E. earl; English

ea. each

EA electronic attack; Endometriosis Association

EAA earth attitude angle; equal areas/equal aspect

EAC external auditory canal

EADB East African Development Bank

EAE experimental allergic encephalitis

EAF effort adjustment factor; experimenter's analysis facility

EAM *Greek* Ethniko Apeleftherotiko Metopo (National Liberation Front)

E & OE errors and omissions excepted

EAP Edgar Allan Poe; Elvis Aron Presley; employee assistance program

EAT earnings after taxes

EB eastbound; Epstein-Barr [virus]; exabyte

E.B. elementary bodies

EBCDIC extended binary coded decimal interchange code

EBE extraterrestrial biological entity

EBIT. earnings before interest and taxes

EBL external blood loss

EBM evidence-based medicine

EbN east by north

EBNF Extended Backus-Naur Form

EBOZ Ebola virus, Zaire strain

E-BPR enhanced bottom pressure recorder

EBRD European Bank for Reconstruction and Development

EBRT external-beam radiation therapy

EbS east by south

EBS emergency broadcast system

E.B.T. examination before trial

e-business electronic business

EBV Epstein-Barr virus

ec emerging company

Ec Ecclesiastes

EC European Community

Ec. Ecuador

.ec Ecuador

ECA Economic Commission for Africa

ECAFE Economic Commission for Asia and the Far East

ECAL electronic calibration

e-cash electronic cash

ECB [acute] exacerbations of chronic bronchitis

Eccl Ecclesiastes

eccl. ecclesiastic; ecclesiastical

Eccles. Ecclesiastes

Eccl. Gk. Ecclesiastical Greek

Eccl. L Ecclesiastical Latin

Ecclus. Ecclesiasticus

ECCM electronic counter-countermeasures

ECCS emergency core cooling system

ECDIN Environmental Chemicals Data and Information Network

ECDIS Electronic Chart Display Information System

ECF extracellular fluid

ECF-A eosinophil chemotactic factor of anaphylaxis

ECFMG Educational Commission for Foreign Medical Graduates

ECFV extracellular fluid volume

ECG electrocardiogram; electrocardiograph

EC-GC electron capture-gas chromatograph

ECHO Exchange Clearing House; Expo Collectors and Historians Organization

ECL emitter-coupled logic

ECLA Economic Commission for Latin America

ECLAC Economic Commission for Latin America and the Caribbean

ECM electronic countermeasures; Emerging Company Marketplace; European Common Market

ECO Economic Cooperation Organization

ECoG electrocorticography

ECOG Eastern Cooperative Oncology Group

ecol. ecology

E. coli Escherichia coli

e-commerce electronic commerce

econ economics (academic course)

econ. economics; economist; economy

ECOR Engineering Committee on Oceanic Resources

ECOSOC Economic and Social [Council]

ECOWAS Economic Community of West African States

ECP extended capabilities port

ECRI Emergency Care Research Institute

ECS electrocerebral silence; environmental control system

ECSC European Coal and Steel Community

ECT electroconvulsive therapy

ECU emergency care unit; European currency unit

Ecua. Ecuador

ECWA Economic Commission for Western Asia

ed education

ED electrical damage; erectile dysfunction; extensive disease

ed. edited by; edition; editor; education

E.D. election district; emergency department

EDA Economic Development Administration; embedded document architecture

EDB ethylene dibromide

Ed.B. *Latin* Educationis Baccalaureus (Bachelor of Education)

EDC estimated date of confinement (pregnancy)

EDD *English Dialect Dictionary*; expected date of delivery

Ed.D. *Latin* Educationis Doctor (Doctor of Education)

EDF Environmental Defense Fund

ED$_{50}$ median effective dose

EDI electronic data interchange

EDIMS Environmental Data and Information Management Systems

EDIS [National Oceanic and Atmospheric Administration] Environmental Data and Information Service

edit. edition; editor

EDL Ethernet data link

EDLIN line editor program

Ed.M. *Latin* Educationis Magister (Master of Education)

EDO extended duration orbiter

EDO RAM extended data out random access memory

EDP electronic data processing

EDR electrodialysis reversal; environmental data record

E-dress electronic address

EDRF endothelium-derived relaxing factor

EdS Specialist in Education

EDS enter day stop order; [National Oceanic and Atmospheric Administration] Environmental Data Service

EDSA Eating Disorders Shared Awareness

EDSP exchange delivery settlement price

EDT Eastern Daylight Time

EDTA ethylenediaminetetraacetic acid

.edu educational institution

educ. educated; education; educational

EE Early English

.ee Estonia

e.e. errors excepted

E.E. electrical engineer; electrical engineering

EEC European Economic Community

EEE eastern equine encephalomyelitis

EEG electroencephalogram; electroencephalograph

EELV evolved expendable launch vehicle

EEMS enhanced expanded memory system

EENT eyes, ears, nose, and throat

EEO equal employment opportunity

EEOC Equal Employment Opportunity Commission

EEP exports enhancement program

EE.UU. *Spanish* Estados Unidos (United States)

EEZ exclusive economic zone

EF efficiency (apartment)

EFA Epilepsy Foundation of America; essential fatty acids

EFF Electronic Frontier Foundation; [National Weather Service] Experimental Forecast Facility

eff. effective; efficiency

effic. efficiency

EFFNCY efficiency (apartment)

EFL English as a foreign language

EFM electronic fetal monitor

EFP exchange for physicals

EFris. East Frisian

EFS exchange of futures for swaps

EFT electronic funds transfer

EFTA European Free Trade Association

EFTS electronic funds transfer system

Eg. Egypt; Egyptian

.eg Egypt

e.g. *Latin* exempli gratia (for example)

EGA enhanced graphics adapter; enhanced graphics array

EGD electrogasdynamics

EGF epidermal growth factor

EGmc East Germanic

EGSE electrical ground support equipment

EGTA ethyleneglycotetraacetic acid

Egypt. Egyptian

egyptol. egyptology

.eh Western Sahara

eHEAL Electronic Health Economics Analysis Letters

EHEC enterohemorrhagic Escherichia coli

eHEL Electronic Health Economics Letters

EHF extremely high frequency

EHHE Environmental Hazards and Health Effects

EHIS Environmental Health Information Services

EHLS [National Center for] Environmental Health's [Division of Environmental Health] Laboratory Sciences

EHO emerging healthcare organization

EHP effective horsepower; electric horsepower

EHPC extended high priority command

EHR Environmental Health Review

EHV extra-high voltage

EHz exahertz

EI echo intensity

EIA Energy Information Administration; environmental impact assessment

EIB European Investment Bank

EIDE enhanced integrated drive electronics

EIEC enteroinvasive Escherichia coli

88 love and kisses (shortwave transmission)

EIK eat-in kitchen

EIMWT Echo Integration-Mid-Water Trawl

e-ink electronic ink

EIS electronic information standards; environmental impact statement

EISA extended industry standard architecture

EIT extreme-ultraviolet imaging telescope

EJ electronic announcer (patterned after DJ)

EJP excitatory junction potential

EKG electrocardiogram; electrocardiograph

EKY electrokymogram

el elevated railroad

EL electroluminescent

el. elevation

E-LAM endothelial-leukocyte adhesion molecule

ELCA Evangelical Lutheran Church of America

ELD electroluminescent display

ELEC electronics

elec. electric; electrical; electrician; electricity

elect. electronic

electr. electricity

elem. element; elementary

elev. elevator; elevation

ELF extremely low frequency

ELH early life history

el-hi elementary and high school

elig. eligible

ELINT electronic intelligence

ELISA enzyme-linked immunoadsorbent assay

Eliz. Elizabethan

ellipt. elliptical; elliptically

ELM electronics module

ELMC electrical load management center

ELN Environmental Librarian's Network

ELSI Ethical, Legal and Social Implications

ELSS extravehicular life support system

ELT emergency locator transmitters

ELV expendable launch vehicle

EM electromagnetic; electron microscope; enlisted man

E.M. Engineer of Mines

EMA Emergency Medicine Assembly

e-mail electronic mail

EMAP Environmental Monitoring and Assessment Program

EMB endometrial biopsy; eosin-methylene blue

EMBBS Emergency Medicine Bulletin Board System

EMC electromagnetic compatibility; electronic media claims

emcee master of ceremonies

emer. emergency; *Latin* emerita (retired female); *Latin* emeritus (retired male)

EMF electromagnetic field; Emergency Medicine Foundation

e.m.f. electromotive force

EMFBI excuse me for butting in

EMFP Ethnic/Racial Minority Fellowship Programs

EMF RAPID Electric and Magnetic Fields Research and Public

Information Dissemination Program

EMG electromyogram

EMGY emergency (shortwave transmission)

EMI educable mentally impaired; electromagnetic interference

EMIC Environmental Mutagen Information Center

EMIT enzyme-multiplied immunoassay technique

EMM expanded memory manager

e-money electronic money

emp emperor; empire

EMP electromagnetic pulse

emp. emperor; empire; empress

e.m.p. *Latin* ex modo praescripto (in the manner prescribed)

EMRA Emergency Medical Response Agency; Emergency Medicine Residents' Association

EMRS Electronic Medical Record System

EMS electrical muscle stimulation; Emergency Medical Service; European Monetary System; expanded memory specification; expanded memory system

EMSC Emergency Medical Services for Children

EMT emergency medical technician

EMT-P emergency medical technician paramedic

emu electromagnetic unit

EMU European Monetary Union; extravehicular mobility unit

EN endocardium

ENA Emergency Nurses Association

ENC Encore

enc. enclosed; enclosure

encl. enclosed; enclosure

ency. encyclopedia

encyc. encyclopedia

encycl. encyclopedia

Encycl. Brit. *Encyclopedia Britannica*

ENDEX environmental data index

endo endocrine

ENDO endometriosis

ENE east-northeast; ethylnorepinephrine

ENFJ Extroversion iNtuition Feeling Judging (Myers-Briggs [personality] Type Indicator)

ENFP Extroversion iNtuition Feeling Perception (Myers-Briggs [personality] Type Indicator)

ENG electronic news gathering; electronystagmogram; electronystagmograph; electronystagmography

eng. engine; engineer; engineering

Eng. England; English

engg. engineering

engin. engineering

engr. engineer; engrave; engraved; engraver; engraving

ENIAC Electronic Numerical Integrator and Computer

enl. enlarged; enlisted

ENMOC El Niño Monitoring Center

ENS ensign

ENSO El Niño/Southern Oscillation

ENT ear, nose, and throat

ENTJ Extroversion iNtuition Thinking Judging (Myers-Briggs [personality] Type Indicator)

entom. entomology

ENTP Extroversion iNtuition Thinking Perception (Myers-Briggs [personality] Type Indicator)

entr. entrance

ENUF enough

env. envelope

environ. environment; environmental

ENW Emergency Nursing World

EO emergency operation; executive officer; executive order

e.o. *Latin* ex officio (by virtue of office)

EOA end of activity

EOB executive office building; explanation of benefits

EOD end of discussion

EOE equal opportunity employer

E.O.E. errors and omissions excepted

EOF end of file

EOG electro-oculography; electro-olfactogram

E.O.H. Equal Opportunity Housing

EOI evidence of insurability

EOL end of line

EOM end of message; end of month; extraocular motion; extraocular movement

EOMB explanation of Medicare benefits

EOMF extraocular motion full; extraocular movement full

EOMI extraocular muscles intact

EOQ end of quarter

EOS earth observation satellite; earth observing system

EOSAT Earth Observation Satellite Company

EOSDIS Earth Observing System Data and Information System

EOT end of thread; end of track; end of transmission

EOU end of user

EOUSA Executive Office for United States Attorneys

EOY end of year

Ep Ephesians

EP electrophotographic; European plan; extended play

EPA eicosapentanoic acid; Environmental Protection Agency

EPAct [National] Energy Policy Act

EPAD electrically powered actuation device

EPAT Early Psychosis Assessment Team

EPC Economic Policy Council; Evidence-based Practice Centers

EPCA Energy Policy and Conservation Act

EPCOT Experimental Prototype Community of Tomorrow

EPCRA Emergency Planning and Community Right-to-Know Act

EPEC enteropathogenic Escherichia coli

Eph. Ephesians

EPHDP Electronic Public Health Development Project

Ephes. Ephesians

EPHIN electron proton helium instrument

EPIC Electronic Privacy Information Center

EPIRB emergency position-indicating radio beacon

Epis. Episcopal; Episcopalian; Epistle

Episc. Episcopal; Episcopalian

Epist. Epistle

EPO [Centers for Disease Control] Epidemiology Program Office; exclusive provider organization

EPP enhanced parallel port

EPR electron paramagnetic resonance; engine-pressure ratio

EPRI Electric Power Research Institute

E-print electronic [pre]print (that is, before publishing in a print journal)

EPROM erasable programmable read-only memory

EPS encapsulated PostScript

E.P.S. earnings per share

EPSF encapsulated PostScript files

EPSP excitatory postsynaptic potential

EPSS electrical power subsystem

EPT excess-profits tax

EPU emergency power unit

e-publishing electronic publishing (on the Internet or the Web)

e-purse electronic purse

EPV extended precision vector

EQ emotional quotient; equalizer; equip (shortwave transmission)

eq. equal; equation; equivalent

E.Q. educational quotient

EQPT equipment (shortwave transmission)

eqq equations

equip. equipment

equiv. equivalence; equivalency; equivalent

Er erbium

ER emergency room

.er Eritrea

ERA earned run average; Economic Regulatory Administration; Equal Rights Amendment; exchange rate agreement

ERASER enhanced recognition and sensing radar

ERB Earth radiation budget

ERBE Earth Radiation Budget Experiment

ERBF effective renal blood flow

ERBS Earth Radiation Budget Satellite

ERC Endometriosis Research Center

ERCP endoscopic retrograde cholangiopancreatography

ERDA Energy Research and Development Administration

ERF Engineering Research Facility

ERG electroretinogram

ERGO Euthanasia Research and Guidance Organization

ERIC Educational Resources Information Center

ERINT extended range interceptor

ERISA Employee Retirement Income Security Act

ERL [National Oceanic and Atmospheric Administration] Environmental Research Laboratories

EROS Earth Resources Observing Satellite

ERP early receptor potential

erron. erroneous; erroneously

ERS Economic Research Service

ert earth Relative Time

ERT estrogen replacement therapy

ERTS Earth Resources Technology Satellite

ERV expiratory reserve volume

Es einsteinium

ES Extension Service

.es Spain

ESA Economics and Statistics Administration; Employment Standards Administration; Endangered Species Act; European Space Agency

ESAD eat shit and die; electronic safe and arm device

ESADMF eat shit and die motherfucker

ESB electrical stimulation of the brain

Esc escape

ESCAP Economic and Social Commission for Asia and the Pacific

ESCWA Economic and Social Commission for Western Asia

ESD electrostatic discharge

Esd. Esdras

ESDI enhanced small device interface

ESDIM [National Oceanic and Atmospheric Administration] Earth System Data and Information Management

Esdr. Esdras

ESDS electrostatic discharge sensitive

ESE east-southeast

ESFJ Extroversion Sensing Feeling Judging (Myers-Briggs [personality] Type Indicator)

ESFP Extroversion Sensing Feeling Perception (Myers-Briggs [personality] Type Indicator)

ESI enhanced serial interface

e-site electronic site (on the Internet or the Web)

Esk. Eskimo

ESL English as a second language

ESM Equipment Support Module

ESMC Eastern Space and Missile Center

ESMR electronic scanning microwave radiometer

ESMTP Extended Simple Mail Transfer Protocol

ESOL English for speakers of other languages

ESOP employee stock-ownership plan

ESP English for Specific Purposes; extrasensory perception

esp. especially

Esq. Esquire

ESR electron spin resonance

Est Esther

EST Eastern Standard Time

est. established; estate; estimate; estimated

Est. Estonia; Estonian

estab. established

e-stamp electronic [postage] stamp

Esth. Esther

ESTJ Extroversion Sensing Thinking Judging (Myers-Briggs [personality] Type Indicator)

e-store electronic store

ESTP Extroversion Sensing Thinking Perception (Myers-Briggs [personality] Type Indicator)

esu electrostatic unit

ESV Earth satellite vehicle

ESWL electrohydraulic shock wave lithotripsy; extracorporeal shock wave lithotripsy

ESWTR [Environmental Protection Agency] Enhanced Surface Water Treatment Rule

Et ethyl

ET Eastern Time; elapsed time; embryo transfer; endotrachial; extraterrestrial

.et Ethiopia

ETA embryo toxicity assay; Employment and Training Administration; estimated time of arrival

e-tailing electronic retailing

et al. *Latin* et alia (and other things); *Latin* et alii (and other people)

ETAW evapotranspiration of applied water

etc. *Latin* et cetera (and so forth)

ETD estimated time of departure

ETDP Expert Tsunami Database for the Pacific

ETEC enterotoxigenic Escherichia coli

ETF embryo toxic factor

Eth. Ethiopia; Ethiopian

ethnol. ethnologist

E3 Electronic Entertainment Expo

ETIC Environmental Teratology Information Center

E-ticket electronic ticket

ETL [National Oceanic and Atmospheric Administration] Environmental Technology Laboratory

ETLA extended three-letter acronym (that is, four letters or more)

ETMS enhanced traffic management system

ETO European theater of operations; exchange traded option

ETP early termination of pregnancy

ETR equal transit rate

Etr. Etruria

e-trader electronic trader (that is, Internet stock trader)

ETS Educational Testing Service

et seq. *Latin* et sequens (and the following one)

et. seqq. *Latin* et sequentia (and the following ones)

ETSR extraterrestrial solar spectral irradiance

ETT endotrachial tube

et ux. *Latin* et uxor (and wife)

ETV educational television

E2 estradiol

ETX end of text

etym. etymological; etymology

Eu europium

EU electronic unit; engineering units; European Union

EUA examination under anesthesia

EUC equatorial undercurrent

EULA end-user license agreement

euphem. euphemistic; euphemistically

Eur. Europe; European

EURAILPASS European Railway Pass

EURATOM European Atomic Energy Community

EUS endoscopic ultrasonography; esophageal ultrasonography

Eutelsat European Telecommunications Satellite Organization

EUV extreme ultraviolet

eV electron volt

ev. evening; evenings

EVA extravehicular activity

eval. evaluation

evan. evangelical; evangelist

evang. evangelical; evangelist

evap. evaporate

eve. evening; evenings

evg. evening

EW emergency ward; enlisted woman

e-wallet electronic wallet

EWGA Executive Women's Golf Association

EWMP efficient water management practice

EWR Newark airport code

EWRP [United States Department of Agriculture] Emergency Wetland Reserve Program

EWTN Eternal Word Television Network

Ex Exodus

ex. examination; example; except; exception; exchange; executive; express; extra

exam examination

exc. excellent; except; exception; excision

Exc. Excellency

excel. excellent

exch. exchange; exchequer

excl. exclamation; excluding; exclusive

exclam. exclamation

exec executive

exec. executor

exerhead someone addicted to physical exercise

exh. exhibit

Ex-Im Export-Import [Bank of the United States]

Eximbank Export-Import Bank [of the United States]

EXLITE extended life tire

Exod. Exodus

exor. executor

exp exploratory; exponent; exponential

exp. expenses; experiment; experimental; expiration; export; express

expat expatriate

expd experienced

expo exposition

expr. expressing; expressive

expt. experiment

exptl. experimental

expwy expressway

expy expressway

exr. executor

exrx. executrix

ext. extension; exterior; external; externally; extinct; extra; extract; extremity

exx. examples

Ez Ezekiel

EZ easy

Ezek. Ezekiel

e-zine electronic fan magazine

Ezk Ezekiel

F

f feminine; focal length; forte; function

F Fahrenheit; fail; false; farad; female; filial generation; fine; fluorine; fog; foul; franc; Friday

f. farthing; fine; folio; following

F. French

f/ f stop (relative aperture of a lens)

FA field artillery; fielding average; football association

f.a. fire alarm

FAA Federal Aviation Administration; free of all average

f.a.a. free of all average

FAACTS Free Aids Advice Counseling Treatment Support [for People with or Affected by AIDS]

FAAGL Foundation of the American Association of Gynecologic Laparoscopists

FAALC Federal Aviation Administration Logistics Center

FAAN Fellow of the American Academy of Nursing

FAATC Federal Aviation Administration Technical Center

fab fabulous

FAC freestanding ambulatory care

fac. facility; facilities; facsimile; faculty

FACCP Fellow of the American College of Chest Physicians

FACD Fellow of the American College of Dentists

FACHE Fellow of the American College of Healthcare Executives

FACMPE Fellow of the American College of Medical Practice Executives

FACNM Fellow of the American College of Nuclear Medicine

FACNP Fellow of the American College of Nuclear Physicians

FACOG Fellow of the American College of Obstetricians and Gynecologists

FACP Fellow of the American College of Physicians

FACR Fellow of the American College of Radiology

FACS Fellow of the American College of Surgeons

FACSM Fellow of the American College of Sports Medicine

FAD fish aggregating device; flavin adenine dinucleotide

F.Adm. fleet admiral

FAF financial aid form

Fah. Fahrenheit

FAHCT Foundation for the Accreditation of Hematopoietic Cell Therapy

Fahr. Fahrenheit

FAHS Federation of American Health Systems

FAIA Fellow of the American Institute of Architects

FAIM Foundation for the Advancement of Innovative Medicine

FALN *Spanish* Fuerzas Armadas de Liberación Nacional (Armed Forces of National Liberation)

fam. family; familiar
FAM Family Channel; Free and Accepted Masons
FAMC Federal Agricultural Mortgage Corporation
FAMOUS French-American Mid-Ocean Undersea Study
FAN Fetal Alcohol Network; Food Allergy Network
f and a fore and aft
fanzine fan magazine
FAO [United Nations] Food and Agriculture Organization
FAQ frequently asked questions [and answers]
FAR Federal Acquisition Regulations
Far. faraday
FARB Federal Assistance Review Board
Farmer Mac Federal Agricultural Mortgage Corporation
FARS Fatal Accident Reporting System; Financial Accounting and Reporting System
FAS Federation of American Scientists; fetal alcohol syndrome; Foreign Agricultural Service
f.a.s. free alongside ship
FASA Federated Ambulatory Surgery Association
FASB Financial Accounting Standards Board
fasc. fascicle
FASC freestanding ambulatory surgery center
FASEB Federation of American Societies for Experimental Biology

FAST flow actuated sediment trap; Food Allergy Survivors Together; fore-aft scanning technique
FAT file allocation table
fath fathom
fax facsimile
FB fullback
F.B. foreign body; freight bill
FBA flexible benefit account
FBB Federal Bulletin Board
FBFM flood boundary floodway map
FBI Federal Bureau of Investigation
FBL fly by light
FBOC Figural Bottle Opener Collectors
FBS fasting blood sugar
FBW fly by wire
fc foot-candle
FC fire control
f.c. follow copy
FCA Farm Credit Administration
FCAP Fellow of the College of American Pathologists
fcap. foolscap
FCC Federal Communications Commission
FCCP Fellow of the College of Chest Physicians
FCCSET Federal Coordinating Council for Science, Engineering, and Technology
FCFS First Come First Served (scheduling method)
FCI Family Care International
FCIA Foreign Credit Insurance Association

FCIC Federal Crop Insurance Corporation

FCIM Federated Council for Internal Medicine

FCL Foldback Current Limiter

FCLB Federation of Chiropractic Licensing Boards

FCN function

FCOJ frozen concentrated orange juice

fcp. foolscap

FCPS Fellow of the College of Physicians and Surgeons

FCRDC [National Cancer Institute] Frederick Cancer Research and Development Center

FCS Fellow of the Chemical Society

FCST Federal Council for Science and Technology

FCV flow control valve

fcy. fancy

FCZ fishery conservation zone

Fd ferredoxin

FD fatal dose; fire department; focal distance; foundation damage

F.D. *Latin* Fidei Defensor (Defender of the Faith)

FDA Food and Drug Administration

FD & C food, drugs, and cosmetics

FDD floppy disk drive

FDDI fiber distributed data interface

FDE Failure Detection Electronics; Flight Dynamics Engineers

FDF flight dynamics facility

FDG 18F-fluorodeoxyglucose

FDHD floppy drive high density

FDIC Federal Deposit Insurance Corporation

FDISK fixed disk [command]

FDLI Food and Drug Law Institute

FDLP Federal Depository Library Program

FDMD Foundation for Depression and Manic Depression

FDNB fluoro-2,4-dinitrobenzene

FDP fibrin/fibrinogen degradation products

FDR formal dining room; Franklin Delano Roosevelt

FDROTFL falling down rolling on the floor laughing

Fe iron

FE field evaluation

FEA Federal Energy Administration; finite element analysis

Feb. February

FEB Federal Executive Board

fec. *Latin* fecit (he or she made or did it)

FEC Federal Election Commission

F.E.C.A. Federal Employees' Compensation Act

fed federal agent

Fed Federal Reserve System

FED field emission device; field-emitting diode

fed. federal; federated; federation

FEDLINK Federal Library and Information Network

fedn. federation

FEDRIP Federal Research in Progress (database)

FEF forced expiratory flow

FEHEM front-end hardware emulator

FEI Federal Executive Institute

FELA Federal Employer's Liability Act

FeLV feline leukemia virus

fem. female; feminine

FEMA Federal Emergency Management Agency

FEOM full extraocular motion; full extraocular movement

FEP front-end processor

FEPA Fair Employment Practices Act

FEPC Fair Employment Practices Commission

FERA Federal Emergency Relief Administration

FERC Federal Energy Regulatory Commission

fess confess

FET federal estate tax; federal excise tax; field-effect transistor; frozen embryo transfer

FETLA further extended three-letter acronym (that is, five letters)

feud. feudal; feudalism

FEV forced expiratory volume

ff fortissimo

FF fast forward

ff. folios; following

FFA free from alongside; Future Farmers of America

FFB Federal Financing Bank; Foundation Fighting Blindness

fff fortississimo

FFP firm-fixed price; fresh frozen plasma

FFR Fellow of the Faculty of Radiologists

FFRDC federally funded research and development center

FFS fee-for-service

FFT fast Fourier transform

FFV First Families of Virginia

FG field goal; fine grain

F.G.A. foreign general average

FGAR N-formylglycinamide ribotide

F.G.F. fibroblast growth factor

FGIS Federal Grain Inspection Service

FGM female genital mutilation

FH family history; Food for the Hungry

FHA Farmers Home Administration; Federal Highway Administration; Federal Housing Administration; forced hot air (furnace); Future Homemakers of America

FHBC Federation of Historical Bottle Clubs

FHBM floodway hazard boundary map

FHC Friends' Health Connection

FHCQ Foundation for Health Care Quality

FHF [International] Federation of Health Funds

FHFB Federal Housing Finance Board

FH₄ tetrahydrofolic acid

FHI Family Health International; Food for the Hungry International

FHLB Federal Home Loan Banks

FHLBB Federal Home Loan Bank Board

FHLMC Federal Home Loan Mortgage Corporation

fhp friction horsepower

FHR fetal heart rate; fetal heart rhythm

FHT fetal heart tone

FHWA Federal Highway Administration

FHx family history

FI fiscal intermediary

.fi Finland

FIA Federal Insurance Administration; feline infectious anemia

FIAT *Italian* Fabbrica Italiana Automobili Torino (Italian Automobile Factory of Turin)

fib fibrillation

FIBS field by information blending and smoothing

FIC Federal Information Centers

FICA Federal Insurance Contributions Act

FICO Financing Corporation

fict. fiction; fictitious

FID free induction decay

fid. fidelity

FIDI Fishery Information, Data, and Statistics Service

FIFA Federation of International Football (that is, soccer) Associations

fi.fa. *Latin* fieri facias (cause [it] to be done)

FIFO first in, first out

FIFRA Federal Insecticide, Fungicide, and Rodenticide Act

50 highway patrol; police

FIG fishing industry grants

fig. figurative; figuratively; figure

FIGLU formiminoglutamic acid

FIGS fully integrated groups

FIIK fucked if I know

FIL father-in-law

FIMA financial management system

FIMIS Fishery Management Information System

fin. finance; financial; finish; finished

Fin. Finland; Finnish

fin indep financially independent

Finn. Finnish

fin sec financially secure

FIO free in and out

FIOS free in and out stowage

FIO2 fraction of inspired oxygen

FIR far infrared

fireplc fireplace

FIRM flood insurance rate map

FIRS Federal Information Relay Service

FIRST Foundation for Ichthyosis and Related Skin Types

1st ed. first edition

FIS Flood Insurance Study; Foundation for Infinite Survival

FISH first in, still here

FIT frequent international traveler

FITB fill in the blank

FITC fluorescein isothiocyanate

FITS flexible image transport system

FIV feline immunodeficiency virus

5-FU fluorouracil

5-HT 5-hydroxytryptamine

50 highway patrol; police

FJ found (shortwave transmission)

.fj Fiji

.fk Falkland Islands

fka formerly known as

F key function key

FKNMS Florida Keys National Marine Sanctuary

fL foot-lambert

FL finished lower level; floor; Florida; focal length

fl. flanker; floor; *Latin* floruit (flourished); flourished; fluid; flute

FLA foreign language acquisition

Fla. Florida

FLAME Family Life and Maternity Education

FLASER forward looking infrared laser radar

fld. field

fl. dr. fluid dram

Flem. Flemish

FLETC Federal Law Enforcement Training Center

Flint. Flintshire

FLIR forward-looking infrared

FLK funny-looking kid

FLL Fort Lauderdale airport code

F/LMR first and last month's rent

flop floating-point operation

flops floating-point operations per second

Flor. Florida

FLOTUS First Lady of the United States

fl. oz. fluid ounce

flr. floor

FLRA Federal Labor Relations Authority

FLS Front Line States

FLSA Fair Labor Standards Act

flu influenza

Fm fermium

FM field manual; field marshal; frequency modulation

fm. fathom; from

.fm Micronesia

FMB Federal Maritime Board

FMC Federal Maritime Commission

FMCS Federal Mediation and Conciliation Service

FMD foot-and-mouth disease

fMet formylmethionine

fMet-tRNA formylmethionyl tRNA

FMHA Farmers Home Administration

FMIS Field Management Information System; Financial Management Information System

FMLA Family Medical Leave Act

fml dr formal dining room

FMN flavin mononucleotide

FMO Flatland Meteorological Observatory

FMP Fisheries Management Plan

FMS financial management service; flight management system

FMV fair market value

FN foreign national

fn. footnote

FNA fine needle aspiration [biopsy]

FNASR first North American serial rights

FNIC Food and Nutrition Information Center

FNLM Friends of the National Library of Medicine

FNMA Federal National Mortgage Association

FNS Food and Nutrition Service

FO field-grade officer; field order; finance officer; flight officer; foreign office

fo. folio

.fo Faeroe Islands

F.O. fuck off

FOA full operational assessment

FOAD fall over and die; fuck off and die

FOAF friend of a friend

foamcrete concrete foam

FOB foreign body

f.o.b. free on board

FOBT fecal occult blood testing

FOC freedom of choice

f.o.c. free of charge

FOCI [National Oceanic and Atmospheric Administration]

Fisheries-Oceanography Coordinated Investigations

FOCUS Fisheries Oceanography Cooperative Users System

FOD foreign object damage

FOE Fraternal Order of Eagles; Friends of the Earth

FOG fiber optic gyro

FOI freedom of information

FOIA Freedom of Information Act

FOK fill or kill order

fol. folio; following

FOLAN Flight Operations Local Area Network

foll. folios; followed

FOMC Federal Open Market Committee

FONSI finding of no significant impact

FOP flight operations plan

FOR free on rail

for. foreign; forest; forestry

f.o.r. free on rail

FORRUM Foundation for Objective Research and Reporting on the Unexplained Mysterious

fort. fortification; fortified

fortif. fortification

FORTRAN formula translator (programming language)

FOS free on steamer

FOSA Federation of Spine Associations

f.o.t. free on truck

FOTCL falling off the chair laughing

4 for

4x4 four-wheel drive

4 C's Conference on College Composition and Communication

4cyl four cylinder

4DDA four-dimensional data assimilation (scheme)

4-H head, heart, hands, and health (program)

4Hyp 4-hydroxyproline

404 not found

401k a retirement savings plan

411 information

4WD four-wheel drive

FoV field of view

f.o.w. first open water

fp fireplace; freezing point

FP family practice; fireplace; flight plan

fp. foolscap

FPA focal plane array; Foreign Press Association

f.p.a. free of particular average

F.P.A. Fair Practices Act; Franklin P. Adams

FPC family practice clinic; Federal Power Commission; fish protein concentrate; Friends Peace Committee

FPCA Family Planning Councils of America

FPGA field programmable gated array

FPI fixed price incentive

FPIA Family Planning International Assistance

fpl fireplace

FPLC fast protein liquid chromatography

fpm feet per minute

FPM focal plane module

FPO fleet post office

FPR fixed price redeterminable

F.P.R. Federal Procurement Regulations

FPRA forward pricing rate agreement

FPRS Federal Property Resources Service

fps feet per second; foot-pound-second; frames per second

FPSS fine pointing sun sensor

FPU floating point unit

FQDN fully qualified domain name

fr fraction

Fr francium

FR family room; *Federal Register*; fire damage

fr. frame; franc; from

Fr. Father; France; Frau; French; Friar; Friday

.fr France

f.r. *Latin* folio recto (right-hand page *or* obverse of page)

F.R. *Federal Register*

FRA Federal Railroad Administration

FRACP Fellow of the Royal Australasian College of Physicians

frag fragment

Frank. Frankish

F.R.A.P. Federal Rules of Appellate Procedure

frat fraternity

FRAXA Fragile X Syndrome Research Foundation

FRB Federal Reserve Board

FRC Federal Records Center; functional reserve capacity

FRCD Family Resource Center on Disabilities

FRCP Fellow of the Royal College of Physicians

F.R.C.P. Federal Rules of Civil Procedure

FRCP(C) Fellow of the Royal College of Physicians (Canada)

FRCP(E) Fellow of the Royal College of Physicians (Edinburgh)

FRCP(I) Fellow of the Royal College of Physicians (Ireland)

FRCS Fellow of the Royal College of Surgeons

FRCS(C) Fellow of the Royal College of Surgeons (Canada)

FRCS(E) Fellow of the Royal College of Surgeons (Edinburgh)

FRCS(I) Fellow of the Royal College of Surgeons (Ireland)

FRD functional requirements document

F.R.D. Federal Rules Decisions

FREIDA Fellowship and Residency Electronic Interactive Database Access System

freq. frequency; frequent; frequentative; frequently

FRF follicle-stimulating hormone-releasing factor

FRG Federal Republic of Germany

FRGS Fellow of the Royal Geographical Society

FRH follitropin-releasing hormone

Fri. Friday

Fris. Frisian

Frisco San Francisco

Frl. Fräulein

FRM fixed rate mortgage

FRMAC Federal Radiological Management Assessment Center

FRN floating rate note

FRNT front

FROM full range of motion; full range of movement

front confrontational

front. frontispiece

frosh freshman

frplc. fireplace

FRS Federal Reserve System; Fellow of the Royal Society

Frs. Frisian

FRSC Fellow of the Royal Society (Canada)

frt. freight

FRTM functional requirements traceability matrix

frwy. freeway

fs film strip

FS Foreign Service; Forest Service

FSA flexible spending account; Food Security Act

FSC Food Safety Consortium

FSD full scale development

FSE fetal scalp electrode; file server Ethernet

FSH follicle stimulating hormone

FSH-RF follicle stimulating hormone-releasing factor

FSH-RH follicle stimulating hormone-releasing hormone

FSI Forensic Science International

FSIS Food Safety and Inspection Service

FSL [National Oceanic and Atmospheric Administration] Forecast Systems Laboratory

FSLIC Federal Savings and Loan Insurance Corporation

FSM flight synchronizer module

FSMB Federation of State Medical Boards [of the United States]

FSO Foreign Service Office

FSS Federal Supply Service; Forensic Science Society

FSSP forward-scattering spectrometer probe

FSTS Federal Secure Telephone Service

FSU former Soviet Union

FSW flight software

FT Fourier transform; free throw

ft. foot; fort; fortification

F/T full time

FTA fun, travel, and adventure; Future Teachers of America

FTA-ABS fluorescent treponemal antibody absorption

FTAM file transfer and access method

FTASB faster than a speeding bullet

FTC Federal Trade Commission

ft-c foot-candle

FTCM Foundation for Traditional Chinese Medicine

FTE full-time equivalent

FTF face-to-face

fth. fathom

FTI free thyroxine index

FTIR Fourier transform infrared radiometer

FTL faster than light

ft-lb foot-pound

FTN finger to nose (neurological test)

FTP File Transfer Protocol

FTRS [National Library of Medicine's] Full-Text Retrieval System

FTS Federal Telecommunications System; Fourier transform spectrometer

FTSG full thickness skin graft

FTT failure to thrive

F2F face-to-face

FTZ free trade zone

FU fouled up; fucked up

F/U follow-up

fubar fouled (*or* fucked) up beyond all reality (*or* recognition *or* repair)

fuc fucose

fuck The claim that *fuck* is an acronym is demonstrably false. It is an old word of Germanic origin.

fud fuddy-duddy

FUD fear, uncertainty, and disinformation; fear, uncertainty, and doubt

FUDR fluorodeoxyuridine

FUDT Newsletter *Forensic Urine Drug Testing Newsletter*

FUF Facing the Uncertain Future (study)

FUO fever of unknown origin

fur. furlong

furn furnished

fut. future; futures

FUTA Federal Unemployment Tax Act

FV fantasy violence

f.v. *Latin* folio verso (on the back of the page)

FVC forced vital capacity

FW filter wheel

FWB four-wheel brake

fwd forward

FWD four-wheel drive; front-wheel drive

FWHM full width at half maximum

FWIW for what it's worth

F-word fuck

FWPCA Federal Water Pollution Control Act

FWS Fish and Wildlife Service

FWV fixed-wing vehicle

fwy freeway

fx fracture

FX foreign exchange; Fox cable TV channel

FXA foreign exchange agreement

FXN function

FY fiscal year

FYA for your amusement

FYEO for your eyes only

FYI for your information

FYROM The Former Yugoslav Republic of Macedonia

FZ Franc Zone

FZS Fellow of the Zoological Society

G

g acceleration of gravity; gram; -ing (shortwave transmission)

G conductance; gauss; gay (as in personal ads); general admission; genitive; German; gigabyte; good; grand (that is, $1000); gravitational constant; guanine

g. gender; gourde; guilder; guinea

G. gulf

<g> grin

ga go ahead

Ga Galatians; gallium

GA general agent; general anesthesia; General Assembly; general average; Georgia; go ahead (shortwave transmission); good afternoon (shortwave transmission)

ga. gauge

.ga Gabon

GAA Gastroenterolgy Administration Assembly

GAAP generally accepted accounting principles

GAAS generally accepted auditing standards

GABA gamma-aminobutyric acid

GAC global area coverage; granular activated carbon

GACT granular activated carbon treatment

GAD glutamate decarboxylase

Gael. Gaelic

GAF gay Asian female; geographic adjustment factor;

global assessment of functioning

GAG Graphic Artists Guild

GAGAS generally accepted government auditing standards

GAL get a life

gal. gallon

Gal. Galatians

gal/cycle gallons per cycle

GALEN Generalized Architecture for Languages, Encyclopaedias, and Nomenclatures [in Medicine]

GALT gut-associated lymphoid tissue

galv. galvanized

GAM gay Asian male

G & A general and administrative [cost]

G & S Gilbert and Sullivan

GAO General Accounting Office

GAP Group for the Advancement of Psychiatry

GAPA ground-to-air pilotless aircraft

gar garden

GAR Grand Army of the Republic

GAS group A streptococci

GASNET Global Anesthesiology Server Network

GASP Group Against Smoking in Public

GATT General Agreement on Tariffs and Trade

GAW Global Atmospheric Watch; guaranteed annual wage

GAWH Global Alliance for Women's Health

gaz. gazette; gazetteer

Gb gigabit

GB gallbladder; gigabyte; government and binding; Great Britain

.gb Great Britain

GBA give better address (shortwave transmission)

GBF gay Black female; Great Books Foundation

GBG gonadal steroid-binding globulin

GBH gamma benzene hexachloride

GBL ground-based laser

GBM gay Black male

Gbps gigabits per second

GBRS generic block recording system

GBS George Bernard Shaw

GBSRN Global Baseline Surface Radiation Network

GByte gigabyte

Gc gigacycle

GC gas chromatograph; gas chromatography; guanine and cytosine (base pair in polynucleic acids)

GCA ground-controlled approach

G.C.B. Knight of the Grand Cross, Order of the Bath

GCC global climatic change; Gulf Cooperation Council

g.c.d. greatest common divisor

GCDIS Global Change Data and Information System

GCF ground communications facility

g.c.f. greatest common factor

GCMD Global Change Master Directory

GC/MS gas chromatography/mass spectrometry

GCPS Global Climate Perspectives System

G-CSF granulocyte colony-stimulating factor

GCT Greenwich civil time

Gd gadolinium

GD geologic division; goddamn; good (shortwave transmission); good for the day [order]

gd. good

.gd Grenada

G.D. grand duchy

GD & R grinning, ducking, and running

GD & T geometric dimensioning and tolerancing

GDB Genome Data Base

GDC General Dental Council

GDI graphic device interface

G.D.I. one who is not a member of a fraternity or sorority (from "goddamned independent")

GDIP General Defense Intelligence Program

gd lkg good-looking

GDP gross domestic product

GDPS global data-processing system

GDR German Democratic Republic

GDS great dark spot; ground data system

GDSIDB Global Digital Sea Ice Data Bank

GDT global descriptor table

Ge germanium

GE gastroesophageal; General Electric; good evening (shortwave transmission)

.ge Georgia (Republic of)

GEBA Global Energy Balance Archive

GEBCO General Bathymetric Chart of the Oceans

GEC global environmental change

GED general equivalency diploma; general educational development

GEENET Global Environmental Epidemiology Network

G-8 Group of 8 (Australia, Canada, EU, Japan, Spain, Sweden, Switzerland, United States)

GEK geomagnetic electrokinetograph

gel gelatin

GELNET Global Health and Environment Library Network

GEM Gemini; ground-effect machine

GEMS Global Environment Monitoring System

gen. gender; general; generally; generator; generic; genitive; genus

Gen. general; Genesis

GENE-TOX Genetic Toxicology

genit. genitive

genl. general

Gen-X Generation X

GEO genetically engineered organism; geosynchronous earth orbit

GEODAS Geophysical Data System

geog. geographic; geography

geogr. geographic; geography

geol. geologic; geological; geology

geom. geometric; geometry

GEOS Geodynamics Experimental Ocean Satellite

GEOSAT Geodetic Satellite

GEOTAIL Geomagnetic Tail Laboratory

G=F grips equal and firm

GER gastroesophageal reflux

ger. gerund

Ger. German; Germany

GERD gastroesophageal reflux disease

Germ. German; Germany

GESS Graphics Executive Support System

GEU gyroscope electronics unit

GeV giga-electron volts

.gf French Guiana

g.f. girl friend

GFCI ground fault circuit interrupter

GFDL [National Oceanic and Atmospheric Administration] Geophysical Fluid Dynamics Laboratory

GFE government-furnished equipment

GFI government-furnished information

G-5 Group of 5 (France, Germany, Japan, United Kingdom, United States)

GFP government-furnished property

GFR glomerular filtration rate

GFWC General Federation of Women's Clubs

GG going (shortwave transmission)

GGPA graduate grade-point average

GGS global geospace science

GH growth hormone

.gh Ghana

GHA Greenwich hour angle

GHAA Group Health Association of America

GHB gamma y-hydroxybutyrate

GHCN Global Historical Climate Network

GHDNet Global Health Disaster Network

GHF gay Hispanic female

GHG greenhouse gas

GHM gay Hispanic male

GHNet Global Health Network

GHQ general headquarters

GHRF growth hormone-releasing factor

GHRH growth hormone-releasing hormone

GHz gigahertz

gi gill

GI galvanized iron; gastrointestinal; general issue; Government Issue

.gi Gibraltar

Gib. Gibraltar

Gibr. Gibraltar

GID general improvement district

GIF graphics interchange format

GIFA Governing International Fisheries Agreement

GIFT gamete intrafallopian tube transfer

gig gigabyte

GIGO garbage in, garbage out

GIH growth hormone inhibiting hormone

GILS Government Information Locator Service

GIN Greenland-Iceland-Norway

GINC Global Information Network on Chemicals

GIP gastric inhibitory polypeptide; gastric inhibitory peptide

GIPME Global Investigation of Pollution in the Marine Environment

GIS Geographic Information System

GISS Goddard Institute for Space Studies

GIT Group Inclusive Tour

GIWIST gee I wish I'd said that

GJF gay Jewish female

GJM gay Jewish male

Gk. Greek

GKA government key access

GL guidelines

gl. gloss

.gl Greenland

Gla 4-carboxyglutamic acid

GLA gamma-linoleic acid

GLAMIS Grants and Loans Accounting and Management Information System

GLAS Goddard Laboratory of Atmospheric Sciences

GLC gas-liquid chromatography

GLCFS Great Lakes Coastal Forecasting System

gld. guilder

GLERL [National Oceanic and Atmospheric Administration] Great Lakes Environmental Research Laboratory

GLFC Great Lakes Fisheries Commission

GLFS Great Lakes Forecasting System

GLG goofy little grin

GLGH good luck and good hunting

GLIN Great Lakes Information Network

gliss. glissando

GLMA Gay and Lesbian Medical Association

G.L.O. General Land Office

GLOBE Global Learning and Observations to Benefit the Environment

G-LOC G[ravity]-induced loss of consciousness

Glos. Gloucestershire

GLOSS Global Sea Level Observing System

gloss. glossary

GLOW gross lift-off weight

Glp 5-oxoproline

gls glass

glu glucose

glutes gluteus muscles

GM general manager; General Motors; good morning (shortwave transmission); grand master

gm. gram

.gm Gambia

GMAC General Motors Acceptance Corporation

GMAN general maneuver

G-man [United States] Government man (FBI agent)

GMAT Graduate Management Admissions Test; Greenwich mean astronomical time

Gmc Germanic

GMC General Motors Corporation; giant molecular cloud

GMCC Geophysical Monitoring for Climatic Change

GMCSF granulocyte-macrophage colony-stimulating factor

GMDSS Global Maritime Distress and Safety System

GME graduate medical education

GMENAC Graduate Medical Education National Advisory Committee

GMIS Grants Management Information System

GMP guanosine monophosphate

GMS Gomori's methenamine-silver stain

gmt. gourmet

GMT Greenwich mean time

GMTA great minds think alike

GMU gyro mechanical unit

GMW gram-molecular weight

gn general; green; guinea

Gn Genesis

GN good night (shortwave transmission); ground network

.gn Guinea

GND ground (shortwave transmission)

gnd. ground

GNI gross national income

GNMA Government National Mortgage Association

GNP geriatric nurse practitioner; gross national product

GnRH gonadotropin-releasing hormone

GO general order

GOES Geostationary Orbiting Environmental Satellite

GOK God only knows

GOLDFISH Generation of Little Descriptions for Improving and Sustaining Health

GOLF global oscillations at low frequency

golf crs. golf course

GOMER get out of my emergency room

GOMOS Global Ozone Monitoring by Occultation of Stars

GOMS Geostationary Operational Meteorological Satellite

GOOS Global Ozone Observing System

GOP Grand Old Party (the Republican Party)

GO PRI send private mail (that is, don't send e-mail)

GOsC General Osteopathic Council

GOT glutamic-oxaloacetic transaminase

GOTFIA groaning on the floor in agony

Goth. Gothic

gour. gourmet

gov. government

Gov. governor

.gov government agency

govt. government

GOWON Gulf Offshore Weather Observing Network

GP general practitioner; general purpose

gp. group

.gp Guadeloupe

GPA grade point average

GPB glossopharyngeal breathing

GPC general purpose computer; gallons per capita

GPCC Global Precipitation Climatology Center

GPCD gallons per capita per day

GPCI geographic practice cost index

gpd gallons per day

gpf gallons per flush

GPF gay professional female; general protection fault

gph gallons per hour

GPI Gingival-Periodontal Index; Graphics Programming Interface

GPIB general purpose interface bus

GPIEM International Marine Environment Award

GPIN Group Practice Improvement Network

gpm gallons per minute

GPM gay professional male

GPO general post office; Government Printing Office

GPPM graphics pages per minute

GPR ground penetrating radar

GPRA Government Performance and Results Act

gps gallons per second

GPS global positioning satellite; global positioning system

GPSG generalized phrase structure grammar

GPT glutamic-pyruvic transaminase

GPWW group practice without walls

GQ general quarters; *Gentlemen's Quarterly*

.gq Equatorial Guinea

GR general relativity

gr. grade; grain; gram; gravity; great; gross; group

Gr. Greece; Greek

.gr Greece

GRA Geriatric Resource Assembly

grad graduate

grad. gradient

gram. grammar

GR & D grinning, running, and ducking

GRAS generally recognized as safe

GRASS Geographic Resources Analysis Support System

Gr. Brit. Great Britain

GRC Government Relations Committee

grdn garden

GRE Graduate Record Examination

GRE-A Graduate Record Exam-Analytical

GR8 great

GRE-Q Graduate Record Exam-Quantitative

GRE-V Graduate Record Exam-Verbal

GRH gonadotropin-releasing hormone

GRIB gridded binary (data format)

GRID Global Resource Information Database

GRM Geophysical Research Mission

grn green

grnd ground

gro. gross

GRP glass-reinforced plastic

grp. group

GRS great red spot

GRT gross register ton

grt. great

GRU *Russian* Glavnoe razvedyvatel'noe upravlenie (Chief Intelligence Directorate)

gr. wt. gross weight

GS general staff; ground speed

GSA General Services Administration; Genetics Society of America; Geological Society of America; Gerontological Society of America; Girl Scouts of America; Great Salinity Anomaly

GSC general staff corps

GSCR group-specific community rating

GSDB Genome Sequence Data Base

GSE geocentric solar ecliptic; ground support electronics; ground support equipment

gse down goose down

G-7 Group of 7 (Canada, France, Germany, Italy, Japan, United Kingdom, United States)

GSFC [National Aeronautics and Space Administration] Goddard Space Flight Center

GSH glutathione

GSL Guaranteed Student Loan

GSM global system for mobile communications

GSO general staff officer

GSR galvanic skin response

GSRIF Goldenhar Syndrome Research and Information Fund

GSSG glutathione disulfide

GST Greenwich sidereal time

GSTT generation-skipping transfer tax

G-suit gravity suit

GSUSA Girl Scouts of the United States of America

GSW gunshot wound

GT Grand Touring; Gran Turismo; gross ton

gt. gilt; great; *Latin* gutta (a drop, as of liquid medicine)

.gt Guatemala

GTAS Generic Testing and Analysis System

Gt. Brit. Great Britain

G.T.C. good 'til canceled

gtd. guaranteed

G-10 Group of 10 (Belgium, Canada, France, Germany, Italy, Japan, Netherlands, Sweden, Switzerland, United Kingdom, United States)

GTG getting (shortwave transmission)

GTN Global Trends Network

GTOS Global Terrestrial Observing System

GTP guanosine triphosphate

GTS gas turbine ship; Global Telecommunications Service

GTT glucose tolerance test

gtt. *Latin* guttae (drops, as of liquid medicine)

GU genitourinary; Guam

.gu Guam

Gua guanine

Guad. Guadelupe

guar. guarantee; guaranteed

Guat. Guatemala

GUD good (shortwave transmission)

GUI graphical user interface

Guin. Guinea

GUT grand unified theory

guttat. *Latin* guttatim (drop by drop)

Guy. Guyana

GV give (shortwave transmission)

g.v. gravimetric volume

GVH graft versus host

GVHR graft versus host reaction

GVW gross vehicular weight

GW gigawatt

.gw Guinea-Bissau

GWF gay White female

GWH gigawatt-hour

GWI Greenhouse Warming Index

GWM gay White male

GWP global warming potential; gross world product

GWTW *Gone with the Wind*

GWU George Washington University

GWVI Gulf War veteran's illnesses

Gy gray

.gy Guyana

gym gymnasium

gym. gymnastics

gyn. gynecology

gyro gyrocompass; gyroscope

GySgt gunnery sergeant

H

h height; hour; Planck's constant

H enthalpy; Hamiltonian; handicapped accessible; haze; henry; heroin; Hispanic; hit; humidity; hydrogen

h. harbor; hard; hardness; high; horn; hundred; husband

ha hectare; hour angle

HA headache; Hydrocephalus Association; hyperalimentation

Ha. Hawaii

h.a. *Latin* hoc anno (this year)

HAA hepatitis-associated antigen

Hab. Habakkuk

hab. corp. *Latin* habeas corpus (a writ to determine whether a prisoner ought to be released)

HACCP hazard analysis critical control point

HACU Hispanic Association of Colleges and Universities

HAF hCG associated factor

HAFOP Health Advocates for Older People

Hag. Haggai

HAIN Health Action Information Network

HAL hardware abstraction layer

HAMSTeRS Haemophilia: A Mutation, Structure, Test, and Resource Site

HAND have a nice day

H & E hemorrhage and exudate

H & P history and physical

HANP Homeopathic Academy of Naturopathic Physicians

HANS Health Action Network Society

HAO Health Action Overseas; high altitude observatory

HAPA Haitian-American Psychiatric Association

HAPFACT Hazardous Air Pollutant Health Effects Fact [Sheets]

HaPI Health and Psychosocial Instruments

HAPI high altitude plasma instrument

HARM high-speed antiradiation missile

HARP Health Administration Responsibility Project

HAV hepatitis A virus

Haw. Hawaiian

HazDat Hazardous [Substance Release/Health Effects] Database

HAZMAT hazardous material

hb halfback

Hb Habakkuk; hemoglobin

H.B. [United States] House [of Representatives] bill

HBcAb antibody to the hepatitis B core antigen

HBcAg hepatitis B core antigen

HbCO carboxyhemoglobin

HBCU historically Black colleges and universities

HBCU/MI historically Black colleges and universities and minority institutions

HBe hepatitis B e antigen

HBE His-bundle electrogram

HBeAb antibody to the hepatitis B e antigen

HBM Her (or His) Britannic Majesty

HBO Home Box Office

H-bomb hydrogen bomb

HBP high blood pressure; hit by pitch

HBR high bit rate

Hb S sickle cell hemoglobin

HBsAb antibody to the hepatitis B surface antigen

HBsAg hepatitis B surface antigen

HBT heterojunction bipolar transistor

HBV hepatitis B virus

HC hard cover [book]

h.c. *Latin* honoris causa (for the sake of honor)

H.C. Holy Communion; House of Commons

HCA heterocyclic amines

HCAA [National] CPA Health Care Advisors Association

HCBP hexachlorobiphenyl

HCC Hubcap Collectors Club; [25-]hydroxycholecalciferol

HCF Hepatitis C Foundation; high-cycle fatigue; Hispanic Christian female

h.c.f. highest common factor

HCFA Health Care Financing Administration

HCFC hydrochlorofluorocarbon

hCG human chorionic gonadotropin

HCH [National] Health Care for the Homeless [Council]

HCIS Health Care Information System

HCL high cost of living

HCLA Health Care Liability Alliance

HCM Hispanic Christian male

HCMA Hypertrophic Cardiomyopathy Association

HCN Health Communication Network

HCP health care practitioner; [Environmental Protection Agency] Habitat Conservation Plan

HCQIP Health Care Quality Improvement Program

HCRES [United States] House [of Representatives] concurrent resolution

HCRMS Health Care Resource Management Society

HCS host computer system; human chorionic somatomammotropic [hormone]; human chorionic somatomammotropin

HCSA Hospital Consultants and Specialists Association

Hct hematocrit

HCUP-3 Healthcare Cost and Utilization Project

HCV hepatitis C virus

HCVD hypertensive cardiovascular disease

Hcy homocysteine

HD hardwood; heating system damage; heart disease; heavy duty; high density; Hodgkin's disease

hd. head

h.d. *Latin* hora decubitus (at bedtime)

HDA hail detection algorithm; Holistic Dental Association

hdbk. handbook

HDCV human diploid cell vaccine; human diploid cell [rabies] vaccine

HDF Hereditary Disease Foundation; hierarchical data format

hdg. heading

HDGECP Human Dimensions of Global Environmental Change

hdkf. handkerchief

HDL high-density lipoprotein

H. Doc. House Document

HDPE high-density polyethylene

hdqrs. headquarters

HDR high dose rate

H. Rept. House [of Representatives] Report

H. Res. House [of Representatives] Resolution

HD-ROM high-density [CD-]ROM

HDS [Office of] Human Development Services

HDSA Huntington's Disease Society of America

HDTV high-definition television

HDV hepatitis D virus

hdwd. hardwood

hdwe. hardware

He helium

HE Her (or His) Excellency; high explosive; His (or Her) Eminence

HealthSTAR Health Services, Technology, Administration, and Research

HEAO high energy astronomy observatory

HEAPS Health Education and Promotion System

HEAST Health Effects Assessment Summary Tables

Heb. Hebrew; Hebrews

Hebr. Hebrew

HED High Energy Detector

HEDIS Health Plan Employer Data and Information Set

HEDM high energy density matter

HEENT head, eyes, ears, nose, and throat

HEL high energy laser; history of the English language

HELM Health and Environment Library Modules

helo helicopter

HELP Health Education Library for People

HEMPAS hereditary erythroblastic multinuclearity associated with positive acidified serum

HEMT high electron mobility transistor

Hep hepatitis

HEPA hamster egg penetration assay; high-efficiency particulate accumulator; high-efficiency particulate air; high-efficiency particulate arresting

HEPI higher education price index

HepNet Hepatitis [Information] Network

her. heraldry

HEV hepatitis E virus

HEW [Department of] Health, Education, and Welfare

hex. hexagon; hexagonal

Hf hafnium

HF high frequency; Hispanic female

hf. half

HFC hydrofluorocarbon

HFI Hepatitis Foundation International

HFMA Healthcare Financial Management Association

HFO heavy fuel oil

hfs hyperfine structure

hg hectogram; hemoglobin

Hg Haggai; mercury

HG High German; Holy Grail

HGA high gain antenna

hgb. hemoglobin

HGED high gain emissive display

HGF hyperglycemic-glycogenolytic factor

hGH human growth hormone

HGH human growth hormone

HGHF/SF hepatocyte growth factor/scatter factor

HGL hydraulic grade line

HGMD Human Gene Mutation Database

HGMIS Human Genome Management Information System

HGPRT hypoxanthine guanine phosphoribosyltransferase

hgt. height

hgwy. highway

HH Her (or His) Highness; His Holiness

HHA home health agency

HHANES Hispanic Health and Nutrition Examination Survey

hhd hogshead

HH.D. *Latin* Humanitatum Doctor (Doctor of Humanities)

HHE Health Hazard Evaluation [Program]

HHFA Housing and Home Finance Agency

HHMI Howard Hughes Medical Institute

HHNA Home Healthcare Nurses Association

HHOK ha-ha, only kidding

HHS [Department of] Health and Human Services

HHT Hereditary Hemorrhagic Telangiectasia [Foundation International]

HHTYAY happy holidays to you and yours

HHV human herpes virus

hi high

HI Hawaii; high intensity; humidity index

H.I. Hawaiian Islands

HIA Hearing Industries Association

HIAA Health Insurance Association of America

Hib Haemophilus influenza type b conjugate (meningitis)

HIB health insurance benefits

HIBCC Health Industry Business Communications Council

HIBR Huxley Institute for Biosocial Research

HIC Health Information Center; Health Insurance Commission

HICPAC Hospital Infection Control Practices Advisory Committee

HID host interface device

HIDA dimethyl iminodiacetic acid; Health Industry Distributors Association

hi-fi high fidelity

HIFO highest in, first out

HIH Her (or His) Imperial Highness

HII health information infrastructure

HIM Her (or His) Imperial Majesty

HIMA Health Industry Manufacturers Association

HiMaTE high mach turbine engine

HIMSS Healthcare Information and Management Systems Society

HIN Health Information Network

Hind. Hindi; Hindustani

HIO health insuring organization

HIP Help for Incontinent People (now **NAFC**: National Association for Continence)

HIPAA Health Insurance Portability and Accountability Act

HIPC health insurance purchasing cooperative

hippo hippopotamus

HIPRA high speed digital processor architecture

HIRA Health Industry Representatives Association

hi-res high resolution

HIRF high intensity radiation field

HIRIS high resolution imaging spectrometer

HIRS Heath Information Resources and Services; high resolution infrared sounder

HIRU Health Information Research Unit

HIS high resolution interferometer spectrometer

hist. historian; historical; history

HISTLINE History [of Medicine On]line

histol. histology

hi-tech high technology

HITH Hospital in the Home

Hitt. Hittite

HIV human immunodeficiency virus

HIVATIS HIV/AIDS Treatment Information Service

HIVD herniated intervertebral disc

HIV- HIV negative

HIV-1 human immunodeficiency virus-1

HIV+ HIV positive

HIV-2 human immunodeficiency virus-2

HJ *Latin* hic jacet (here lies)

HJR House [of Representatives] joint resolution

HK housekeeping

.hk Hong Kong

hl hectoliter

H.L. House of Lords

HLA human leukocyte antigen; human lymphocyte antigens

HLC heavy lift capability

hld. hold

HLI Human Life International

HLL high level [computer] language

HLMS high latitude monitoring station

HLPS hot liquid process simulator

hlqn. harlequin

HLS *Latin* hoc loco situs (laid in this place); holograph letter signed

HLV heavy lift vehicle

hm hectometer

HM Her (or His) Majesty; him (shortwave transmission); Hispanic male

hm. home

.hm Heard and McDonald Islands

HMA high memory area

HMAS Her (or His) Majesty's Australian Ship

HMBS Her (or His) Majesty's British Ship

HMC Her (or His) Majesty's Customs

HMCS Her (or His) Majesty's Canadian Ship

HMD [National Library of Medicine] History of Medicine Division

HMF Her (or His) Majesty's Forces

HMG human menopausal gonadotropin

HMG-CoA *-hydroxy-*-methylglutaryl-CoA

HMMWV high mobility multipurpose wheeled vehicle

HMO health maintenance organization

HMPAO hexametazimepropyleneamine oxime; hexamethylpropyleneamine oxime

HMRI Hospital Medical Records Institute

HMS Her (or His) Majesty's Ship

HMSO Her (or His) Majesty's Stationery Office

HN head nurse

.hn Honduras

HNA Hospice Nurses Association

HNGR hangar

HNL Honolulu airport code

hnRNA heterogeneous nuclear RNA

hny honey

Ho holmium; Hosea

ho. house

H.O. head office

HOC hydrophobic organic compound

HOCA high osmolar contrast agent

HOCM high osmolar contrast medium

HOH hard of hearing

HOI Health Outcomes Institute

hol holiday

hom. homily; homonym

HOMES Huron, Ontario, Michigan, Erie, Superior (mnemonic device for remembering the Great Lakes)

homie homeboy

hon honey

HON Health on the Net [Foundation]

hon. honor; honorable; honorary

Hon. Honduras; honorable; honorary

Hond. Honduras

hood neighborhood

HOP high oxygen pressure

HOPE Health Opportunity for People Everywhere

hor. horizontal

hor. decub. *Latin* hora decubitus (at bedtime)

horol. horology

horr. horticulture

hor. som. *Latin* hora somni (at the hour of sleep—that is, at bedtime)

hort. horticultural; horticulture

Hos. Hosea

hosp. hospital

HOST Healthcare Open Systems and Trials

HOTO health of the oceans

HOV high-occupancy vehicle

HOW home owners warranty

hp horsepower

HP high pressure; Hewlett-Packard [Company]

HPA high power amplifier

HPBW half-power band width

HPC high pressure compressor

HPD hourly precipitation data

HPE holoprosencephaly

HPF highest possible frequency; Hispanic professional female

HPFS high performance file system

hPG human pituitary gonadotrophin

HPGL Hewlett-Packard Graphics Language

HPI history of present illness

HPIB Hewlett-Packard Interface Bus

HPL human placental lactogen

HPLC high pressure liquid chromatography; high performance liquid chromatography

HPM high power microwave; Hispanic professional male

HP-MSOGS high performance-molecular sieve oxygen generation system

HPO healthcare purchasing organization; hospital provider organization

HPPA Hospital Purchaser-Provider Agreement

HPPC health plan purchasing cooperatives

HPS Hanta virus Pulmonary Syndrome; Heath Physics Society; high-pressure steam; high-protein supplement

HPSA health professional shortage area

HPSG head-driven phrase structure grammar

HPSLT high power semiconductor laser technology

HPT high pressure turbine; home pregnancy test

HPV human papillomavirus; human-powered vehicle

H. pylori Helicobacter pylori

HQ headquarters

HR heart rate; home run; human relations; human resources

hr. hour

Hr. Herr

.hr Croatia

h.r. home run

H.R. home rule; House of Representatives

HRA Health Resources Administration

h.r.a. health risk assessment

HRCT high resolution computed tomography

HRD human resources director

H.R.E. Holy Roman Empire

H. Rept. House Report

H. Res. House Resolution

HREX Human Radiation Experiments [Information Management System]

HRG Health Research Group

HRH Her (or His) Royal Highness

HRIR high resolution infrared radiometer

hrly. hourly

HRPT high resolution picture transmission

HRQL health-related quality of life

HRS [Environmental Protection Agency] Hazardous Ranking System; high resolution spectrometer; High Resolution; Human Resources Society

hrs. hours

HRSA [United States] Health Resources and Services Administration

HRt hard-return

HRT hormone replacement therapy

hrzn horizon

Hs hassium

HS high school; his (shortwave transmission)

h.s. *Latin* hora somni (at the hour of sleep—that is, at bedtime)

HSA health service agreement

HSAL high speed algebraic logic

HSB hue, saturation, and brightness

HSCT high speed civil transport

HSDB Hazardous Substances Data Bank

hse. house

HSG hysterosalpingogram

HSGT high speed ground transit

HSH Her (or His) Serene Highness

HSI Health Services International; Hispanic-serving institution; hyperspectral imaging

HSIK how should I know

HSIO high speed input/output

HSLC Health Sciences Libraries Consortium

HSMHA Health Services and Mental Health Administration

hsp heat shock proteins

HSPC Health and Science Policy Committee

HSQB Health Standard and Quality Bureau

HSRPROJ Health Services Research Projects [in Progress]

HSS Hospital Shared Services

HSSTD Historical Sea Surface Temperature Dataset

HST Harry S. Truman; Hawaii-Aleutian Standard Time; Hubble Space Telescope; hypersonic transport

HST&M History of Science, Technology, and Medicine

HSTAR Health Services/Technology Assessment Research

HSTAT Health Services/Technology Assessment Texts

HSV herpes simplex virus

ht height

Ht hypertension

HT halftime; halftone; high tension; high tide

.ht Haiti

h.t. *Latin* hoc titulo (this title, under this title)

HTA health technology assessment

HTH hope this helps

HTHL horizontal takeoff, horizontal landing

HTLV human T-cell lymphotropic virus

HTLV-I T-cell lymphotrophic virus type I; human lymphotropic virus, type 1

HTLV-II T-cell lymphotrophic virus type II; human lymphotropic virus, type 2

HTLV-III human T-cell lymphotropic virus type III

HTM hypertext markup

HTML Hypertext Markup Language

HTN hypertension

hTRT human telomerase reverse transcriptase

Hts. heights

http Hypertext Transfer Protocol

HTVL horizontal takeoff; vertical landing

HTWS Hawaii Tsunami Warning System

hU dihydrouridine

.hu Hungary

HUAC House Un-American Activities Committee

HUD [Department of] Housing and Urban Development

HUGO Human Genome Organization

humies humanists

Hung. Hungarian; Hungary

HUS hemolytic uremic syndrome

HV half-value; have (shortwave transmission); high voltage

h.v. *Latin* hoc verbo (this word)

H.V. high velocity; high voltage

HVA homovanillic acid

HVAC heating, ventilating, and air-conditioning

HVD hypertensive vascular disease

HVL half-value layer

HVPS high voltage power supply

hvy. heavy

HW hardware; hardwood; high water; hot water; how (shortwave transmission)

H/W hot water

HWC Hurricane Warning Center

HWCI hardware configuration item

HWD height x width x depth

HWM high-water mark

HWO Hurricane Warning Office (National Weather Service)

HWP height/weight [are] proportional

hwy. highway

hx [medical] history

hyd. hydraulics; hydrostatics

hydro. hydroelectric

Hyp hypoxanthine; hydroxyproline

hyp. hypotenuse; hypothesis; hypothetical

hyperbol. hyperbolically

hyph. hyphenated

hypo hypodermic [injection]; sodium hyposulfite; sodium thiosulfate

hypoth. hypothesis

HyTech hypersonic technology

Hz hertz

I

i imaginary unit

I current; ice; incomplete; institute; intelligence; interstate; iodine; isospin; 1

i. interest; intransitive

I. island; isle

IA Iowa

Ia. Iowa

i.a. *Latin* in absentia (in absense)

IAA indoleacetic acid

IAACN International and American Associations of Clinical Nutritionists

IAAF International Amateur Athletic Federation

IAB Internet Architecture Board

IABO International Association of Biological Oceanography

IABP International Arctic Buoy Program

IAC in any case

IACI International Association for Craniofacial Identification

IACP International Academy of Compounding Pharmacists

IACPO Inter-American Council of Psychiatric Organizations

IACS International Association of Chemical Societies

IAD Washington Dulles International airport code

IADB Inter-American Defense Board; Inter-American Development Bank

IADR International and American Associations for Dental Research

IAE in any event

IAEA International Atomic Energy Agency

IAF Inter-American Foundation

IAFP International Association for Financial Planning

IAG International Association of Geodesy

IAGA International Association of Geomagnetism and Aeronomy

IAGD Illinois Academy of General Dentistry

IAGLR International Association for Great Lakes Research

IAHE International Alliance of Healthcare Educators

IAHS International Association of Hydrological Sciences

IAI Inter-American Institute [for Global Change Research]

IAIMS Integrated Advanced Information Management System

IALMH International Academy of Law and Mental Health

IAM International Association of Machinists

IAMA International Arts Medicine Association

IAMAP International Association of Meteorology and Atmospheric Physics

IAMAW International Association of Machinists and Aerospace Workers

IAMSLIC International Association of Aquatic and Marine Science Libraries and Information Centers

IANAL I am not a lawyer

IANC International Anatomical Nomenclature Committee

I & D incision and drainage

I & O intake and output

I & T integration and test

IAP international airport; International Association of Pancreatology

IAPA International Association of Physicians in Audiology

IAPAC International Association of Physicians in AIDS Care

IAPM International Association of Medical Prosthesis Manufacturers

IAPSO International Association for the Physical Sciences of the Ocean

IARC International Agency for Research on Cancer

IARCC Interagency Arctic Research Coordination Committee

IARCH Institute of Action Research for Community Health

IARU International Amateur Radio Union

IAS indicated air speed

IASC Inter-American Society for Chemotherapy

IASD interatrial septal defect

IASIA Institute for Advanced Studies in Immunology and Aging

IASO International Association for the Study of Obesity

IASOSFRGDOH International Amalgamated Society of Searchers for Rare, Greasy, Dirty Old Hubcaps

IASP International Association for Suicide Prevention; International Association for the Study of Pain

IASPEI International Association of Seismology and Physics of the Earth's Interior

IASSMD International Association for the Scientific Study of Mental Deficiency

IATA International Air Transport Association

IATTC Inter-American Tropical Tuna Commission

IAU International Association of Universities; International Astronomical Union

IAVCEI International Association of Volcanology and Chemistry of the Earth's Interior

IAVH International Association of Veterinary Homeopathy

IB In bond; incendiary bomb

ib. *Latin* ibidem (in the same place)

IBA International Bar Association

I-bahn infobahn (that is, information superhighway)

I band isotropic band

IBC International Bathymetric Chart; iron-binding capacity

IBD inflammatory bowel disease

IBEC International Bank for Economic Cooperation

IBF International Boxing Federation

IBG interblock gap

ibid. *Latin* ibidem (in the same place)

IBIS Interactive BodyMind Information System

IBM International Business Machines [Corporation]

IBMTR International Bone Marrow Transplant Registry

IBNR incurred but not reported

I-Bond inflation-indexed [United States government savings] bond

IBR infectious bovine rhinotracheitis

IBRD International Bank for Reconstruction and Development

IBS Irritable Bowel Syndrome

IBT immunobead binding test

IBV infectious bronchitis virus

IBY International Biological Year

IC immediate constituent; integrated circuit; I see

ICA International Cancer Alliance; International Chiropractors Association; International Cooperative Alliance; Interstitial Cystitis Association

ICAAC Interscience Conference on Antimicrobial Agents and Chemotherapy

ICACGP International Commission on Atmospheric Chemistry and Global Pollution

ICAEL Intersocietal Commission for the Accreditation of Echocardiography Laboratories

ICAF Industrial College of the Armed Forces

ICAMI International Committee Against Mental Illness

ICAM-1 intercellular adhesion molecule-1

ICAN International Children's Anophthalmia Network

ICAO International Civil Aeronautics Organization

ICARE International Cancer Alliance for Research and Education

ICAS integrated circuit applications specifications

ICAVL Intersocietal Commission for the Accreditation of Vascular Laboratories

ICBM intercontinental ballistic missile

ICBW I could be wrong

ICC Indian Claims Commission; International Chamber of Commerce; Interstate Commerce Commission

ICCH International Commodities Clearing House

ICCHHH International Club for Collectors of Hatpins and Hatpin Holders

ICCS International Classification of Clinical Services

ICD interface control document; International Classification of Diseases

ICDA *International Classification of Diseases*, Adapted [for Use in the United States]

ICDO International Classification of Diseases for Oncology

ICE Institute for Christian Economics; internal-combustion engine; International Cultural Exchange

Ice. Iceland; Icelandic

ICEA International Childbirth Education Association

ICEDOC International Committee for Establishment and Development of Oncology Centers

Icel. Iceland; Icelandic

ICEM Intergovernmental Committee for European Migration; International Conference on Emergency Medicine

ICES International Council for the Exploration of the Seas

ICF intracellular fluid

ICFTU International Confederation of Free Trade Unions

ICGA International Carnival Glass Association

ICHNA International Child Health Nursing Alliance

ICHP Institute for Child Health Policy

ICHPPC International Classification of Health Problems in Primary Care

ICHSRI International Clearinghouse of Health System Reform Initiatives

ichth. ichthyology

ichthyol. ichthyology

ICI intracervical insemination

ICIC International Cancer Information Center

ICIDH International Classification of Impairments, Disabilities, and Handicaps

ICIDH-2 International Classification of Impairments, Activities, and Participation

ICIRN International Council on Information Resources for Nursing

ICJ International Court of Justice

ICLARM International Center for Living Aquatic Resources Management

ICLEI International Council for Local Environmental Initiatives

ICLRN Interagency Council on Library Resources for Nursing

ICM Intergovernmental Committee for Migration

ICMJE International Committee of Medical Journal Editors

ICML International Congress on Medical Librarianship

ICMP Internet Control Message Protocol

ICMS International Center for Medical Specialties

ICNAF International Convention of the Northwest Atlantic Fisheries

ICNIRP International Commission on Non-Ionizing Radiation Protection

ICO International Coffee Organization

I/CO installation and check-out

ICOCBW I could, of course, be wrong

ICOI International Congress of Oral Implantologists

ICP intracranial pressure

ICPA International Chiropractic Pediatric Association

ICPC International Classification of Primary Care

ICPD International Conference on Population and Development

ICPO International Criminal Police Organization

ICQ I seek you

ICRC International Committee of the Red Cross

ICRDB International Cancer Research Databank Branch

ICRIN Injury Control Resource Information Network

ICRM International Red Cross and Red Crescent Movement

ICRP International Commission on Radiological Protection

ICRSDT International Committee on Remote Sensing and Data Transmission

ICRU International Commission on Radiation Units [and Measurements]

ICRW International Center for Research on Women

ICS intercostal space; International Cloning Society

ICSC International Chemical Safety Cards

ICSEAF International Commission for the Southeast Atlantic Fisheries

ICSEM International Commission for the Scientific Exploration of the Mediterranean Sea

ICSH interstitial cell-stimulating hormone

ICSI International Commission on Snow and Ice; intracytoplasmic sperm injection

ICSPRO [United Nations] Inter-Secretariat Committee on Scientific Programs Relating to Oceanography

ICSU International Council of Scientific Unions

ICSW International Council on Social Welfare

ICT internal cold target

ICTP International Center for Theoretical Physics

I-ctus. *Latin* jurisconsultus (one learned in the law)

ICU intensive care unit

ICV interdecadal climate variability

ICW in connection with (shortwave transmission); Intracoastal Waterway

ICZM integrated coastal zone management

ID Idaho; identification; insect damage; Intelligence Department

id. *Latin* idem (the same)

Id. Idaho

.id Indonesia

i.d. inner diameter; inside diameter; internal diameter

I.D. infecting dose

IDA International Development Association; Institute for Defense Analyses

Ida. Idaho

IDAA International Diabetic Athletes Association

IDB Inter-American Development Bank; intermediary dealer broker

IDC International Data Company; International Diabetes Center

IDCA [United States] International Development Cooperation Agency

IDD interface design document

IDDD international direct distance dialing

IDDM insulin-dependent diabetes mellitus

IDE integrated disk electronics; integrated drive electronics; interface design enhancement

IDEA Individuals with Disabilities Education Act

IDEAS Information on Disability–Equipment Access Service

IDF Immune Deficiency Foundation; International Diabetes Federation

IDG International Data Group

IDHS Intelligence Data Handling System

IDIC infinite diversity in infinite combinations

IDIDAS Interactive Digital Image Display and Analysis System

IDIQ indefinite delivery, indefinite quantity

IDL interactive data language; intermediate density lipoprotein

IDP integrated data processing; international driving permit

IDR incremental design review

IDS integrated delivery system; Internet Dermatology Society

IDSA Infectious Disease Society of America

IDU injection drug user

IE Indo-European

I E inspiratory expiratory

.ie Ireland

I.E. industrial engineer; industrial engineering

i.e. *Latin* id est (that is)

IEA International Energy Agency

IEC International Electrotechnical Commission

IEEE Institute of Electrical and Electronics Engineers

IEF International Eye Foundation

IEH Institute for Environment and Health

IEP initial enrollment period; isoelectric point

IEPA International Early Psychosis Association

IEPC Individual Education Planning Committee; Interagency Emergency Planning Commission

IERC International Enuresis Research Center

IESS Integrated Electromagnetic System Simulator

IETF Internet Engineering Task Force

IETM Interactive Electronic Technical Manual

IEVS Income Eligibility Verification Systems

IF infertility; intracytoplasmic sperm injection; interferon; intermediate frequency

I/F interface

IFA International Federation on Aging

IFAD International Fund for Agricultural Development

IFAP Industrial Foundation for Accident Prevention

I.F.B. invitation for bids

IFBD International Foundation for Bowel Dysfunction (now **IFFGD**: International Founda-

tion for Functional Gastrointestinal Disorders)

IFC International Finance Corporation

IFCC International Federation of Clinical Chemistry

IFCTU International Federation of Christian Trade Unions

IFEH International Federation of Environmental Health

iff if and only if

IFF identification, friend or foe

IFFGD International Foundation for Functional Gastrointestinal Disorders

IFFS International Federation of Fertility Societies

IFGE International Federation of Gynecologic Endoscopists

IFGR International Foundation for Genetic Research

IFIAS International Federation of Institutes for Advanced Study

IFIC International Food Information Council

IFIP International Federation for Information Processing

IFJ International Federation of Journalists

IFMP International Federation for Medical Psychotherapy

IFMSA International Federation of Medical Students' Associations

IFMSS International Federation of Multiple Sclerosis Societies

IFN interferon

IFN-α interferon alpha

IFN-β interferon beta

IFN-γ interferon gamma

IFO identified flying object

IFOV instantaneous field of view

IFPOS International Federation of Pediatric Orthopaedic Societies

IFPRI International Food Policy Research Institute

IFPS International Federation of Psychoanalytic Societies

IFR instrument flight rules

IFRCS International Federation of Red Cross and Red Crescent Societies

IFRRO International Federation of Reproduction Rights Organizations

IFS Information Fatigue Syndrome; International Foundation for Science

IFST Institute of Food Science and Technology

IFUFOCS Institute for UFO Contactee Studies

Ig immunoglobulin

IG inspector general

IgA immunoglobulin A

IGA integrated graphics array

IGADD Inter-Governmental Authority on Drought and Development

IGBP International Geosphere-Biosphere Program

IGBT Insulated Gate Bipolar Transistor

IGC International Geological Congress

IgD immunoglobulin D

IGDOD Inspector General, Department of Defense

IgE immunoglobulin E

IGF insulin-like growth factor

IgG immunoglobulin G

IgM immunoglobulin M

IGM intergalactic medium

ign. ignition

IGOM integrated global ocean monitoring

IGOSS Integrated Global Ocean Services System

IGP igneous and geothermal processes

IGS inner Gulf shelf

IGY International Geophysical Year

IH infectious hepatitis

IHA Indian Housing Authority; Integrated Healthcare Association

IHAS ideopathic hypertrophic aortic stenosis

IHC Internet Healthcare Coalition

IHCF Inherited High Cholesterol Foundation; International Healthy Cities Foundation

IHDS Integrated Health Delivery System

IHEA International Health Economics Association

IHGP International Human Genome Project

IHGT Institute for Human Gene Therapy

IHHRR International Health Human Resources Registry

IHI Index to Health Information; Institute for Healthcare Improvement

IHM [National Library of Medicine] Images from the History of Medicine

IHO integrated healthcare organization

IHOC International Healthcare Opportunities Clearinghouse

IHOP International House of Pancakes

ihp indicated horsepower

IHPO International Health Program Office

IHPP Intergovernmental Health Policy Project

IHPR Institute of Health Promotion Research

IHPS Integrated Healthcare Practice Society

IHR Institute of Historical Review; Internet Health Resources

IHS Indian Health Service; Institute of Health Sciences; Jesus

IHW Internet Health Watch

II illegal immigrants

IIA Institute of Internal Auditors

IIASA International Institute for Applied Systems Analysis

IIB International Investment Bank

IIE Institute of Industrial Engineers

IIFS International Institute of Forensic Science

III Insurance Information Institute

IIP International Institute of Parasitology

IIR Imaging Infrared

IIRC if I recall correctly

IIRCAID if I recall correctly and I do

IIRV improved interrange vector

IITA Information Infrastructure Technology Applications

IITF Information Infrastructure Task Force

IJP inhibitory junction potential

IL Illinois; interlanguage (that is, a not fully acquired second or foreign language)

.il Israel

ILA International Longshoremen's Association

ILAR Institute for Laboratory Animal Research

ILBRT endoluminal brachytherapy

ILC International Law Commission

ILGWU International Ladies' Garment Workers' Union

ill. illustrated; illustration

Ill. Illinois

illus. illustrated; illustrated by; illustration; illustrator

ILM Industrial Light and Magic

ILO International Labor Organization

IL-1 interleukin-1

IL-1ra interleukin 1 receptor antagonist

ILS instrument landing system

IL-2 interleukin-2
ILYA incompletely launched young adult
IM immediately (shortwave transmission); immunoassay; intermediate modeling; intramuscular
I.M. intramural
IMA International Monovision Association
IMAGE Integrated Molecular Analysis of Genomes and their Expression
IMAO in my arrogant opinion
IMAP image map
IMAP4 Internet Messaging Access Protocol [version] 4
IMC instrument meteorological conditions
IMCDO in my conceited dogmatic opinion.
IMCO in my considered opinion; Intergovernmental Maritime Consultative
IMD intermodulation distortion
IME in my experience
IMF International Monetary Fund
IMGT immunogenetics [database]
IMHO in my honest opinion; in my humble opinion
IMI International Market Index
IMIA International Medical Informatics Association
imit. imitation; imitative; imitatively
IML Ring International Medical Libraries Ring
IMM interactive multimedia

immed. immediately
IMMI Index of Medieval Medical Images in North America
immun. immunity; immunization
immunol. immunology
IMNERHO in my never even remotely humble opinion
IMNSHO in my not so humble opinion
IMO in my opinion; International Maritime Organization; International Meteor Organization
imp impression
IMP instrument mounting platform
imp. imperative; imperfect; imperial; import; imported; importer; imprimatur
imper. imperative; imperatively
imperf. imperfect; imperforate
impers. impersonal; impersonally
improv improvisation
IMS Information Management Society; information management system; Institute of Museum Services
IMSL International Mathematics and Statistics Library
IMT interactive media training
IMU inertial measurement unit
IMV in my view; intermittent mandatory ventilation
in inch
In indium
IN Indiana
.in India

inc. including; income; incomplete; increase

Inc. Incorporated

INCB International Narcotics Control Board

incho. inchoative

INCIID International Council on Infertility Information Dissemination

incl. including; inclusive

incog. incognita; incognito

incr. increase

IND investigational new drug

ind. independence; independent; index; indigo; industrial; industry

in d. *Latin* in dies (daily)

Ind. India; Indian; Indiana; Indies

Ind.E. industrial engineer; industrial engineering

indef. indefinite; indefinitely

indic. indicative; indicator

indie independent

indiv. individual

individ. individual

indn. indication

Indon. Indonesia; Indonesian

indus. industrial; industry

INF intermediate-range nuclear forces

inf. infantry; inferior; infinitive; infinity; information; *Latin* infra (below)

infin. infinitive

INFJ Introversion iNtuition Feeling Judging (Myers-Briggs [personality] Type Indicator)

infl. inflected; influenced

info information

INFO International Fortean Organization

INFOCLIMA World Climate Data Information Referral Service

info-dense informationally dense

infomercial information commercial

INFOSEC Information Security

INFP Introversion iNtuition Feeling Perception (Myers-Briggs [personality] Type Indicator)

infra dig *Latin* infra dignitatem (beneath [one's] dignity)

ing. inguinal

INH isonicotinic acid hydrazide

INI International Nursing Index

INIA International Institute on Aging

INIT initialization

init. initial

Inmarsat International Maritime Satellite Organization

INO Institute for Naval Oceanography

inorg. inorganic

INP International News Photo

INPFC International North Pacific Fisheries Commission

INPHO Information Network for Public Health Officials

INPO in no particular order

in pr. *Latin* in principio (in the beginning)

inq. inquiry

INQUA International Union for Quaternary Research

INR International Normalized Ratio

I.N.R.I. *Latin* Iesus Nazarenus Rex Iudaeorum (Jesus of Nazareth, King of the Jews)

Ins insert key

INS Immigration and Naturalization Service; inertial navigation system; International News Service

ins. inches; inspector; insulation; insurance

INSAT Indian Geostationary Satellite

INSCOM [United States Army] Intelligence and Security Command

insol. insoluble

insp. inspected; inspector

inst. current month; instant; institute; institution; institutional

instr. instruction; instructor; instrument; instrumental

int. intelligence; intercept; interest; interim; interior; interjection; intermediate; internal; international; interval; interview; intransitive

int. cib. *Latin* inter cibos (between meals)

intel intelligent

INTELSAT International Telecommunications Satellite

intens. intensive

inter. interjection; intermediate

interj. interjection

InterNIC Internet Network Information Center

interp. interpreter

INTERPOL International Criminal Police Organization

interrog. interrogative; interrogatively

INTJ Introversion iNtuition Thinking Judging (Myers-Briggs [personality] Type Indicator)

intl. international

intnl international

INTP Introversion iNtuition Thinking Perception (Myers-Briggs [personality] Type Indicator)

intr interested; interested in

intr. intransitive

INTRAH International Training in Health

intrans. intransitive; intransitively

intro introduction

intro. introduction; introductory

introd. introduction

INV in vitro fertilization

inv. invented; invention; inventor; investment; invoice

INVG investigate (shortwave transmission)

IO Intraocular

.io British Indian Ocean Territory

I/O input/output

IOA International Ostomy Association

IOC International Olympic Committee

IOF International Oceanographic Foundation

IOL intraocular lens

IOLTA interest on lawyers' trust accounts

IOM Index and Options Market; International Organization for Migration

IOMP International Organization for Medical Physics

ION Institute of Nutrition

Ion. Ionic

IOOF Independent Order of Odd Fellows

IOP input output processor; intraocular pressure

IOR immature oocyte retrieval

IORT intraoperative ratio

IOSG International Oncology Study Group

IOSH Institution of Occupational Safety and Health

IOU a note of debt (from "I owe you")

IOVS *Investigative Ophthalmology and Visual Science*

IOW in other words

IP image processor; intellectual property; Internet Protocol

i.p. isoelectric point

IPA International Phonetic Alphabet; International Phonetic Association; isopropyl alcohol

IPAA International Patient Advocacy Association

IPCC [United Nations] Intergovernmental Panel on Climate Change

IPCS International Program on Chemical Safety

IPD information processing division

IPEH International Physicians for Equitable Healthcare

IPEMB Institution of Physics and Engineering in Medicine and Biology

IPF idiopathic pulmonary fibrosis; interstitial pulmonary fibrosis

IPFSC International Pacific Salmon Fisheries Commission

IPHC International Pacific Halibut Commission

IPHIR interplanetary helioseismology with irradiance observations

I-phone Internet telephony

ipm inches per minute

IPM integrated pest management; interprogram messaging

IPN integrated provider network

IPng Internet Protocol, next generation

IPO initial public offering

IPOD International Program of Ocean Drilling

IPOS International Psycho-Oncology Society

IPPB intermittent positive pressure breathing

IPPD integrated product and process development

IPPF International Planned Parenthood Federation

IPPNW International Physicians for the Prevention of Nuclear War

IPPV intermittent positive pressure ventilation

IPRAF International Plastic, Reconstructive, and Aesthetic Foundation

IPRAS International Confederation for Plastic, Reconstructive, and Aesthetic Surgery

iPrSGal isopropylthiogalactoside

ips inches per second

IPS inertial pointing system; interplanetary scintillation

IPSA Institute for Psychological Study of the Arts

IPSP inhibitory postsynaptic potential

IPTG isopropylthiogalactoside

IP₃ inositol 1,4,5-trisphosphate

IPTS International Practical Temperature Scale

IPU Integrated Power Unit

IPV injectable poliovirus vaccine

IPWSO International Prader-Willi Syndrome Organization

IPX Internet packet exchange

IPX/SPX Internet packet exchange/sequenced packet exchange

IQ intelligence quotient; intelligent equalizer

.iq Iraq

i.q. *Latin* idem quod (the same as)

Ir iridium

IR information retrieval; infrared

Ir. Irish

.ir Iran

IRA individual retirement account; Irish Republican Army

IRAC infrared array camera

IRAN individual retirement annuity

IR&D independent research and development

IRB Institutional Review Board

IRBM intermediate-range ballistic missile

IRC Internet Relay Chat

I.R.C. Internal Revenue Code

IRCM Infrared Countermeasures

IRD interface requirements document; international radiation detector

I.R.D. income in respect of decedent

IrDA infrared data association

Ire. Ireland

IRECA International Rescue and Emergency Care Association

IRG interrecord gap

IRH Institute for Reproductive Health

IRI immunoreactive insulin; ionospheric research instrument

IRICP International Research Institute for Climate Prediction

irid. iridescent

IRIS Integrated Risk Information System

IRL in real life

IRM Information Resources Management

IRMC Information Resources Management College

IRMFI I reply merely for information

IRMO Information Resources Management Office

IRMS Information Resources Management Service

IRMVS Institute for Reparative Medicine and Vascular Surgery

IRO International Refugee Organization

IROC International Rose O'Neill Club

iron. ironic; ironical; ironically

IRP Integrated Resource Planning

IRPA International Radiation Protection Association; International Retinitis Pigmentosa Association

IRPTC International Register of Potentially Toxic Chemicals

IRR interrange ratio

irreg. irregular; irregularly

IRQ interrupt request

I.R.Q. open data line (from "interrupt request")

IRS infrared spectrograph; Internal Revenue Service

IRSA International Rett Syndrome Association

IRSC Internet Resources for Special Children

IRST infrared search and track

IRU inertial reference unit

IRV inspiratory reserve volume; interrange vector

Is Isaiah

Is. island; isle; Israel

IS information services

.is Iceland

I/S information systems

ISA Industry Standard Architecture; International Standards Association

Isa. Isaiah

ISAC International Society for Analytical Cytology

ISACCD International Society for Adult Congenital Cardiac Disease

ISAD International Society of Abortion Doctors

ISAKOS International Society of Arthroscopy, Knee Surgery, and Orthopaedic Sports Medicine

ISAM indexed sequential access method

ISAP Internet Self-Assessment in Pharmacology

ISAS Institute of Space and Astronautical Science

ISBN International Standard Book Number

ISC International Seismological Center; International Society of Chemotherapy

ISCAIC International Symposium on Computing in Anesthesia and Intensive Care

ISCAIP International Society for Child and Adolescent Injury Prevention

ISCB International Society for Clinical Biostatistics

ISCD International Society for Computerized Dentistry

ISD International Society of Differentiation

ISDA International Swaps and Derivatives Association

ISDN integrated services digital network

ISEA International Society of Exposure Analysis

ISEE International Society for Environmental Epidemiology; International Society for the Enhancement of Eyesight

ISFJ Introversion Sensing Feeling Judging (Myers-Briggs [personality] Type Indicator)

ISFP Introversion Sensing Feeling Perception (Myers-Briggs [personality] Type Indicator)

ISH isolated systolic hypertension

ISHBR International Society of Hepato-Biliary Radiology

ISHN Industrial Safety and Hygiene News

ISHTAR Inner Shelf Transfer and Recycling

ISI Instrument/Spacecraft Interface

ISICR International Society for Interferon and Cytokine Research

ISKO International Society for Knowledge Organization

isl. island

ISLCBS International Seal Label and Cigar Band Society

ISM interstellar medium

ISMA International Securities Market Association

ISMC International Symposium on Medicinal Chemistry

ISMP Institute for Safe Medication Practices

ISN integrated service network; International Society of Nephrology

ISNA Intersex Society of North America

ISNCC International Society of Nurses in Cancer Care

ISNG International Society of Nurses in Genetics

ISO in search of; International Organization for Standardization (technically not an initialism—term is based on the prefix *iso-*, from the Greek *isos*, meaning 'equal'); intraseasonal atmospheric oscillation

ISOM International Society for Orthomolecular Medicine

ISONG International Society of Nurses in Genetics

ISOO International Society of Online Ophthalmologists

ISP Internet service provider

ISPD International Society for Peritoneal Dyalisis

ISPE International Society for Pharmacoepidemiology

ISPO International Society for Preventive Oncology

ISQua International Society for Quality [in Health Care]

ISR interrupt service routine

Isr. Israel; Israeli

ISRS International Society of Refractive Surgery

iss. issue

ISS integrated sensor system; International Skeletal Society

ISSC International Social Science Council

ISSN International Standard Serial Number

ISSSEEM International Society for the Study of Subtle Energies and Energy Medicine

IST insulin shock therapy

ISTAHC International Society of Technology Assessment in Health Care

isth. isthmus

ISTJ Introversion Sensing Thinking Judging (Myers-Briggs [personality] Type Indicator)

ISTM International Society of Travel Medicine

ISTP Index to Scientific and Technical Proceedings; Introversion Sensing Thinking Perception (Myers-Briggs [personality] Type Indicator)

ISTR I seem to recall

ISTSS International Society for Traumatic Stress Studies

ISV International Scientific Vocabulary

ISWYM I see what you mean

ISY International Space Year

IT information technology

It. Italian; Italy

.it Italy

ITA initial teaching alphabet; International Trade Administration

ITAA International Transactional Analysis Association

ital. italic; italicize; italics

Ital. Italian; Italic

ITAR International Traffic in Arms Regulations

ITC International Touring Car; International Trade Commission

ITCZ Intertropical Convergence Zone

ITER International Toxicity Estimates for Risk

ITI intratubal insemination

ITIC International Tsunami Information Center

itin. itinerary

ITM in the money

ITO International Trade Organization

ITOS Improved TIROS Operational Satellite

ITP idiopathic thrombocytopenic purpura; inosine 5c-triphosphate; Interactive Testing in Psychiatry

ITPR infrared temperature profile radiometer

ITQ individual transferable quota

ITS intelligent tutoring system

ITSFWI if the shoe fits, wear it

ITT International Telephone and Telegraph

ITU International Telecommunication Union

ITU-T International Telecommunications Union–Telecommunication

ITV instructional television

ITWS Integrated Terminal Weather System

IU international unit

IUB International Union of Biochemistry

IUBMB International Union of Biochemistry and Molecular Biology

IUBS International Union of Biological Sciences

IUCD intrauterine contraceptive device

IUCN International Union for Conservation of Nature [and Natural Resources]

I/UCRC Industry/University Cooperative Research Center

IUD intrauterine device

IUE International Ultraviolet Explorer

IUGG International Union of Geodesy and Geophysics

IUGR intrauterine growth retardation

IUGS International Union of Geological Sciences

IUI intrauterine insemination

IUP intrauterine pregnancy

IUPAC International Union of Pure and Applied Chemistry

IUPHAR International Union of Pharmacology

IUSS [United States Navy] Integrated Underwater Surveillance System

IV intravenous; intravenously

I-V intraventricular

IVAS International Veterinary Acupuncture Society

IVB intraventricular block

IVC inferior vena cava; intravaginal culture

IVD intervertebral disc

IVF in vitro fertilization

IVF-ET in vitro fertilization and in vivo transfer of the embryo

IVHS Intelligent Vehicle Highway System

IVIg intravenous immunoglobulin

IVP intravenous pyelography; intravenous pyelogram

IVU intravenous urogram

IW index word; isotopic weight

i.w. inside width

I-way information superhighway (that is, the Internet)

IWBNI it would be nice if

IWC International Whaling Commission

IWHC International Women's Health Coalition

IWRA International Water Resources Association

IWS instrument work station

IWT internal warm target

IWW Industrial Workers of the World

IX it is (shortwave transmission)

IXC interexchange carrier

IYFEG insert your favorite ethnic group

IYSWIM if you see what I mean

J

j current density; joule

J jack; Jewish (as in personal ads)

J. Japanese; Journal; judge; justice

JA joint account; judge advocate; Junior Achievement

Ja. January

Jac. *Latin* Jacobus (James)

JAG judge advocate general

JAL Japan Airlines

Jam. Jamaica

JAMA *Journal of the American Medical Association*

Jan. January

Jap. Japan; Japanese

JAP *derogatory* Jewish American Princess

Jas. James

jato jet-assisted takeoff

Jav. Javanese

JAWF Joint Agriculture-Weather Facility

JAYCEES Junior Chamber of Commerce

Jb Job

JBF just been fucked (that is, disheveled)

JBS John Birch Society

JC Jesus Christ; Julius Caeser; Junior College; juvenile court; member of Junior Chamber of Commerce

JCAHO Joint Commission on Accreditation of Health Organizations

JCAHPO Joint Commission on Allied Health in Ophthalmology

J.C.B. *Latin* Juris Canonici Baccalaureus (Bachelor of Canon Law)

JCC Jewish Community Center

J.C.D. *Latin* Juris Canonici Doctor (Doctor of Canon Law)

JCEWS Joint Command, Control, and Electronic Warfare School

JCL Job Control Language

J.C.L. *Latin* Juris Canonici Licentiatus (Licentiate in Canon Law)

JCMHC Joint Commission on Mental Health of Children

JCMIH Joint Commission on Mental Illness and Health

JCOG Japanese Clinical Oncology Group

JCS Joint Chiefs of Staff

JCSOS Joint and Combined Staff Officer School

Jct. junction

Jd Jude

JD Justice Department; juvenile delinquent

J.D. Jack Daniel's [bourbon whiskey]; *Latin* Juris Doctor (Doctor of Jurisprudence)

JdFR Juan de Fuca Ridge

Jdt. Judith

Je Jeremiah

Je. June

JEDA Joint Environmental Data Analysis Center

Jer. Jeremiah

jerry geriatric

JFK John Fitzgerald Kennedy; New York's John F. Kennedy airport code

JFYI just for your information

jg junior grade

Jg Judges

JGB Japanese Government bonds

Jgs Judges

JHVH Jehovah

JHWH Jehovah

JIC just in case

JICST Japan International Center of Science and Technology

jiff jiffy (that is, a very brief period of time)

JIFSAN Joint Institute for Food Safety and Applied Nutrition

JIT just in time

JITMT [United States–]Japan Industry and Technology Management Training

JJ judges; justices

JJA June-July-August

Jl Joel

Jl. July

J-list journalist

Jm James

.jm Jamaica

Jn John

JND just noticeable difference

Jno. John

J.N.O.V. *Latin* judicium non obstante veredicto (judgment notwithstanding verdict)

jnr. junior

jnt. joint

Jo. Joel

.jo Jordan

J/O jack off

joc. jocular; jocularly

jockumentary jock documentary film

JOOC just out of curiosity

JOOTT just one of those things

Jos Joshua

Jos. Joseph

Josh. Joshua

jour. journal; journalist; journeyman

JOVIAL Jules' own version of the international algorithmic language

JP jet propulsion

Jp. Japanese

.jp Japan

J.P. justice of the peace

JPEG Joint Photographic Experts Group

JPL Jet Propulsion Laboratory

Jpn. Japan

Jr Jeremiah

jr. junior

Jr. journal; Junior

JRA juvenile rheumatoid arthritis

JRC Junior Red Cross

Js. James

JSC Johnson Space Center

J-school journalism school

J.S.D. *Latin* Juris Scientiae Doctor (Doctor of Juristic Science)

JSTARS Joint Surveillance and Target Attack Reconnaissance System

JT joint tenants, joint tenancy

jt. joint

JTC3A Joint Tactical Command, Control, and Communications Agency

JTR Joint Travel Regulation

JTU Jackson Turbidity Unit

Ju. June

JUCO junior college
Jud. Judith
J.U.D. *Latin* Juris Utriusque Doctor (Doctor of Common and Canon Laws)
Judg. Judges
Jul. July
jun. junior
Jun. June
Junc. junction
juv. juvenile
juvie juvenile
JV junior varsity
JWARS Joint Warfare Simulation
jwlr. jeweler
Jy. July

K

k karat; 1000
K kaon; Kelvin; kicker; kilobyte; kindergarten; king; Kings; knight; 1,000; 1,024 (the closest number to 1,000 that is a power of 2—used for certain measurements, such as bytes); potassium; strikeout
k. kopek; krona; krone
ka cathode
Ka kilo amperes
KAMT Keeping Abreast of Medical Transcription
Kan. Kansas
Kans. Kansas
K:A ratio ketogenic-antiketogenic ratio
Karmen Karlsruhe-Rutherford Medium Energy Neutrino [Experiment]

kat katal
KAZ Kazakhstan
kb kilobar
Kb kilobit
KB kilobyte; king's bishop; knowledge base
K.B. King's Bench
kbar kilobar
KBE Knight Commander of the Order of the British Empire
Kbps kilobits per second
KByte kilobyte
kc kilocurie; kilocycle
KC Kansas City
K.C. King's Counsel; Knights of Columbus
kcal kilocalorie
K.C.B. Knight Commander of the Order of the Bath
KCBT Kansas City Board of Trade
kcl kilocalorie
KCRT keyboard CRT
kc/s kilocycles per second
KD kiln-dried; knocked down
KDP key decision point
.ke Kenya
KEAS knots equivalent airspeed
KEGG Kyoto Encyclopedia of Genes and Genomes
KEK *Japanese* Koh-Ene-Ken (an abbreviation for a Japanese name of the National Laboratory for High Energy Physics)
KEN [National Mental Health Services] Knowledge Exchange Network
Ken. Kentucky
Ker. Kerry

keV kiloelectron unit
KEW kinetic energy weapon
keypal Internet penpal
KFC Kentucky Fried Chicken
kg kilogram
kG kilogauss
.kg Kyrgyzstan
K.G. Knight of the Order of the Garter
KGAL kilogallon(s)
KGB *Russian* Komitet Gosudarstvennoj Bezopasnosti (Committee for State Security)
kgf kilogram force
kgm. kilogram
kg-m kilogram-meter
KGRA known geothermal resource area
Kgs. Kings
KGZ Kyrgyzstan
KH Kelvin-Helmholtz
.kh Cambodia
KHN Knoop hardness number
KHYF know how you feel
kHz kilohertz
.ki Kiribati
KIA killed in action
kilo kilogram
KISS Keep it simple, stupid!
kit kitchen
kitch kitchen
kJ kilojoule
KJ knee jerk (reflex)
KJV King James Version
KKK Ku Klux Klan
KKt king's knight
kl kiloliter
KLA Kosovo Liberation Army
km kilometer

.km Comoros
km/h kilometers per hour
kmph kilometers per hour
kmps kilometers per second
KN king's knight
kn. knot
.kn Saint Kitts and Nevis
KNF model Koshland-Némethy-Filmer model
knowbot knowledge robot
Knt. knight
KO knockout
K of C Knights of Columbus
K of P Knights of Pythias
KOOKS Keep Our Own Kids Safe
Kor. Korea; Korean
kosh kosher (that is, acceptable or up-to-date)
KP king's pawn; kitchen police
.kp Democratic People's Republic of Korea
kPa kilopascal
kpc kiloparsec
kph kilometers per hour
KPNO Kitt Peak National Observatory
kpps kilo pulses per second
Kr krypton
KR king's rook
kr. krona; krone
.kr Republic of Korea
K ration [Ancel Benjamin] Keys ration
KS Kansas; Kaposi's sarcoma; Knee Society
KSC Kennedy Space Center
kt kiloton
kT kiloton
Kt knight

kt. karat; knight; knot

K/T Cretaceous-Tertiary event (that is, comet or meteorite that hit earth 65 million years ago)

ktch kitchen

K-12 kindergarten through twelfth grade

K2K KEK to Kamioka [physics experiment]

KUB kidneys, ureter, bladder

Kuw. Kuwait

kV kilovolt

kVp kilovolts peak

kW kilowatt

KW know (shortwave transmission)

.kw Kuwait

KWBC National Weather Service Telecommunications Gateway

kWh kilowatt-hour

kW-hr kilowatt-hour

KWIC keyword in context

KY Kentucky

Ky. Kentucky

.ky Cayman Islands

.kz Kazakhstan

L

l length; liter

L 50; lambert; [coarse/ suggestive] language (television rating); large; Latino (as in personal ads); left; lesbian (as in personal ads)

l. lake; land; late; line; lira

L. Lake; Latin; Licentiate; Linnaean; Lodge

La lanthanum

LA linoleic acid; Louisiana

La. Louisiana

.la Laos

L.A. Latin America; Legislative Assembly; Local Agent; Los Angeles

lab laboratory

Lab Labrador retriever

lab. label; labor; laboratory; laborer

Lab. Labrador

LAC LaCrosse encephalitis; large area coverage; local area coverage

LACI lipoprotein-associated coagulation inhibitor

lacq. lacquered

LAD leukocyte adhesion deficiency; leukocyte antibody detection assay

LADAR light amplification for detection and ranging

LAES Latin American Economic System

LaF Louisiana French

LAIA Latin American Integration Association

LAK lymphokine activated killer [cells]

LAM Lymphagioleiomyomatosis

lam. laminated

Lam. Lamentations

LAN local area network

Lancs. Lancashire

LANDSAT land satellite

lang. language

LANL Los Alamos National Laboratory

LANTIRN low altitude navigation and targeting infrared for night

LAO left anterior oblique [projection]

lap laparotomy

LAP leukocyte alkaline phosphatase

LaRC Langley Research Center

LARP live-action role playing

LAS League of Arab States

LASCO large angle spectrometric coronagraph; [white] light and spectrometric coronagraph

laser light amplification by stimulated emission of radiation

LASIK laser assisted in-situ keratomileusis

lat. lateral; latitude

Lat. Latin; Latvia; Latvian

l.a.t. local apparent time

LATS long-acting thyroid stimulator

LAV lymphadenopathy-associated virus

lav. lavatory

LAVH laparoscopic-assisted vaginal hysteroscopy

LAWN local area wireless network

LAWS laser atmospheric wind sounder

LAX Los Angeles airport code

laun laundry room

LAUP laser-assisted uvulopalatoplasty

LB Labrador; linebacker

lb. *Latin* libra (pound)

.lb Lebanon

LBBY lobby

LBD laser beam detector

LBF Lactobacillus bulgaricus factor

LBJ Lyndon Baines Johnson

LBNL Lawrence Berkeley National Laboratory

LBO leveraged buyout

LBP low back pain

LBS land-based sources [of marine pollution]

lbs. *Latin* librae (pounds)

lc lowercase

LC landing craft; Library of Congress; living children; low consumption

.lc Saint Lucia

l.c. lowercase

L.C. leading cases; Lord Chancellor; Lower Canada

L/C letter of credit

LCA life cycle assessment

LCAT lecithin-cholesterol acyltransferase

LCC life cycle cost

LCCG Lung Cancer Cooperative Group

LCD liquid crystal display

l.c.d. least common denominator

L.Cdr. lieutenant commander

LCI landing craft, infantry

LCL less-than-carload lot

l.c.m. least common multiple

LCM landing craft, mechanized

LCMS Lutheran Church Missouri Synod

L.Cpl. lance corporal

LCS landing craft support; liquid crystal shutter

LCSG Lung Cancer Study Group

LCT land conservation trust; landing craft, tank; local civil time

L/cycle liters per cycle

LD laser disk; learning disability; learning disabled; lethal dose; light drinker; limited disease

ld. lead; load

Ld. limited; limited company; lord

LDB liquidity data bank; [Genetic] Location Database

LDC less developed country

ldg. landing; loading

LDH lactate dehydrogenase; lactic dehydrogenase

LDL low-density lipoprotein

L-dopa levodopa

LDPE low-density polyethylene

LDR low-dose rate

ldr. leader

LDRR Laboratory of Diagnostic Radiology Research

L.D.S. Latter-Day Saints

LDT local descriptor table

LDu. Low Dutch

LE left end; lower extremity

lea. league

Leaps long-term equity anticipation securities

Leb. Lebanon

LEC local exchange carrier

lect. lecture

lectr. lecturer

LED light-emitting diode; low energy detector

LEEP loop electrocautery excision procedure

LEF Life Extension Foundation

leg. legal; legate; legato; legislation; legislative; legislature

legis legislation; legislative; legislature

legit legitimate

Leics. Leicestershire

L8R later

LEM lunar excursion module

LEO Leo; low earth orbit

LEP limited English proficiency

LES lower esophageal sphincter

LET linear energy transfer

Lev. Leviticus

Levit. Leviticus

lex. lexicon

lf line feed; lightface

LF ledger folio

L.F. Law French

L-F low frequency

LFA left frontoanterior (position); Lupus Foundation of America

LFD linear finite difference

LFG lexical functional grammar

LFP left frontoposterior (position); low frequency prediction

L.Fr. Law French

LFT liver function test

LG left guard; Low German

lg. language; large; long

LGA low gain antenna

LGB laser-guided bomb

lge. large

LGk Late Greek

LGM last glacial maximum; little green men

L>R left greater than right

lgstc linguistic

lgstcs linguistics

LH liquid hydrogen; luteinizing hormone

l.h. left hand

LHA Lincoln Highway Association

L.H.D. *Latin* Litterarum Humanorum Doctor (Doctor of Humane Letters, Doctor of Humanities)

LHeb Late Hebrew

LH/FSH-RF luteinizing hormone/follicle stimulating hormone-releasing factor

LHNCBC Lister Hill National Center for Biomedical Communications

LHRF luteinizing hormone releasing factor

LHRH luteinizing hormone releasing hormone

LH2 liquid hydrogen

L.H.W.C.A. Longshore and Harbor Workers' Compensation Act

LHX liquid hydrogen

li link

Li lithium

.li Liechtenstein

L.I. Long Island

lib liberation

LIB Libra; library

lib. liberal; liberalism; librarian; library

Lib. Liberia

libr library

lic license

LID poor operator (shortwave transmission)

lidar light detecting and ranging (laser radar)

Liech. Liechtenstein

Lieut. Lieutenant

LIF Lifetime (cable television channel)

LIFO last in, first out

lig ligation

Li-Ion lithium-ion [battery]

lim limit

LIM Lotus Intel Microsoft [expanded memory specification]

Lim. Limerick

LIME laser induced microwave emissions

limo limousine

lin. lineal; linear

LINAC linear accelerator

Lincs. Lincolnshire

LINES long interspersed elements

ling. linguistics

lino linoleum

LION low energy ion and electron instrument

lipo liposuction

LIPS linear inferences per second

liq. liquid; liquor

LISP List Processing (computer language)

LISW Licensed Independent Social Worker

lit literature (academic course)

LIT leukocyte immunization therapy

lit. liter; literal; literally; literary; literature

Lit.B. *Latin* Litterarum Baccalaureus (Bachelor of Letters, Bachelor of Literature)

lit crit literary criticism

Lit.D. *Latin* Litterarum Doctor (Doctor of Letters, Doctor of Literature)

lith. lithograph; lithography

Lith. Lithuania; Lithuanian

litho lithograph

litho. lithograph; lithography

lithog. lithograph; lithography

Lit.M. *Latin* Litterarum Magister (Master of Letters, Master of Literature)

Litt.B. *Latin* Litterarum Baccalaureus (Bachelor of Letters, Bachelor of Literature)

Litt.D. *Latin* Litterarum Doctor (Doctor of Letters, Doctor of Literature)

Litt.M. *Latin* Litterarum Magister (Master of Letters, Master of Literature)

liv. living [room]

L.J. law journal; law judge

Lk Luke

lk. like

Lk. lake

.lk Sri Lanka

LKS liver, kidneys, and spleen

LL lending library; limited liability; lower left

ll. laws; leaves; lines

L.L. Late Latin; Law Latin

LLAP live long and prosper

LLAT lysolecithin-lecithin acyltransferase

L.Lat. Law Latin

LL.B. *Latin* Legum Baccalaureus (Bachelor of Laws)

LLBA *Linguistics and Language Behavior Abstracts*

LLC logical link control

LL.D. *Latin* Legum Doctor (Doctor of Laws)

LLDC least developed country

LLE left lower extremity

LLETZ large loop excision of transformation zone (of the cervix of the uterus)

LLJ low level jet

LLL La Leche League; left lower lobe

LLLI La Leche League International

LLLTV low light level television

LL.M. *Latin* Legum Magister (Master of Laws)

LLNL Lawrence-Livermore National Laboratory

LLQ left lower quadrant

LLWAS Low Level Windshear Alert System

lm lumen

Lm Lamentations

LM Legion of Merit; lunar module

LMA local management association

LMDS local multipoint distribution service

LME large marine ecosystem; Late Middle English

LMG light machine gun

L/min liters per minute

LMP last menstrual period

LMR living marine resource

LMT licensed massage therapist; local mean time

ln natural logarithm

Ln. lane

LNA alpha-linoleic acid

lndg. landing

lndry. laundry

LNG liquefied natural gas

LNPF lymph node permeability factor

LN2 liquid nitrogen

lo low

LO love olympics (that is, sex with the intent to procreate)

LOA left occipitoanterior (position); letter of agreement; limited operational assessment

l.o.a. length overall

LOBT local on-board time

LOC laxatives of choice; level of consciousness; loss of consciousness

loc. location; locative

LOCA low osmolar contrast agent

LOCIS Library of Congress Information System

loc. cit. *Latin* loco citato (in the place cited)

LOCM low osmolar contrast medium

LOCS Land-Ocean-Climate Satellite

LOE Late Old English

LOF lube, oil, and filter [change]

log. logic

logo logotype

LOL laughing out loud; little old lady

Lond. London

L1 language one (that is, first or native language)

long. longitude

Long. Longford

LONI Library of Neuropsychological Information

LOOM Loyal Order of Moose

LOP left occipitoposterior (position)

loq. *Latin* loquitur (speaks)

loran long range radio aid to navigation

LORCS League of Red Cross and Red Crescent Societies

lo-res low resolution

LOROPS long range oblique optical system

LOS law of the sea; length of stay; line of scrimmage; line of sight; loss of signal

LOT left occipitotransverse (position)

LOWR lower

LOX liquid oxygen

LP limited partnership; liquid petroleum; liquid propane; long-playing [record]; Lower Peninsula [of Michigan] lumbar puncture

LPBT Ladies Professional Bowlers Tour

LPC Licensed Professional Counselor; low pressure chamber

162 | LPD

LPD low probability of detection; luteal phase defect

Lpf liters per flush

LPG liquefied petroleum gas

LPGA Ladies Professional Golf Association

LPH lipotropic hormone

lpi lines per inch

lpm lines per minute

LPN licensed practical nurse

LPO left posterior oblique (position)

LPS lipopolysaccharide

LPV long period variable

LQ letter quality

Lr lawrencium

LR living room; lower right; low rate

.lr Liberia

L.R. law reports

L/R left/right

L.R.A. *Law Reports Annotated*

LRB liquid rocket booster

LRC longitude rotation convention

LRCP Licentiate of the Royal College of Physicians

LRCP(E) Licentiate of the Royal College of Physicians (Edinburgh)

LRCP(I) Licentiate of the Royal College of Physicians (Ireland)

LRCS Licentiate of the Royal College of Surgeons

LRCS(E) Licentiate of the Royal College of Surgeons (Edinburgh)

LRCS(I) Licentiate of the Royal College of Surgeons (Ireland)

LRF Leukemia Research Foundation; luteinizing hormone-releasing factor

LRFA Lymphoma Research Foundation of America

LRFPS Licentiate of the Royal Faculty of Physicians and Surgeon

lrg. large

LRH luteinizing hormone-releasing hormone

LRP live role playing

LRT light-rail transit

LRTI lower respiratory tract infection

LRV light-rail vehicle

LS level sensor; lumbosacral

.ls Lesotho

L.S. *Latin* locus sigilli (the place of the seal)

LSA left sacroanterior (position); Leukemia Society of America; Linguistic Society of America

LSAT Law School Admissions Test

LSB least significant bit

LSC least significant character

LSD least significant digit; lysergic acid diethylamide

L.S.D. pounds, shillings, and pence

LSF line spread function

LSG large-scale geostrophic

LSI large-scale integration

LSO landing signal officer; London Symphony Orchestra

LSOA Longitudinal Study of Aging

LSP least significant portion; left sacroposterior (position)

L/S ratio lecithin/sphingomyelin ratio

LSS lifesaving service; life-support system

LST landing ship, tank; left sacrotransverse (position); local sidereal time; local solar time

lt left

LT left tackle; leukotriene; long ton

lt. light

Lt. lieutenant

.lt Lithuania

l.t. local time

LTC long-term care

Lt. Col. lieutenant colonel

Lt. Comdr. lieutenant commander

Ltd. limited; limited company

Lt. Gen. lieutenant general

Lt. Gov. lieutenant governor

LtH left-handed

LTH luteotropic hormone

L.Th. Licentiate in Theology

lthr. leather

LTJG lieutenant junior grade

l.t.l. less than truckload

LTM long-term memory

LTMSH laughing 'til my sides hurt

LTOP lease-to-ownership plan

LTOT long-term oxygen therapy

LTP lunar transient phenomenon

LTR long-term relationship

ltr. letter; lighter

LTS launch telemetry station; launch tracking system

L2 language two (that is, second or foreign language)

Lu lutetium

.lu Luxembourg

lub. lubricant; lubricating

lube lubricant; lubricate

LUE left upper extremity

LUF luteinized unruptured follicle

LUL left upper lobe

LUQ left upper quadrant

LUT local user terminal

Luth. Lutheran

luv love

lux luxurious

Lux. Luxembourg

Lv Leviticus

LV leave (shortwave transmission); left ventricle

lv. leave; livre

.lv Latvia

LVET left ventricular ejection time

LVF left ventricular function

LVH left ventricular hypertrophy

lvl level

LVN licensed vocational nurse

LVPS low voltage power supply

LVRS lung volume reduction surgery

LVT landing vehicle tracked

LW longwave; low water

LWD low-water data

LWIR long wavelength infrared

LWL length at water line; load water line

LWM low-water mark

LWOP lease with option to purchase

LWR light water reactor

lwr. lower

LWV League of Women Voters

lx lux

.ly Libya

lymph. lymphocyte

lyr. lyric

lytes electrolytes

lytic osteolytic

LZ landing zone

LZW Lempel-Ziv-Welch [algorithm]

M

m masculine; mass; meter; minute; modulus

M em; Maccabees; Mach number; male; married (as in personal ads); medium; megabyte; mellow; metal; middle [term]; million; molar; molarity; moment; Monday; month; more (shortwave transmission); [heart] murmur; mutual inductance; 1000

m. manual; married; *Latin* meridies (noon); meridian; mile; morning

M. majesty; mark; master; medieval; mill; minim; Monsieur

mA milliampere

MA Marijuana Anonymous; Maritime Administration; Massachusetts; mature audience; medical assistance; mental age

.ma Morocco

M.A. *Latin* Magister Artium (Master of Arts)

MAA macroaggregated albumin; master-at-arms; Medical Artists' Association

MAAC maximum allowable actual charge

MAB monoclonal antibody

M.A.B.E. Master of Agricultural Business and Economics

MAC maximum allowable cost; membrane attack complex; military airlift command; minimal alveolar concentration; minimal anesthetic concentration;

Mac. Maccabees; Macedonia; Macedonian

MACAP Major Appliance Consumer Action Program

Macc. Maccabees

Maced. Macedonia; Macedonian

mach. machine; machinery; machinist

MACHO massive astrophysical compact halo object

macro macroinstruction

MACTIS Marine and Coastal Technology Information Service

MAD mutually assured destruction

Mad. Madagascar; madam

MADD Mothers Against Drunk Driving

MADER Management of Atmospheric Data for Evaluation and Research

MAE moves all extremities

M.A.E. Master of Aeronautical Engineering; Master of Art Education; Master of Arts in Education

M.A.Ed. Master of Arts in Education

MAESA Measurements for Assessing the Effects of Stratospheric Aircraft

MAEW moves all extremities well

MAF macrophage-activating factor; million acre-feet

mag magazine

mag. magnet; magnetism; magneto; magnitude

maglrv magnetic levitation [train]

M.Agr. Master of Agriculture

mahog. mahogany

MAI Mycobacterium avium-intracellulare; [World Trade Organization] Multilateral Investment Agreement

maint. maintenance

Maj. major

Maj. Gen. major general

Mal. Malachi; Malawi; Malawian; Malay; Malaysia; Malaysian

M.A.L.S. Master of Arts in Liberal Studies; Master of Arts in Library Science

MAN Metropolitan Area Network

man. manual

Man. Manitoba

M & A mergers and acquisitions

M & I municipal and industrial

M & S modeling and simulation

man. pr. *Latin* mane primo (early morning, first thing in the morning)

MANS Microcosm Autonomous Navigation System

MANTIS Manual, Alternative, and Natural Therapy Index System

manuf. manufacture; manufacturer

manufac. manufacture

MAO monoamine oxidase

MAOI monoamine oxidase inhibitor

MAP modified American plan

M-appeal man appeal

MAPS measuring air pollution from space; mesoscale analysis and prediction system

MAPI [Microsoft's] Messaging Application Programming Interface

MAPs microtubule-associated proteins

MAPS Meteorological and Aeronautical Presentation System

MAPW Medical Association for Prevention of War

mar. maritime; married

Mar. March

MAR major acquisition review; Mid-Atlantic Ridge

MARAD Maritime Administration

MARC machine readable cataloging

March. marchioness

Marecs Maritime European Communications Satellite

MARF Medical Acupuncture Research Foundation

marg. margin; marginal

MARIC Marine Resources Information Center

Mart. Martinique

MARV maneuverable reentry vehicle

MAS mobile atmospheric spectrometer

masc. masculine

maser microwave amplification by stimulated emission of radiation

MASH Mobile Army Surgical Hospital

maspin mammary associated serine protease inhibitor

Mass. Massachusetts

MAST military antishock trousers

mat. matinee

M.A.T. Master of Arts in Teaching

MATC maximum acceptable toxicant concentration

math mathematics

math. mathematical; mathematician

Matt. Matthew

MATV master antenna television

MATZ military air traffic zone

MAU multistation access unit

MAV micro air vehicle

MAWS missile approach warning system

max maximum

MAX Cinemax

max. maximum

MAXX Maximum Access to Diagnosis and Therapy (The Electronic Library of Medicine)

mayo mayonnaise

mb millibar

Mb megabit

MB Manitoba; megabyte

M.B. *Latin* Medicinae Baccalaureus (Bachelor of Medicine)

M.B.A. Master of Business Administration

MBAA Mortgage Bankers Association of America

MBAS methylene blue active substance

MBC maximum breathing capacity

M.B.C.I. Medical Books for China International

mbd million barrels per day

MBD minimal brain dysfunction

MBDA Minority Business Development Agency

MBE molecular beam epitaxy

M.B.E. Member of the Order of the British Empire

MBFR mutual and balanced force reduction

MBHO Managed Behavioral Healthcare Organization

Mbits/s megabits per second

MBL marine boundary layer

MBNA Monument Builders of North America

MBO management by objective

Mbone multicast backbone

Mbps megabits per second

MBR master bedroom

MBret. Middle Breton

MBS mortgage-backed security; Mutual Broadcasting System

MBT mother's blood type

MBTA Massachusetts Bay Transit Authority

MBTI Myers-Briggs [personality] Type Indicator

MBV model-based vision

Mbyte megabyte

mc millicurie

Mc Maccabees; megacycle

MC Marine Corps; Maritime Commission; Master Card; Medical Corps; megacycle; Member of Congress

.mc Monaco

M.C. master of ceremonies

m/c miscarriage

MCA microchannel architecture; middle cerebral artery; motorcycle accident

MCAT Medical College Admissions Test

MCC mid-course correction; Midwest Climate Center; Mission Control Center

MCCA Medicare Catastrophic Coverage Act

MCD minimum cost design

mcf thousand cubic feet

mcg microgram

MCGA multicolor graphics array

MCH mean corpuscular hemoglobin

M.Ch. Magister Chirurgiae, Master of Surgery

MCHB Maternal and Child Health Bureau

MCHC mean corpuscular hemoglobin concentration

MCHPRC Maternal and Child Health Policy Research Center

mCi millicurie

MCI (formerly) Microwave Communications Inc.

MCIC Managed Care Information Center

MCL Marine Corps League; [Environmental Protection Agency] maximum contaminant level

M.C.L. Master of Civil Law; Master of Comparative Law

MCLG [Environmental Protection Agency] maximum contaminant level goal

MCM mechanical current meter; multichip module

MCMI Millon clinical multiaxial inventory

MCN molecular and cellular neuroscience

MCO managed care organization

MCP male chauvinist pig; microchannel plate

MCPI medical consumer price index

MCPO master chief petty officer

MCP-1 monocyte chemoattractant protein-1

MCR medical cost ratio; metabolic clearance rate

MCS mesoscale convective system; multiple chemical sensitivity

M-CSF macrophage colony-stimulating factor

MCT metal-oxide-semiconductor controlled transistor

MCV mean corpuscular volume; mesoscale convectively generated vortices

Md mendelevium

MD Maryland; Medical Department; Middle Dutch; muscular dystrophy

Md. Maryland

M.D. *Latin* Medicinae Doctor (Doctor of Medicine)

.md Moldova

m/d months after date

MDA methylenedioxy amphetamine; monochrome display adapter; Muscular Dystrophy Association

MDa. Middle Danish

M-day mobilization day

MDC more developed country

MDD major depressive disorder

MDE motor drive electronics

MDF Macular Degeneration Foundation

MDI multiple document interface

m. dict. *Latin* more dicto (as directed)

M.Div. Master of Divinity

Mdm. Madam

MDMA methylenedioxy-methamphetamine

MDNCF monocyte-derived neutrophil chemotactic factor

mdnt. midnight

MDR minimum daily requirement

M.D.S. Master of Dental Surgery

mdse. merchandise

mds rm maid's room

MDT Mountain Daylight Time

MDu. Middle Dutch

ME Maine; medical examiner; Middle English

Me. Maine

M.E. mechanical engineer; mechanical engineering; mining engineer; mining engineering; mission engineer

meas. measurable; measure

mech. mechanical; mechanics; mechanism

MECO main engine cutoff

med medical

MED [Office of] Medical [Services] (State)

med. medial; median; medication; medicine; medieval; medium

Med. Mediterranean

M.Ed. Master of Education

MEDEA Measurements of Earth Data for Environmental Analysis

medfly Mediterranean fruit fly

Med. Gk Medieval Greek

Med. Gr. Medieval Greek

Medicaid medical aid insurance

Medicare medical care insurance

Medit. Mediterranean

Med. L Medieval Latin

MEDLARS Medical Literature Analysis and Retrieval System

Med. Lat. Medieval Latin

MEDLINE MEDLARS Online

meds medications

MEDS Meteorological and Environmental Data Services

meg megabyte; megohm

MEG magnetoencephalogram

MEGO my eyes glaze over

MEI Medicare Economic Index

MEK methyl ethyl ketone

MELICA medium energy ion composition analyzer

MEM [Eagle's] minimum essential medium

mem. member; memoir; memorandum; memorial

memo memorandum

MEMS microelectromechanical systems

M.Eng. Master of Engineering

mep mean effective pressure

MEP member of the European Parliament

MEPED medium energy proton and electron detector

mEq milliequavalent

MEQ/L milliequivalents per liter

mer. meridian

merc. mercantile; mercury; Mercury

Mercosur *Spanish* Mercado Común del Cono Sur (Southern Cone Common Market)

MES main engine start

MESA microsurgical epididymal sperm aspiration

MeSH Medical Subject Headings

MESI modified, exclusive, shared, and invalid [data]

Messrs. Messieurs

Met New York Metropolitan Opera Company; New York Metropolitan Opera House

MET metabolic equivalent

met. metaphysics; metropolitan

metal. metallurgic; metallurgy

metall. metallurgic; metallurgy

metaph. metaphor; metaphoric; metaphysics

METCON Metropolitan Consortium for Minorities in Science and Engineering

meteor. meteorological; meteorology

meteorol. meteorology

meth methamphetamine

Meth. Methodist

metHb methemoglobin

metMb metmyoglobin

METO Middle East Treaty Organization

mets metastasis

METs metabolic equivalents

METSAT meteorological satellite

MeV million electron-volts

MEWA multiple employer welfare arrangements

Mex. Mexican; Mexico

Mex. Sp. Mexican Spanish

mezz. mezzanine

mf medium frequency; mezzo forte

mF millifarad

MF medium frequency; Middle French

M.F. mother fucker

M.F.A. Master of Fine Arts

MFCMA Magnuson Fishery Conservation and Management Act

MFD multifunction display
mfd. manufactured
mfg. manufacture; manufacturing; manufactured
M.F.H. Master of Fox Hounds
MFIB Medicare Fraud Investigations Branch
MFIC National Fraud Information Center
MFJ married filing jointly
MFlem. Middle Flemish
MFM modified frequency modulation
MFN most-favored nation
MFP major frame pulse; mean free path; mobile flux platform
mfr. manufacture; manufacturer
MFS Medicare fee schedule
mg milligram
Mg magnesium
MG machine gun; major general; military government
.mg Madagascar
MGA monochrome graphics adapter
MGB *Russian* Ministerstvo Gosudarstvennoj Bezopasnosti (Ministry of State Security)
mgd million gallons per day
MGE media generation element; Minneapolis Grain Exchange
MGES Multispecialty Group Executive Society
MGk Middle Greek
MG/L milligrams per liter
mgm milligram
MGM Metro-Goldwyn-Mayer
MGMA Medical Group Management Association

mgmt. management
MGP matrix Gla protein
mgr. manager
Mgr. Monseigneur; Monsignor
MGS Mars Global Surveyor
mgt. management
MGySgt master gunnery sergeant
mh millihenry
MH Medal of Honor; mental health
.mh Marshall Islands
MHA Mental Health Association
M.H.A. Master of Hospital Administration
MHAUS Malignant Hyperthermia Association of the United States
MHBFY my heart bleeds for you
MHC major histocompatibility complex; Mental Health Commission
MHD magnetohydrodynamic
MHG Middle High German
M.H.L. Master of Hebrew Literature
MHN Mental Health Net
MHOTY my hat's off to you
MHS message handling system; Military Health System
MHSS Military Health Services System
MHW mean high water
MHz megahertz
Mi Micah
MI mentally impaired; Michigan; military intelligence; mode indicator; multiple intelligences; myocardial infarction

mi. mile; mill

MIA Miami airport code; missing in action

MIB Medical Information Bureau

MIC military-industrial complex; minimal inhibitory concentration

Mic. Micah

MICA medical intensive care unit; mentally ill chemical abuser; mentally ill chronic abuser

Mich. Michigan

MICIS Midwestern Climate Information System

MICLP Medical Informatics Cultural Literacy Project

MICR magnetic ink character recognition

micro. microcomputer; microprocessor; microscopic

microbiol. microbiology

mid middle

M.I.D. minimal infecting dose

MIDI musical instrument digital interface

Midn. midshipman

MIF migration-inhibitory factor

MIGA Multilateral Investment Guarantee Agency

MIH melanotropin release-inhibiting hormone

mil million

MIL military; mother-in-law

mil. military; militia

.mil military organization

milit. military

MILO magnetically insulated line oscillator

MILSTAR military strategic and tactical relay satellite

MIM *Mendelian Inheritance in Man*

mim. mimeograph

MIME multipurpose Internet mail extensions

mimeo mimeograph

MIMIC microwave/millimeter wave monolithic integrated circuit

min. mineralogy; minim; minimum; mining; minister; minor; minute

Minn. Minnesota

MINURSO *French* la Mission des Nations Unies pour l'organisation d'un référendum au Sahara occidental (United Nations Mission for the Referendum in Western Sahara)

MIO minimal identifiable odor

MIP monthly investment plan

MIPS million instructions per second

MIr Middle Irish

MIR microwave imaging radiometer

MIRA Media Image Resource Alliance

MIRP Manipulated Information Rate Processor

MIRV multiple independently targeted reentry vehicle

MIS management information services; management information system; manager of information services

misc. miscellaneous

MISR multiangle imaging spectrometer

Miss. Mississippi

mistr. mistranslation; mistranslating

mit mitigating circumstance

MIT Massachusetts Institute of Technology

MIT/LL Massachusetts Institute of Technology–Lincoln Laboratory

MIZ marginal ice zone

Mk Mark

MK make (shortwave transmission); menaquinone

mk. mark; markka

.mk Macedonia

mks meter-kilogram-second

mksA meter-kilogram-second-ampere

MKSAP Medical Knowledge Self-Assessment Program

MK-7 menaquinone-7

MK-6 menaquinone-6

mkt. market

mktg. marketing

ml milliliter

mL millilambert

Ml Malachi

ML Medieval Latin; Middle Latin

.ml Mali

MLA Medical Library Association; Member of the Legislative Assembly; Modern Language Association

MLC Marginal Line Calculus [Index]

MLD median lethal dose; minimum lethal dose

MLDT mean logistics delay time

MLE midline episiotomy

MLF multilateral force

MLG Middle Low German

MLI multilayer insulation

Mlle Mademoiselle

Mlles Mesdemoiselles

mlRNA messenger-like RNA

MLS Multiple Listing Service

M.L.S. Master of Library Science

MLSS mixed liquor suspended solids

MLV medium launch vehicle

MLVSS mixed liquor volatile suspended solids

MLW mean low water

mm millimeter

MM mesoscale model

.mm Myanmar

m.m. *Latin* mutatis mutandis (with the necessary changes)

M.M. Messieurs

MMC Marine Mammal Commission

MMCC Medicare Managed Care Contract

Mme Madame

Mmes Mesdames

mmf magnetomotive force

MMH monomethyl hydrazine

mmHg millimeters of mercury

MMIC monolithic microwave integrated circuit

MMM mesoscale and microscale meteorology

MMMT malignant mixed müllerian tumor; malignant mixed mesodermal tumor

mmol millimole

MMPA Marine Mammal Protection Act

MMPI Minnesota Multiphasic Personality Inventory

MMR measles, mumps, rubella

MMS Minerals Management Service

MMT multiple mirror telescope

MMU manned maneuvering unit

MMW millimeter wave

MMX multimedia extensions

Mn manganese

MN magnetic north; Minnesota

.mn Mongolia

MNC multinational corporation

MND motor neuron disease

MNDA Motor Neurone Disease Association

mngr. manager

MNP Microcom Network Protocol

MnSOD manganese superoxide dismutase

MNT medical nutrition therapy

Mo molybdenum

MO magnetooptical; medical officer; Missouri; *Latin* modus operandi (way of working)

mo. month

Mo. Missouri

.mo Macau

M.O. mail order; money order

MOA market opportunity analysis; memorandum of agreement

MoAb monoclonal antibody

MOB medical office building

MOBA Museum of Bad Art [of Boston]

moc moccasin

MOC market on close [order]

mod modern

MOD mesiodistocclusal

mod. moderate; moderato; modern; modulo; modulus

Mod. Da. Modern Danish

modem modulator demodulator

Mod. Du. Modern Dutch

Mod. E. Modern English

Mod. Fr. Modern French

Mod. G Modern German

Mod. Gk. Modern Greek

Mod. Gr. Modern Greek

Mod. Heb. Modern Hebrew

Mod. Icel. Modern Icelandic

modif. modification

Mod. Ir. Modern Irish

MODIS moderate [resolution] imaging spectroradiometer

Mod. L. Modern Latin

Mod. Prov. Modern Provençal

Mod. Skt Modern Sanskrit

MOF magneto-optical filter

MOG Metropolitan Opera Guild

Moho Mohorovicic discontinuity

MOIL Marine Operations and Instrumentation Laboratory

MOL Manned Orbital Laboratory

mol. molecular; molecule

mol. wt. molecular weight

MOM Militia of Montana; milk of magnesia

m.o.m. middle of month

MOMA Museum of Modern Art

MOMV manned orbital maneuvering vehicle

mon. monastery; monetary

Mon. Monday

Mong. Mongolia

mono monaural; mononucleosis; monophonic

Mont. Montana

MOO Milkbottles Only Organization; MUD, object oriented

MOPA master oscillator power amplifier

MOR middle-of-the-road; monthly operating review

mor. morocco; mortar

Mor. Morocco; Moroccan

mor. dict. *Latin* more dicto (as directed)

MORE Minority Outreach Research and Education

MorF male or female

morn. morning

morph metamorphose; morphine

morph. morphological; morphology

mor. sol. *Latin* more solito (as usual, as customary)

MOS metal-oxide semiconductor; military occupational specialty

mos. months

M.O.S. member of the opposite sex

MOSFET metal oxide semiconductor field effect transistor

MOST magneto-optical storage technology

mot. motion

MOTAS member of the appropriate sex

MOTOS member of the opposite sex

MOTSS member of the same sex

MOTV manned orbital transfer vehicle

MOU memorandum of understanding

Mountie mounted policeman; member of the Royal Canadian Mounted Police

MOVE Mobility Opportunities Via Education

MOW movie of the week

MOZ Mozambique

Moz. Mozambique

mp melting point; mezzo piano

MP member of Parliament; military police; military police [officer]; mounted police

.mp Northern Mariana Islands

m.p. *Latin* modo praescripto (in the manner prescribed)

MPA microscopic particulate analysis

M.P.A. Master of Public Accounting; Master of Public Administration

MPAA Motion Picture Association of America

MPC Multimedia Personal Computer

MPCA The Media Photographers' Copyright Agency

MPD maximum permissible dose; minimum peripheral dose

MPE malignant pleural effusion

M.P.E. Master of Public Education

MPEG Moving Picture Experts Group

MPer. Middle Persian

mpg miles per gallon

mph miles per hour

M.P.H. Master of Public Health

M.Phil. master of philosophy

MPI marine pollution incident

MPLC Motion Picture Licensing Corporation

Mpls. Minneapolis

mpm meters per minute

MPM malignant pleural mesothelioma; microwave power module

MPN most probable number

MPP massively parallel processor

MPPDA Medicine-Pediatrics Program Directors Association

MPR mannose-6-phosphate receptors; monthly program review

MPRSA Marine Protection, Research, and Sanctuaries Act

mps meters per second

MPS Medical Protection Society; mononuclear phagocyte system

MPX multiplex

.mq Martinique

MQP mandatory quote period

mr milliradian

mR milliroentgen

MR medium rate; metabolic rate

Mr. mister (Used as a courtesy title for a man)

.mr Mauritania

MRAA Mental Retardation Association of America

MRC Medical Research Council

MRCP Member of the Royal College of Physicians

MRCP(E) Member of the Royal College of Physicians (Edinburgh)

MRCP(I) Member of the Royal College of Physicians (Ireland)

MRCS Member of the Royal College of Surgeons

MRCS(E) Member of the Royal College of Surgeons (Edinburgh)

MRCS(I) Member of the Royal College of Surgeons (Ireland)

MRCVS Member of the Royal College of Veterinary Surgeons

MRD minimal reacting dose

M.R.E. Meals Ready to Eat

mrem millirem

MRF medium-range forecast; melanotropin-releasing factor

MRH melanotropin-releasing hormone

MRI machine-readable information; magnetic resonance imaging; Mystery Readers International

MRIPS Multimodality Radiological Image Processing System

MRMC Medical Research Modernization Committee

mRNA messenger RNA

MRO Medical Review Officer

MROCC Medical Review Officer Certification Council

MRP material requirements planning

Mrs. Used as a courtesy title for a married or widowed woman (from "mistress")

MRS medical review systems

MRSA methicillin-resistant Staphylococcus aureus

ms manuscript; millisecond; mitral stenosis

Ms Used as courtesy title for a woman, regardless of marital status (a blend of "Miss" and "Mrs.")

MS mass spectrometer; mass spectrometry; Microsoft; microwave scanner; Mississippi; multiple sclerosis

Ms. Miss/Mrs.

.ms Montserrat

M.S. *Latin* Magister Scientiae (Master of Science)

MSA management services agreement; medical savings account; methane sulfonic acid; Metropolitan Statistical Area

M.S.A. Master of Science in Agriculture

MSB most significant bit; most significant byte

MSC most significant character

M.Sc. *Latin* Magister Scientiae (Master of Science)

MSCI Morgan Stanley Capital Index

MSD most significant digit

MS-DOS Microsoft Disk Operating System

msec millisecond

MSEN Multiple Sclerosis Education Network

MSF Multiple Sclerosis Foundation

MSFC Marshall Space Flight Center; Medical Students for Choice

MSG monosodium glutamate

msg. message

Msgr. Monseigneur; Monsignor

M.Sgt. master sergeant

MSH melanocyte-stimulating hormone

MSHA Mine Safety and Health Administration

MSI minority-serving institution; multispectral imager

M.S. in L.S. Master of Science in Library Science

M16 model 16 [rifle]

MSJ message (shortwave transmission)

MSKCC Memorial Sloan-Kettering Cancer Center

MSL maximum stress load; mean sea level

M.S.L. mean sea level

MSLT Multiple Sleep Latency Test

MSN Microsoft Network; MSNBC

M.S.N. Master of Science in Nursing

MSNBC Microsoft/National Broadcasting Company

MSO management service organization

MSP most significant portion

MSPB Merit Systems Protection Board

MSR measure (shortwave transmission); monthly status report

MSRC Marine Sciences Research Center

mss manuscripts

MSS management support system; message switching system; multispectral scanner

MSS. Manuscripts

MSSD Model Secondary School for the Deaf

MST mesosphere-stratosphere-troposphere; Mountain Standard Time

mstr. br. master bedroom

M.S.T.S. Military Sea Transportation Service

MSU microwave sounding unit

MSUD Maple Syrup Urine Disease

MSw. Middle Swedish

M.S.W. Master of Social Welfare; Master of Social Work

Mt Matthew; meitnerium

MT empty; machine translation; megaton; Montana; Mountain Time

mt. maintenance

Mt. mount; mountain

.mt Malta

M.T. metric ton

MTA material transfer agreement; message transfer agent, Metropolitan Transportation Authority

MTB Materials Transportation Bureau

MTBE methyl tertiary butyl ether

MTBF mean time between failures

mtc. maintenance

MTCR Missile Technology Control Regime

MTD maximum tolerated dose

mtDNA mitochondrial deoxyribonucleic acid

MTF modulation transfer function

mtg. meeting; mortgage

mtge. mortgage

mth. month

mthly. monthly

MTL Montreal

Mtn. mountain

MTO Mediterranean Theater of Operations

MTPPI Medical Technology and Practice Patterns Institute

MTPR miniature temperature pressure recorder

MTR magnetic tape recorder; miniature temperature recorder

MTS Musculoskeletal Tumor Society

Mts. mountains

MTSO mobile telephone switching office

MTTR mean-time-to-restore; mean-time-to-repair

MTU maximum transmission unit

MTV Music Television

MU multiple unit

.mu Mauritius

m.u. mouse unit

MUD multiuser dimension; multiuser domain; multiuser dungeon

MUDOS [Digital Research's] Multiuser Distributed Operating System

MUFON Mutual UFO Network, [Inc.]

multi-CSF multicolony-stimulating factor

mun. municipal

muni municipal bond

munic. municipal

Mur muramic [acid]

mus. museum; music; musical; musician

Mus.B. *Latin* Musicae Baccalaureus (Bachelor of Music)

Mus.D. *Latin* Musicae Doctor (Doctor of Music)

Mus.Dr. *Latin* Musicae Doctor (Doctor of Music)

Mus.M. *Latin* Musicae Magister (Master of Music)

mux multiplexer

mV millivolt

MV mean variation; megavolt; mitral valve

.mv Maldives

MVA motor vehicle accident

MVD *Russian* Ministerstvo Vnutrennikh Del (Ministry of Internal Affairs)

MVP most valuable player; mitral valve prolapse

MVPS medical volume performance standard; Medicare volume performance standard

MVR mitral valve replacement

MVS [IBM's] Multiple Virtual System

MVV maximum voluntary ventilation

mW milliwatt

MW megawatt; microwave; Middle Welsh

.mw Malawi

MWC model Monod-Wyman-Changeux model

MWe megawatts electric

MWF Monday-Wednesday-Friday

MWS major weapon system; microwave spectrometer

MWSR microwave water substance radiometer

mx metastases

Mx maxwell

MX Merry Christmas; motocross

.mx Mexico

mxd. mixed

My. May

.my Malaysia

m.y. million years

MYA million years ago

myc. mycological; mycology

mycol. mycological; mycology

MYOB Mind your own business!

myth. mythological; mythology

mythol. mythological; mythology

.mz Mozambique

N

n indefinite number; neuter; neutron; new; normal; note

N en; knight; name; needs improvement; Newton; New York Stock Exchange; nitrogen; no (shortwave transmission); nominative; noon; north; northern; noun; not (shortwave transmission)

n. footnote; *Latin* natus (born); net; note; noun

N. Norse

Na Nahum; sodium

NA Narcotics Anonymous; Native American (as in personal ads)

Na. Nahum

.na Namibia

n.a. *Latin* non allocatur (it is not allowed)

N.A. North America; not allowed; not applicable; not available

N/A not applicable; not available

NAA National Academy on Aging; National Aeronautic Association; Neurosciences Administration Assembly

NAACCR North American Association of Central Cancer Registries

NAACP National Association for the Advancement of Colored People

NAADD National Association on Alcohol, Drugs and Disability

NAAF National Alopecia Areata Foundation

NAAFA National Association to Advance Fat Acceptance

NAAP National Association of Activity Professionals

NAAR National Alliance for Autism Research

NAAWP National Association for Advancement of White People

NAB National Association of Broadcasters; New American Bible

NABCO National Alliance of Breast Cancer Organizations

nabe neighborhood

NABIS Northern Alberta Brain Injury Society

NABR National Association for Biomedical Research

NAC National Advisory Council; National AIDS Clearinghouse

NACA National Advisory Committee for Aeronautics

NACAA National Association of Consumer Agency Administrators

NACB National Academy of Clinical Biochemistry

NACC North Atlantic Cooperation Council

NACCHO National Association of County and City Health Officials

NACD National Association of Computer Dealers

NACHRI National Association of Children's Hospitals and Related Institutions

NACoA National Association for Children of Alcoholics

NACOA National Advisory Committee on Oceans and Atmosphere

NACS National Association of College Stores

NACU National Association of Colleges and Universities

NAD National Academy of Design; National Association of the Deaf; nicotinamide adenine dinucleotide; no acute distress

N.A.D. no appreciable disease

NADA National Automobile Dealers Association

NADC Naval Air Development Center

NADF National Adrenal Diseases Foundation

NADH nicotinamide adenine dinucleotide (reduced form)

NADL National Association of Dental Laboratories

NADONA/LTC National Association of Directors of Nursing Administration in Long Term Care

NADP nicotinamide adenine dinucleotide phosphate

NADPH nicotinamide adenine dinucleotide phosphate (reduced form)

NAD+ nicotinamide adenine dinucleotide (oxidized form)

NADP+ nicotinamide adenine dinucleotide phosphate (oxidized form)

nads testicles (from "gonads")

NADS National Association for Down Syndrome; *Newsletter of the American Dialect Society*

NADT National Association for Drama Therapy

NAE National Academy of Engineering

NAELA National Academy of Elder Law Attorneys

NAEMSE National Association of Emergency Medical Service Educators

NAEMSP National Association of Emergency Medical Service Physicians

NAEMT National Association of Emergency Medical Technicians

NAEP National Assessment of Educational Progress

NAEPP National Asthma Education and Prevention Program

NAER National Association for Emergency Response

NAF National Abortion Foundation; National Anxiety Foundation; National Ataxia Foundation; neutrophil activating factor

NAFA Nordic Association for Andrology

NAFAC National Association for Ambulatory Care

NAFC National Association for Continence

NAFO Northwest Atlantic Fisheries Organization

N. Afr. North Africa; North African

NAFTA North American Free Trade Agreement

NAG N-acetylglutamate

NAGARA National Association of Government Archives and Records Administrators

Nah. Nahum

NAHAT National Association of Health Authorities and Trusts

NAHB National Association of Home Builders

NAHC National Association for Home Care

NAHDO National Association of Health Data Organizations

NAHN National Association of Hispanic Nurses

NAHQ National Association of Health Quality

NAHS North American Hyperthermia Society

NAIA National Association of Intercollegiate Athletes

NAIC National Aging Information Center; National Association of Insurance Commissioners

Nairu nonaccelerating inflation rate of unemployment

NAK negative acknowledgment

Nam Vietnam

NAM National Association of Manufacturers

N. Am. North America; North American

NAMA National Alliance of Methadone Advocates

NAMCP National Association of Managed Care Physicians

NAMCS National Ambulatory Medical Care Survey

NAME National Association of Miniature Enthusiasts

N. Amer. North America; North American

NAMES National Association for Medical Equipment Services

NAMH National Association for Mental Health

NAMI National Alliance for the Mentally Ill

NAMIEP National AIDS Minority Information and Education Program

NAMSS National Association Medical Staff Services

NAMT National Association for Music Therapy

NANAD National Association of Anorexia Nervosa and Associated Disorders

NANBNC hepatitis non-A, non-B, non-C hepatitis

NANC neuron nonadrenergic, noncholinergic neuron

NAND NOT AND (logical operator)

NANDA North American Nursing Diagnosis Association

N & V nausea and vomiting

NANMT National Association of Nurse Massage Therapists

NANN National Association of Neonatal Nurses

NANOS North American Neuro-Ophthalmology Society

NANPRH National Association of Nurse Practitioners in Reproductive Health

NAOMA National Acupuncture and Oriental Medicine Alliance

NAON National Association of Orthopaedic Nurses

NAOTD National Alliance of the Disabled

NAP neutrophil activating protein

NAPA National Association of Performing Artists

NAPAFASA National Asian Pacific American Families Against Substance Abuse

napalm naphthene + palmitate

NAPAP National Acid Precipitation Assessment Program

NAPBC National Action Plan on Breast Cancer

NAPCAN National Association for Prevention of Child Abuse and Neglect

NAPCRG North American Primary Care Research Group

NAPE National Association of Physicians for the Environment

NAPH National Association of Public Hospitals and Health Systems

naph. naphtha

NAPHO National Association of Physician Hospital Organization

NAPHSIS National Association for Public Health Statistics and Information Systems

NAPIA National Association of Professional Insurance Agents

NAPNAP National Association of Pediatric Nurse Associates and Practitioners

NAPNES National Association for Practical Nurse Education and Service

NAPS National Association of Personnel Services

NAPSA North American Pediatric Subspecialty Association

NAPWA National Association of People Living with HIV/AIDS

NAR National Association of Realtors

nar. narrow

NARA National Archives and Records Administration

NARAL National Abortion and Reproductive Rights Action League

narc narcotics agent

narc. narcotic; narcotics

narco narcotics agent

NARCOMS North American Research Consortium on Multiple Sclerosis

NAREB National Association of Real Estate Boards

NARFE National Association of Retired Federal Employees

NARHP National Adolescent Reproductive Health Partnership

NARIC National Rehabilitation Information Center

NARMC North Atlantic Regional Medical Center

NARP National Association of Railroad Passengers

NARPPS National Association of Rehabilitation Professionals in the Private Sector

narr. *Latin* narratio (narrative, that is, declaration in a legal action); narrator

NARSAD National Alliance for Research on Schizophrenia and Depression

NAS National Academy of Sciences; National Airspace System; naval air station; no added salt; nonindigenous aquatic species

NASA National Aeronautics and Space Administration

NASAA North American Securities Administrators Association

NASA DFRC National Aeronautics and Space Administration–Dryden Flight Research Center

NASCAR National Association for Stock Car Auto Racing

NASCI North American Society for Cardiac Imaging

NASD National Association of Securities Dealers

NASDAQ National Association of Securities Dealers Automated Quotation System

NASEMSD National Association of State Emergency Medical Service Directors

NaSGIM National Study of Graduate Education in Internal Medicine

NASK nuclear attack survival kit

NASL North American Soccer League

NASM National Academy of Sports Medicine; National Air and Space Museum

NASN National Association of School Nurses

NASOG National Association of Specialist Obstetricians and Gynaecologists

NASP National Aerospace Plane

NASPGN North American Society for Pediatric Gastroenterology and Nutrition

NASS National Agricultural Statistics Service; North American Spine Society

NASTAT North American Society of Teachers of the Alexander Technique

NASUCA National Association of State Utility Consumer Advocates

NASW National Association of Science Writers; National Association of Social Workers

nat. national; native; natural

natch naturally

NATE National Association of Teachers of English

NATICH National Air Toxics Information Clearinghouse

natl. national

NATO North Atlantic Treaty Organization

Nau. Nauru

naut. nautical

NAV net asset value

nav. naval; navigable; navigation

Nav. Navajo

N.A.V Net asset value

navaid navigation aid

NAVAIR Naval Air [Systems command headquarters]

NAVH National Association for the Visually Handicapped

navig. navigation

NAVS North American Vegetarian Society

NAVSAT navigation satellite

NAVTA North American Veterinary Technician Association

NAWAS National Warning System

NAWC Naval Air Warfare Center

NAWHO National Asian Women's Health Organization

NAWHP National Association of Women's Health Professionals

Nazi *German* Nationalsozialistische [deutsche Arbeiter-Partei] (National Socialist [German Workers' Party])

Nb niobium; Numbers

NB New Brunswick; northbound

Nb. Numbers

n.b. *Latin* nota bene (note well)

NBA National Basketball Association; National Boxing Association

NBAC National Bioethics Advisory Commission

NBC National Broadcasting Company

NBCC National Board for Certified Counselors; National Breast Cancer Coalition

NBCCEDP National Breast and Cervical Cancer Early Detection Program

NBCDI National Black Child Development Institute

NBCHN National Board for Certification of Hospice Nurses

NBD no big deal

NbE north by east

nbg no bloody good

NBME National Board of Medical Examiners

NBNA National Black Nurses Association

NBNSC National Board of Nutrition Support Certification

NBOME National Board of Osteopathic Medical Examiners

NBP National Braille Press

NBS National Biological Survey; National Bureau of Standards (now **NIST**, National Institute of Standards and Technology)

NBT nitroblue tetrazolium

NBT test nitroblue tetrazolium test

NBVF National Burn Victim Foundation

NbW north by west

NC network computer; no charge; no credit; noncallable; Nordic Council; normocephalic; North Carolina

.nc New Caledonia

N.C. North Carolina

NCAA National Collegiate Athletic Association

NCADD National Council on Alcoholism and Drug Dependence

NCADI National Clearinghouse for Alcohol and Drug Information

NCADV National Coalition Against Domestic Violence

NCAHF National Council Against Health Fraud

NCAI National Coalition for Adult Immunization

N.Cal New Caledonia

NCALI National Clearinghouse for Alcohol Information

NCAR National Center for Atmospheric Research

N.Car. North Carolina

NCATA National Coalition of Arts Therapies Associations

NCATT no comment at this time

NCB National Cooperative Bank

NCBDE National Certification Board for Diabetes Educators

NCBE National Clearinghouse on Bilingual Education

NCBI National Center for Biotechnology Information

NCC National Coordinating Committee; National Council of Churches

NCCA National Commission for the Certification of Acupuncturists

N.C.C.A. *Negligence and Compensation Cases Annotated*

NCCAN National Center on Child Abuse and Neglect

NCCAOM National Certification Commission for Acupuncture and Oriental Medicine

NCCDPHP National Center for Chronic Disease Prevention and Health Promotion

NCCE National Coalition for Consumer Education

NCCF National Childhood Cancer Foundation

NCCIDSA North Central Chapter Infectious Diseases Society of America

NCCLS National Committee for Clinical Laboratory Standards

NCCMHC National Council of Community Mental Health Centers

NCCN National Comprehensive Cancer Network

NCCP National Center for Children in Poverty

NCCPA National Commission on Certification of Physician Assistants

NCCS National Children's Cancer Society; National Coalition for Cancer Survivorship

NCD National Council on Disability

N.C.D. *Latin* nemine contradicente (no one dissenting)

NCDA National Cheerleading and Dance Association

NCDB National Cancer Data Base

NCDC National Climatic Data Center

NCDRH National Center for Devices and Radiological Health

NCEH National Center for Environmental Health

NCEHIC National Center for Environmental Health and Injury Control

NCEMCH National Center for Education in Maternal and Child Health

NCEMI National Center for Emergency Medicine Informatics

NCEP National Centers for Environmental Prediction; National Cholesterol Education Program

NCEPOD National Confidential Enquiry into Perioperative Deaths

NCF no clean flux

NCFC National Council of Farmer Cooperatives

NCFR National Council on Family Relations

NCFST National Center for Food Safety and Technology

NCGR National Center for Genome Research

NCH National Center for Homeopathy

NCHC National Coalition on Health Care

NCHE National Center for Health Education

NCHEC National Commission for Health Education Credentialing

NCHGR National Center for Human Genome Research

NCHP National Council of Hospice Professionals

NCHS National Center for Health Statistics

NCHSR National Center for Health Services Research [and Health Care Technology Assessment]

NCHSTE National Consortium of Health Science and Technology Education

NCHSTP National Center for HIV, STD, and TB Prevention

NCI National Cancer Institute

NCIC National Cancer Institute of Canada; National Cartographic Information Center

NCID National Center for Infectious Diseases

NCIPC National Center for Injury Prevention and Control

NCIS Naval Criminal Investigative Service

NCJRS National Criminal Justice Reference Service

NCL National Consumers League

NCLF National Children's Leukemia Foundation

NCM National Coastal Monitoring

NCND National Center for Nutrition and Dietetics

NCO noncommissioned officer

NCOA National Council on the Aging

NCOD National Coming Out Day

NCOFF National Center on Fathers and Families

NCP [Environmental Protection Agency] National Contingency Plan; [Novell's] NetWare Core Protocol

NCPC National Capital Planning Commission

NCPCA National Committee to Prevent Child Abuse

NCPIE National Council on Patient Information and Education

NCPOA National Chronic Pain Outreach Association

NCQA National Committee for Quality Assurance

NCQHA National Committee for Quality Health Care

NCRA National Cancer Registrars Association

NCRP National Council on Radiation Protection [and Measurements]

NCRR National Center for Research Resources

NCRW National Council for Research on Women

NCS National Cemetery System; National Center for Stuttering

NCSA National Center for Supercomputing Applications

NCSBN National Council of State Boards of Nursing

NCSC National Council of Senior Citizens

NC-17 No children under 17 admitted

NCTE National Council of Teachers of English

NCTM National Council of Teachers of Mathematics

NCTR National Center for Toxicological Research

NCUA National Credit Union Administration

n.c.v. no commercial value

NCWS noncommunity water system

NCYD National Center for Youth with Disabilities

Nd neodymium

ND North Dakota; Notre Dame

n.d. no date [of publication]

N.D. Doctor of Naturopathy; North Dakota

N/D no drinking/drugs; non drinker

NDA New Drug Application

NDACAN National Data Archive on Child Abuse and Neglect

N.Dak. North Dakota

NDB nondirectional beacon

NDDF National Drug Data File

NDDIC National Digestive Diseases Information Clearinghouse

NDE near-death experience

NDEA National Defense Education Act

NDEI National Diabetes Education Initiative

NDEP National Diabetes Education Program

NDGA National Depression Glass Association

NDI National Death Index

NDIC National Diabetes Information Clearinghouse

NDIS network driver interface specification

NDMA Nonprescription Drug Manufacturers Association

NDMDA National Depressive and Manic-Depressive Association

NDMS National Disaster Medical System

NDP New Democratic Party [of Canada]; nucleoside diphosphate

NDR nondestructive readout

NDRI Naval Dental Research Institute

NDRO nondestructive readout

NDSC National Down Syndrome Congress

NDSS National Down Syndrome Society

NDT nondestructive testing

NDU National Defense University

NDVI normalized difference vegetation index

Ne Nehemiah; neon

NE Nebraska; New England; northeast; northeastern; not equal to

Ne. Nehemiah

.ne Niger

NEA National Education Association; National Endowment for the Arts; Nuclear Energy Agency

NEB *New English Bible*

Neb. Nebraska

NEbE northeast by east

NEbN northeast by north

Nebr. Nebraska

nebul. nebula

NEC Nuclear Energy Commission

NED *New English Dictionary* (now **OED**, *Oxford English Dictionary*)

NEDARC National Emergency [Medical Services for Children] Data Analysis Resource Center

NEEP negative end-expiratory pressure

NEIC National Earthquake Information Center

NEIS National Earthquake Information Service

neg. negative; negotiable

NegAM negative amortization

negl. negligible

NEH National Endowment for the Humanities

Neh. Nehemiah

NEHA National Environmental Health Association

NEHAP National Environmental Health Action Plan

NEHEP National Eye Health Education Program

NEI National Eye Institute

n.e.i. not elsewhere included

NEIC National Electronic Information Corporation

NEJM *New England Journal of Medicine*

NEL National Engineering Laboratory

NEMA National Emergency Medicine Association

nem con *Latin* nemine contradicente (no one contradicting)

nem diss *Latin* nemine dissentiente (no one dissenting)

NEMPAC National Emergency Medicine Political Action Committee

NEMSA National Emergency Medical Service Alliance

neo newborn (from "neonate")

NEP New Economic Policy; non-English proficient

Nep. Nepal

NEPA National Environmental Policy Act

NEPP National Early Psychosis Project

NERL National Exposure Research Laboratory

NES National Enuresis Society

n.e.s. not elsewhere specified

NESDIS National Environmental Satellite, Data and Information Services

NESDRES National Environmental Data Referral Service

NESS National Environmental Satellite Service

NEST non-surgical embryonic selective thinning

Net Internet

NET National Educational Television

.net network provider

Neth. Netherlands

netiquette [Inter]net etiquette

NeuAc N-acetylneuraminic acid

neur. neurological; neurology

neurol. neurology; neurosurgery

neut. neuter; neutral

Nev. Nevada

NewEng. New England

Newf. Newfoundland

Newfie resident of Newfoundland; Newfoundland (breed of dog)

New Hebr. New Hebrides

New Test. New Testament

New Zeal. New Zealand

NEX Navy exchange

NEXRAD [National Weather Service] Next Generation Weather Radar

NF National Formulary; neurofibromatosis; Newfoundland; no funds

.nf Norfolk Island

n/f no funds

NFA National Futures Association

NFB National Federation for the Blind

NFC National Finance Center; National Football Conference

NFCC National Foundation for Consumer Credit

NFCVP National Funding Collaborative on Violence Prevention

NFD network flow diagrams

NFDC National Flight Data Center

NFED National Foundation for Ectodermal Dysplasias

NFFR National Foundation for Facial Reconstruction

NFG no fucking good

NFI National Fisheries Center

NFIA National Families in Action

NFID National Foundation for Infectious Diseases

NFL National Football League

NFIP National Flood Insurance Program

Nfld. Newfoundland

NFNA National Flight Nurses Association

NFP natural family planning

NFPA National Flight Paramedics Association

NFPRHA National Family Planning and Reproductive Health Association

NFr. Northern French

NFris. Northern Frisian

NFS National Forest Service; network file system

NFW no fucking way

ng nanogram

NG National Guard; natural gas; newsgroup; no good; nose guard

.ng Nigeria

n.g. no good; not good

NGB National Guard Bureau

NGDC National Geophysical Data Center

NGF National Golf Foundation; nerve growth factor

NGk. New Greek

NHeb. New Hebrew

NGI Next Generation Internet

ngm nanogram

NGNA National Gerontological Nursing Association

NGO nongovernmental organization

NGRI not guilty by reason of insanity

NGS National Genealogical Society; National Geodetic Survey; National Geographic Society

NGSP National Glycohemoglobin Standardization Program

NGU nongonococcal urethritis

NGVD National Geodetic Vertical Datum

NH New Hampshire; Northern Hemisphere

N.H. New Hampshire

NHAAP National Heart Attack Alert Program

NHANES National Health and Nutrition Examination Survey

NHBPEP National High Blood Pressure Education Program

NHC National Health Council; National Hurricane Center

NHCSSP National Health Care Skill Standards Project

NHDS National Hospital Discharge Survey

N.Hebr. New Hebrides

NHeLP National Health Law Program

NHES National Health Examination Survey

NHF National Hemophilia Foundation

NHGRI National Human Genome Research Institute

NHHCS National Home and Hospice Survey

NHI National Health Insurance; National Highway Institute

NHIC National Health Information Center

NHIK National Health Information Knowledgebase

NHIRC National Health Information Resource Center

NHIS National Health Interview Survey

NHL National Hockey League

NHLBI National Heart, Lung, and Blood Institute

NHLBI OEI National Heart, Lung, and Blood Institute Obesity Education Initiative

NHMRC National Health and Medical Research Council

NHNA New Hampshire Nurses' Association

NHO National Hospice Organization

NHPC Natural Holistic Pet Care

NHPF National Health Policy Forum

NHPI National Health Provider Inventory

NHPRC National Historical Publications and Records Commission

NHRC Naval Health Research Center

NHS National Health Service; National Honor Society

NHSA National Healthcare Staffing Association

NHSC National Health Service Corps

NHSDA National Household Survey on Drug Abuse

NHTSA National Highway Traffic Safety Administration

Ni nickel

NI night (shortwave transmission)

.ni Nicaragua

NIA National Institute on Aging

NIAAA National Institute on Alcohol Abuse and Alcoholism

NIAD National Institute of Art and Disabilities

NIAID National Institute of Allergy and Infectious Diseases

NIAMS National Institute of Arthritis and Musculoskeletal and Skin [Diseases]

NIB National Industries for the Blind; Nordic Investment Bank

NIC National Ice Center; National Institute of Corrections; network interface card; newly industrializing country

Nic. Nicaragua; Nicaraguan

NiCad nickel-cadmium [battery]

NICBDAT nothing is certain but death and taxes

NICD National Information Center on Deafness

NICE National Institute for Consumer Education

NFIC National Fraud Information Center

NICHCY National Information Center for Children and Youth with Disabilities

NICHHD National Institute of Child Health and Human Development

NICHSR National Information Center on Health Services Research [and Health Care Technology]

NICK Nickelodeon (cable television channel)

NICO National Insurance Consumer Organization

NICWA National Indian Child Welfare Association

NIDA National Institute on Drug Abuse

NIDCD National Institute on Deafness and Other Communication Disorders

NIDDK National Institute of Diabetes and Digestive and Kidney [Diseases]

NIDDM non-insulin-dependent diabetes mellitus

NIDR National Institute of Dental Research

NIDRR National Institute on Disability and Rehabilitation Research

NIE National Institute of Education; newly industrializing economy

NIEHS National Institute of Environmental Health Sciences

NIFO next in, first out

NIG National Institute of Genetics

Nig. Nigeria; Nigerian

nightie nightgown

nighty nightgown

NIGMS National Institute of General Medical Sciences

NIH National Institutes of Health

NIHB National Indian Health Board

NIHECS National Institutes of Health Electronic Computer Store

NII National Information Infrastructure

NIJ National Institute of Justice

NIK Nickelodeon channel

NIL nothing, I have nothing for you (shortwave transmission)

NIMBY not in my backyard

NiMH nickel-metal hydride [battery]

NIMH National Institute of Mental Health

NIMR National Institute for Medical Research

NIMS National Infant Mortality Survey

NIMTO not in my term of office

NINDS National Institute of Neurological Disorders and Stroke

NINE National Institute of Nutritional Education

911 emergency

NINR National Institute of Nursing Research

NIOSH National Institute for Occupational Safety and Health

NIOSHTIC National Institute for Occupational Safety and Health Technical Information Center

NIP National Immunization Program

NIPAW National Inhalants and Poisons Awareness Week

NIPC National Inhalant Prevention Coalition

NIPF National Incontinentia Pigmenti Foundation

NIPS National Institute for Physiological Sciences

NIR near infrared

N. Ir Northern Ireland; Northern Irish

NIRA National Industrial Recovery Act

N. Ire. Northern Ireland

NIRS National Institute of Radiological Science

NIS Naval Investigative Service; network information service; Newly Independent States

NIST National Institute of Standards and Technology

NISU National Injury Surveillance Unit

NIT National Intelligence Test; National Invitational Tournament

nitro nitroglycerin

NIV noninvasive ventilation

NJ New Jersey

N.J. New Jersey

NK none known; not known

NKA no known allergy; now known as

nkat nanokatal

NKCF National Keratoconus Foundation

NKDA no known drug allergy

NKF National Kidney Foundation

NKSF natural killer cell stimulating factor

NKUDIC National Kidney and Urologic Diseases Information Clearinghouse

NKVD *Russian* Narodnyj Kommissariat Vnutrennikh Del (People's Commissariat of Internal Affairs)

NL National League; new line; New Latin

.nl Netherlands

n.l. *Latin* non licet (not permitted); *Latin* non liquet (not clear)

NLADA National Legal Aid and Defender Association

NLDTD National Library of Digital Theses and Dissertations

Nle norleucine

NLF National Liberation Front

NLGHA National Lesbian and Gay Health Association

NLM National Library of Medicine

NLM SIS National Library of Medicine Specialized Information Services

NLN National League for Nursing

NLO nonlinear optics

NLQ near letter quality

NLRA National Labor Relations Act

NLRB National Labor Relations Board

NLSC National Logistics Supply Center

NLT night letter

NLTN National Laboratory Training Network

NLY newly

nm nanometer; nautical mile; nuclear magneton

nM nanomolar

NM New Mexico; neuromuscular

N.M. New Mexico

NMA National Medical Association

NMC National Marine Center; National Meteorological Center

NMCHC National Maternal and Child Health Clearinghouse

NMCS National Military Command System

NMCUES National Medical Care Utilization and Expenditure Survey

NMDA N-methyl D-aspartate excitotoxic amino acid

NMDC National Medical Device Coalition

NMES National Medical Expenditure Survey

N.Mex. New Mexico

NMF National Marfan Foundation

NMFI National Master Facility Inventory

NMFS National Marine Fisheries Service

NMHA National Mental Health Association

NMHC nonmethane hydrocarbon

NMHF National Mental Health Foundation

NMHID National Mental Health Institute on Deafness

NMHS National Mental Health Strategy

NMI no middle initial

NMIHS National Maternal and Infant Health Survey

NMIMC Naval Medical Information Management Center

NMIS Network Medical Information Services

NML National Measurement Laboratory

NMRDC Naval Medical Research and Development Command

NMMSA National Minority Medical Suppliers Association

NMN nicotinamide mononucleotide

NMP nucleoside 5c-monophosphate

NMPIS National Marine Pollution Information Systems

NMR nuclear magnetic resonance

NMS National Mortality Survey

NMSS National Multiple Sclerosis Society

NMT Nordic Mobile Telephone

NMU National Maritime Union

nn. footnotes; names; notes; nouns

NNBA National Nurses in Business Association

NNDSS National Notifiable Diseases Surveillance System

NNE north-northeast

NNFF National Neurofibromatosis Foundation

NNHS National Nursing Home Survey

NNHSF National Nursing Home Survey Followup

NN/LM National Network of Libraries of Medicine

NNM NASDAQ National Market [System]

NNR National Narcolepsy Registry

NNS National Natality Survey

NNSA National Nurses Society on Addictions

NNSDO National Nursing Staff Development Organization

NNT nearest neighbor tool (mathematical method)

NNW north-northwest

No nobelium

no. north; northern; number

.no Norway

NOAA National Oceanic and Atmospheric Administration

NOAASIS National Oceanic and Atmospheric Administration Satellite Information System

NOAH Network of Animal Health

NOAO National Optical Astronomy Observatories

NOARL Naval Ocean and Atmosphere Research Laboratory

NOB notes over bonds

NOCIRC National Organization of Circumcision Information Resource Centers

NOCR Network for Oncology Communication and Research

noct. maneq. *Latin* nocte maneque (at night and in the morning)

No.Dak. North Dakota

NODC National Oceanographic Data Center

NODD NORD Orphan Drug Designation [Database]

NOE nuclear Overhauser effect

NOED *New Oxford English Dictionary*

NOF National Osteoporosis Foundation

NOFAS National Organization on Fetal Alcohol Syndrome

NOHARMM National Organization to Halt the Abuse and Routine Mutilation of Males

NOHIC National Oral Health Information Clearinghouse

NOHSCP [Environmental Protection Agency] National Oil and Hazardous Substances Contingency Plan

n.o.i.b.n. not otherwise indexed by name

noir film noir

NOL net operating loss

NOLF Nursing Organization Liaison Forum

nolo nolo contendere

nol. pros. nolle prosequi

NOLTP National Organization of Lung Transplant Patients

nom. nominative

NOMAD Navy Oceanographic Meteorological Association

NOMIC National Organization for Mentally Ill Children

NoMSG National Organization Mobilized to Stop Glutamate

non nonsmoking (area of restaurant)

noncom noncommissioned officer

non obs. *Latin* non obstante (notwithstanding)

non obst. *Latin* non obstante (notwithstanding)

non pros. *Latin* non prosequitur (he or she does not follow up)

non seq. *Latin* non sequitur (it does not follow)

nonstand. nonstandard

non-U non upper class

NOP not operational; not our publication

n.o.p. not otherwise provided for

NOPE network operations engineer

NOR NOT OR (logical operator)

Nor. Norman; north; northern; Norway; Norwegian

NORAD North American Aerospace Defense Command; (formerly) North American Air Defense Command

Noraid Irish Northern Aid Committee

NORC naturally occurring retirement community

NORD National Organization for Rare Disorders

Norf. Norfolk

NORIF nonstimulated oocyte retrieval in (office) fertilization

norm standard; model; pattern

norm. normal

Norm. Norman

NORML National Organization for the Reform of Marijuana Laws

north. northern

Northumb. Northumbrian

N or V nausea or vomiting

Norw. Norway; Norwegian

NOS National Ocean Service; network operating system

nos. numbers

n.o.s. not otherwise specified

NOSB National Organic Standards Board

NOSS National Oceanic Satellite System

NO synthase nitric oxide synthase

NOTT Nocturnal Oxygen Therapy Trial

Notts. Nottinghamshire

nov. novelist

Nov. November

N.O.V *Latin* non obstante veredicto (notwithstanding the verdict)

NOVA Nurses Organization of Veterans Affairs

NOW National Organization for Women

N.O.W. account negotiable order of withdrawal account

Nox nitrogen oxide

NOx nitrous oxide

NOYB none of your business

n.p. no pagination; no place [of publication]

Np neptunium

NP neuropsychiatry; not palpable; noun phrase; nurse practitioner

.np Nepal

N.P. notary public

NPA National Pediculosis Association; National Perinatal Association; National Prostate Association

NPACE Nurse Practitioner Association for Continuing Education

n. pag. no pagination

NPC National Petroleum Council

NPCMCH National Parent Consortium on Maternal and Child Health

NPCR National Program of Cancer Registries

NPDES [Environmental Protection Agency] National Pollutant Discharge Elimination System

NPDWR [Environmental Protection Agency] National Primary Drinking Water Regulations

NPF National Parkinson Foundation; National Psoriasis Foundation

n.p.f. not provided for

NPG negative population growth

NPI National Provider Identifier

NPL [Environmental Protection Agency] National Priorities List ("Superfund" List)

n. pl. plural noun

NPM National Poetry Month

NPN nonprotein nitrogen

NPND National Parent Network on Disabilities

n.p.o. *Latin* non per os (not by mouth); *Latin* nil per os (nothing by mouth)

NPPC National Pork Producers Council

NPPHCN National Progressive Primary Health Care Network

NPPSIS National Parent to Parent Support and Information System

NPPV noninvasive positive pressure ventilation

NPR National Public Radio

NPRH Nurse Practitioners in Reproductive Health

Nps nitrophenylsulfenyl

NPS National Park Service; nonpoint source [pollution]

NPT Nonproliferation Treaty

NPTN National Pesticides Telecommunications Network

NPV negative pressure ventilation

nr near

NR not rated; number (shortwave transmission)

.nr Nauru

N.R. nonresident; not reported

NRA National Recovery Administration; National Rifle Association; Naval Reserve Association

NRAO National Radio Astronomy Observatory

NRC National Research Council; [United States Coast Guard] National Response Center; Nuclear Regulatory Commission

NRCC National Registry in Clinical Chemistry

NRCCSA National Resource Center on Child Sexual Abuse

NRCS Natural Resources Conservation Service

NRDC Natural Resources Defense Council

NREM non-rapid eye movement

NREMT National Registry of Emergency Medical Technicians

NREN National Research and Education Network

NRG energy

NRHA National Rural Health Association

NRID National Registry of Interpreters for the Deaf

NRL Naval Research Laboratory

NRMP National Resident Matching Program

NRN no reply necessary

nRNA nuclear RNA

NRO National Reconnaissance Office

NRPF National Retinitis Pigmentosa Foundation (now Foundation Fighting Blindness)

NRSP National Remote Sensing Program

NRT [Environmental Protection Agency] National Response Team; near real-time

NRTA National Retired Teachers Association

NRWA National Rural Water Association

NRZ nonreturn [to] zero

NRZ-L nonreturn [to] zero level

ns nanosecond

Ns nimbostratus

NS New Style (calendar); nonsmoking [section]; normal saline; no smoking [allowed]; Nova Scotia; nuclear sclerosis; nuclear ship

n.s. new series; not specified

n/s not sufficient

N/S nonsmoker

NSA National Security Agency; National Skating Association; National Ski Association; National Standards Association; National Stroke Association; National Student Association; nonsurgical sperm aspiration

NSAC National Society for Autistic Children

NSAID nonsteroidal antiinflammatory drug

NSAW National Sleep Awareness Week

NSAWI National Substance Abuse Web Index

NSB National Science Board

NSBRI National Space Biomedical Research Institute

NSC NASDAQ Small Capitalization; National Safety Council; National Security Council; Neuroscience Center

NSCLC non-small cell lung cancer

NSDWR National Secondary Drinking Water Regulations

NSE National Stock Exchange

nsec nanosecond

NSF National Science Foundation; National Sleep Foundation; not sufficient funds

n.s.f. not sufficient funds

NSFG National Survey of Family Growth

NSG Nuclear Suppliers Group

NSGC National Society of Genetic Counselors, Inc.

NSIDC National Snow and Ice Data Center

NSILA nonsuppressible insulin-like activity

NSMS National Sheet Music Society

NSO National Solar Observatory

NSP neurological shellfish poisoning

NSPCA National Society for the Prevention of Cruelty to Animals

NSPHPC National Survey of Personal Health Practices and Consequences

NSPS [Environmental Protection Agency] New Source Performance Standards

NSR nasoseptal reconstruction

NSSA National Sjogren's Syndrome Association

NSSDC National Space Science Data Center

NSSFC National Severe Storms Forecast Center

NSSLHA National Student Speech Language Hearing Association

NST non-stress test

NSTA National Science Teachers Association

NSTC National Science and Technology Council

NSTL National Space Technology Laboratories

NSVD normal spontaneous vaginal delivery

NSW New South Wales

NT New Testament; Northwest Territories

nt. night

NTDBWY nice to do business with you

NTDRA National Tire Dealers and Retreaders Association

NTF National Turkey Federation

NTG nitroglycerin; nothing (shortwave transmission)

Nthb. Northumberland

NTIA National Telecommunications and Information Administration

NTID National Technical Institute for the Deaf

NTIS National Technical Information Service

NTMI nontransmural myocardial infarction

NTNG nontoxic nodular goiter

NTP Network Time Protocol

n.t.p. normal temperature and pressure

NTR nuclear thermal rocket

NTS nucleus tractus solitarii

NTSB National Transportation Safety Board

NTSC National Television Standards Committee

NTU nephelometric turbidity unit

nt.wt. net weight

NTYMI now that you mention it

NTZ Neutral Zone

.nu Niue

n.u. name unknown

Nuc nucleoside

NUG necrotizing ulcerative gingivitis

NUI notebook user interface

nuke a nuclear device or weapon; a nuclear-powered electric generating plant

num. number; numeral

Num. Numbers

numb. numbered

numis. numismatic; numismatics

Num Lock numeric lock key

NV Nevada; never (shortwave transmission); not voting

N-V neurovascular

Nva norvaline

NVCA National Valentine Collectors Association

N/V/D nausea-vomiting-diarrhea

NVG Night Vision Goggles

NVHA National Voluntary Health Agencies

NVIC National Vaccine Information Center

NVS nonvolatile solids

NVSS nonvolatile suspended solids

NW northwest; northwestern; now (shortwave transmission)

NWAV(E) New Ways of Analyzing Variation (in English and other languages)

NWB non-weight-bearing

NWbN northwest by north

NWbW northwest by west

NWC National War College

NWDA National Wholesale Druggists Association

NWDC National Wildlife Defense Council

NWHIC National Women's Health Information Center

NWHRC National Women's Health Resource Center

NWIC National Water Information Clearinghouse

NWO New World Order

NWP numerical weather prediction

NWR National [Oceanic and Atmospheric Administration] Weather Radio; National Wildlife Refuge [System]

NWRC National Women's Resource Center

NWS National Weather Service

NWSFO National Weather Service Forecast Office

NWT Northwest Territories

n.wt. net weight

NWU National Writers Union

NX next (shortwave transmission)

NY New York

N.Y. New York

NYBID New York [interbank] bid [rate]

NYBOR New York [interbank] offered rate

NYC New York City

NYCE New York Cotton Exchange

NYCTMI now you come to mention it

NYFE New York Futures Exchange

NYMEX New York Mercantile Exchange

NYP not yet published

NYS New York State

NYSE New York Stock Exchange

NYT *New York Times*

.nz New Zealand

N.Z. New Zealand

n_0 Loschmidt's number

O

o *Latin* octarius (pint); octavo; ohm

O old; Oriental (as in personal ads, but usually **A**, Asian); out; outstanding

0. ocean; Ohio

OA office automation; Office of Administration; operations agreement; Ophthalmology Assembly

o/a on or about

OAA Obstetric Anaesthetists Association; Otolaryngology Administration Assembly

OAL over-all length

OAM [National Institute of Health] Office of Alternative Medicine

O & M operations and maintenance

OAO orbiting astronomical observatory

OAPC Office of Alien Property Custodian

OAPEC Organization of Arab Petroleum Exporting Countries

OAPP Office of Adolescent Pregnancy Programs

OAR [National Oceanic and Atmospheric Administration Office of] Oceanic and Atmospheric Research

OAS Organization of American States

OASDHI Old Age, Survivors, Disability, and Health Insurance

OASDI Old Age, Survivors' and Disability Insurance

OASIS Obstetric Anesthesia Safety Improvement Study; Online Asperger Syndrome Information and Support

OASTP Office of the Assistant Secretary for Technology Policy

OATUS on a totally unrelated subject

OAU Organization of African Unity

OAUS on an unrelated subject

ob obvious

OB obstetric; obstetrics; obstetrician

ob. *Latin* obiit (he or she died); *Latin* obiter (incidentally); oboe

Ob. Obadiah

O.B. off Broadway

OBC on board computer

O.B.E. Order of the British Empire

OBGA Obstetrics and Gynecology Assembly

OB/GYN obstetrician/gynecologist; obstetrics/gynecology

Obie O.B. (that is, off Broadway)

OBIGGS on-board inert gas generating system

obit obituary

obit. *Latin* obitus (death, that is, obituary)

obj. object; objective

obl. oblique; oblong

obno obnoxious

OBO order book official

o.b.o. or best offer

OBOGS on-board oxygen generation system

OBRA Omnibus Budget Reconciliation Act

OBS organic brain syndrome

obs. obscene; observation; observatory; obsolete; obstetrics

OBS/GYN obstetrics/gynecology

obstet. obstetric; obstetrics

OBT on-board time

obv. obverse

Oc. ocean

OC open-captioned

o.c. *Latin* opere citato (in the work cited)

O.C. Officer Commanding; Old Catholic; Orphan's Court

o/c overcharge

OCA Obsessive Compulsive Anonymous

OCAS Organization of Central American States

OCC Options Clearing Corporation

occ. occident; occidental; occupation

occas. occasional; occasionally

OCD obsessive compulsive disorder

oceanogr. oceanography

OCF Obsessive-Compulsive Foundation

OCHAMPUS Office of Civilian Health and Medical Program of the Uniformed Services

OCO one cancels the other order

OCorn. Old Cornish

OCP obligatory contour principle; oral contraceptive pill

OCR Office of Civil Rights; optical character reader; optical character recognition

OCRM Office of Coastal Resource Management

OCS Office of Community Services; Officer Candidate School; Old Church Slavonic

OCSE Office of Child Support Enforcement

OCST Office of Commercial Space Transportation

oct. octavo

Oct. October

OC-VU ocean view

OD overdose

o.d. *Latin* oculus dexter (right eye); olive drab; on demand; outside diameter

O.D. Doctor of Optometry; officer of the day; overdraft; overdrawn

ODA official development assistance

ODBC open database connectivity

ODI open data-link interface

ODM oil debris monitoring

ODP ozone depletion potential

ODPHP Office of Disease Prevention and Health Promotion

Oe oersted

OE Old English

OECD Organization for Economic Cooperation and Development

OECS Organization of Eastern Caribbean States

OED *Oxford English Dictionary*

OEM original equipment manufacturer

OEMP Office of Environmental Monitoring and Prediction

OEO Office of Economic Opportunity

OEP Office of Emergency Preparedness; Office of Environmental Policy; open enrollment period

OER officer efficiency report

OES Office of Employment Security

OETA original estimated time of arrival

OF Oriental female; outfield; outfielder

OFA Office of Family Assistance; Orthopedic Foundation for Animals

ofc office

OFCC Office of Federal Contract Compliance

OFCCP Office of Federal Contract Compliance Programs

off. office; officer; official

offic. official

OFM Office of Financial Management

O.F.M. Order of Friars Minor

OFP Office of Family Planning

OFPP Office of Federal Procurement Policy

OFr Old French

OFR Office of the Federal Register

ofr. offer

OFris. Old Frisian

OFS office (shortwave transmission)

OG officer of the guard

OGE Office of Government Ethics

OGOD one gene, one disorder

OGPS Office of Grants and Program Systems

OGPU *Russian* Obedinennoe Gosudarstvennoe Politcheskoe Upravlenie (United State Political Administration)

OH off hand; Ohio; open house (real estate)

OHD organic heart disease

OHG Old High German

OHI Oral Hygiene Index

OHI-S Simplified Oral Hygiene Index

OHMO Office of Health Maintenance Organizations

OHMS On Her (or His) Majesty's Service

OHRE Office of Human Radiation Experiments (Department of Energy)

OI Office of Investigator; optimum interpolation

OIC Office of Independent Counsel; oh, I see

OIE Overseas Investment Exchange

OIF Osteogenesis Imperfecta Foundation

OIG Office of Inspector General

OIP official index period

OIr. Old Irish

OIS Osteopathic Information Service

OIT Office of International Trade

OIt. Old Italian

OJ orange juice

OJJDP Office of Juvenile Justice and Delinquency Prevention

OJP Office of Justice Programs

OJT on-the-job training

OK Oklahoma

O.K. oll korrect

Okie Oklahoman

Okla. Oklahoma

OL Old Latin

OLB offensive linebacker; outside linebacker

Old Ch. Slav. Old Church Slavonic

OLE object linking and embedding

oleo oleomargarine

OLFrank. Old Low Frankish

OLG Old Low German

OLI/HMD Online Images from the History of Medicine Division

OLR outgoing longwave radiation

OLS ordinary least squares

OLSNA Orthopaedic Laser Society of North America

OM Oriental male; outcomes management

Om. Oman

.om Oman

O.M. Order of Merit

OMA Occupational Management and Budget

OM&R operations, maintenance, and replacement

OMB Office of Management and Budget

OMD *Online Medical Dictionary*

OMEC Online Medical Employment Center

OMG Object Management Group

OMH Office of Minority Health

OMH-RC Office of Minority Health Resource Center

OMIM Online Mendelian Inheritance in Man

OMIS Office of Management and Information Systems

omn. hor. *Latin* omni hora (every hour)

OMNI Organizing Medical Networked Information

OMO Office of Marine Operations

OMP oligo-N-methylmorpholinium propylene oxide; orotidylic acid; orotidylate; orotidine 5c-monophosphate

OMPA octamethyl pyrophosphoramide

OMS orbital maneuvering system; organic mental syndrome; outcomes management system

OMT object modeling technique

ON Old Norse; Ontario

ONC open network computing

ONFr. Old Northern French

ONI Office of Naval Intelligence

ONNA oh no, not again

ONR Office of Naval Research

ONS Oncology Nursing Society

Ont. Ontario

OO object-oriented

OOA out of area

OOB out of bed

OOD officer of the deck

OODP object-oriented data processing

OOF other official flows

OOH *Occupational Outlook Handbook*

OOI out of interest

OOP object-oriented programming; out of print

OOPL object-oriented programming language

OOTB out of the box (that is, brand new)

op operation; operative; operator; opportunity

Op operation; op[tical] art

OP observation post; operate (shortwave transmission); operator (shortwave transmission); out of print; outpatient

op. opus

o.p. out of print

O.P. Order of Preachers

O/P out of print

OPA Office of Population Affairs; Orthopedic Practice Assembly

OPANAL *Spanish* Organismo para la Proscripción de las Armas Nucleares en la América Latina [y el Caribe] (Agency for the Prohibition of Nuclear Weapons in Latin America and the Caribbean)

OPC organic photoconductor

op. cit. *Latin* opere citato (in the work cited)

OPDIN Ocean Pollution Data Center

OPEC Organization of Petroleum Exporting Countries

Op-Ed opposite the editorial page

OPEN Online Public Education Network

OPers. Old Persian

OPFI Office of Program and Fiscal Integrity

OPg. Old Portuguese

OPHS Office of Public Health and Science

ophthalm. ophthalmology

OPI overall performance index

OPIC Overseas Private Investment Corporation

OPK ovulation predictor kit

OPL [White House] Office of Public Liaison

OPM Office of Personnel Management

OPO organ procurement organization

OPol. Old Polish

opp. opposed; opposite

oppies older professional parents

oppo opposition research

OPPTS [Environmental Protection Agency] Office of Prevention, Pesticides, and Toxic Substances

OProv. Old Provençal

OPRR Office for Protection from Research Risks

OPruss. Old Prussian

OPS Ophthalmic Photographers' Society

opt. optative; optical; optional

OPV oral poliovirus vaccine

OR operating room; operations research; Oregon; owner's risk

Or. Oregon

ORA Orthopaedic Rehabilitation Association

ORBD~NRC Osteoporosis and Related Bone Diseases ~ National Resource Center

orch. orchestra

ORD Chicago O'Hare airport code; [National Institutes of Health] Office of Rare Diseases; optical rotatory dispersion

ord. order; ordinal; ordinance; ordnance

ordn. ordnance

Ore. Oregon

Oreg. Oregon

org. organic; organization; organized

.org organization

ORHP Office of Rural Health Policy

orig. origin; original; originally

Ork. Orkney Islands

ORM Office of Regional Management

ornith. ornithologic; ornithological; ornithology

ORNL Oak Ridge National Laboratory

OROM optical read-only memory

ORP ordinary, reasonable, and prudent

ORR Office of Refugee Relief; Office of Refugee Resettlement

ORS Orthopaedic Research Society

ORSA Operations Research Society of America

O-R system oxidation reduction system

orth. orthopedic; orthopedics

ORTHO American Orthopsychiatric Association

ORuss. Old Russian

ORV off-road vehicle

Os osmium

OS Old Saxon; operating system; out of stock

o.s. *Latin* oculus sinister (left eye); old series; out of stock

O.S. Old Style (calendar); ordinary seaman

OSA obstructive sleep apnea; Optical Society of America

O.S.A. Order of Saint Augustine

O.S.B. Order of Saint Benedict

OSC Office of Space Communications; Office of Special Counsel

OSCAR Orbiting Satellite Carrying Amateur Radio

OSCE Organization on Security and Cooperation in Europe

OSD operational system development

OSDBU Office of Small and Disadvantaged Business Utilization

OSE Operations Simulations Engineer

OSEP Office of Special Education Programs

OSERS Office of Special Education and Rehabilitative Services

OSF Office of Space Flight

O.S.F. Order of Saint Francis

OSGR Office of State Government Relations

OSH Office on Smoking and Health

OSHA Occupational Safety and Health Administration

OSHRC Occupational Safety and Health Review Commission

OSI open system interconnection; out of stock indefinitely

OSM Office of Surface Mining [Reclamation and Enforcement]

OSN Ocular Surgery News

OSO Orbiting Solar Observatory

OSp. Old Spanish

OSS Office of Space Science; Office of Strategic Services

OSSA Office of Space Science and Applications

OSSD Office of Space Systems Development

OST ocean surface temperature

OSTP Office of Science and Technology Policy

OS/2 [IBM] Operating System Two

O.S.U. Order of Saint Ursula

OSV object-subject-verb

OSw. Old Swedish

OT occupational therapy; offensive tackle; Office of Telecommunications; Office of Transportation; Old Testament; optical thickness; optimality theory; overtime

O.T. old terminology

OTA Office of Technology Assessment; Office of Technical Assistance; Orthopaedic Trauma Association

OTAA Office of Trade Adjustment Assistance

OT&E operational testing and evaluation

OTB off-track betting

OTC Officers' Training Corps; over-the-counter

OTEC ocean thermal energy conversion

OTH over the horizon

OTHB over the horizon backscatter

OTL out to lunch

OTO otolaryngology

OTOH on the other hand

otol. otology

OTR Occupational Therapist, Registered; other (shortwave transmission)

O.T.R. *offensive* on the rag (that is, menstruating)

OTS Office of Thrift Supervision; Officers' Training School

OTT over the transom

OTTH on the third hand

OTurk. Old Turkish

OTV orbital transfer vehicle

O.U. *Latin* oculus uterque (each eye; both eyes)

OUI operation [of motor vehicle while] under influence [of liquor or drugs]

OUP Oxford University Press

OUR oxygen utilization rate

OV orbital vehicle; over (short-wave transmission)

OVC Office for Victims of Crime

OVI Office of Voluntarism Initiatives

OVS object-verb-subject

OW Old Welsh; one way

OWBO Office of Women's Business Ownership

OWelsh Old Welsh

OWH [Centers for Disease Control and Prevention] Office of Women's Health

OWI Office of War Information; operating [a vehicle] while intoxicated

OWL Orthopaedic Web Links

Ox. Oxford

Oxbridge Oxford and Cambridge [Universities]

Oxfam Oxford Committee for Famine Relief

Oxon *Medieval Latin* Oxonia (Oxford, Oxfordshire); *Latin* Oxoniensis; (of Oxford)

OXT oxytocin

OY optimum yield

oz. ounce; ounces

oz. ap. apothecaries' ounce

oz. av. avoirdupois ounce

ozs. ounces

oz. t. troy ounce

P

p momentum; piano (musical direction); proton; punctuation

P pale; parental generation; parity; parking available; pass; pawn; Peter; petite; phosphorus; pressure; professional (as in personal ads); punter

p. page; part; participle; past; penny; peseta; peso; pint; pipe; pole; population; principal; purl

p- para-

pa pulmonary artery

Pa pascal; protactinium

PA Palestinian Authority; Pennsylvania; physician assistant; professional association; public affairs

Pa. past

.pa Panama

p.a. per annum

P.A. physician's assistant; power of attorney; press agent; prosecuting attorney; public-address system

PAA Pediatric Administration Assembly

PABA para-aminobenzoic acid

PAC political action committee

Pac. Pacific

Pacif. Pacific

PACOR packet processor

PACS picture archiving and communication system

PAC-10 Pacific Athletic Conference

PACU post anesthesia care unit

PAD packet assembler/disassembler; pressure anomaly detection

PADC Pennsylvania Avenue Development Corporation

PADS planned arrival and departure system; *Publications of the American Dialect Society*

PAF platelet-aggregating factor

PaG. Pennsylvania German

PAGE polyacrylamide gel electrophoresis

PAH p-aminohippuric acid; polararomatic hydrocarbon; polycyclic aromatic hydrocarbon

PAHCOM Professional Association of Health Care Office Managers

PAHO Pan American Health Organization

PAI Population Action International

PAIGE Patient Instruction Generator

PAIR Professional Association of Interns and Residents

PAIS Public Affairs Information Service

Pak. Pakistan; Pakistani

Paki *offensive* Pakistani

PAL phase alternation line; Police Athletic League

Pal. Palestine; Palestinian

paleogr. paleography

paleont. paleontology

PALS pediatric advanced life support

pam. pamphlet

PAMA Pan American Medical Association

PAMM Program Against Micronutrient Malnutrition

PAMs polyacrylamides

PAN peroxyacetyl nitrate

Pan. Panama; Panamanian

P & A percussion and auscultation

P and H postage and handling

p & i principle and interest

P and L profit and loss

P & S purchase and sale

P & W *Poets & Writers Magazine*

pano panoramic

PAO Pediatric Assessment Online

PAP peroxidase antiperoxidase complex

PAPP p-aminopropiophenone

pa. ppl passive participle; past participial

pa. pple passive participle; past participial

PAPS adenosine 3c-phosphate 5c-phosphosulfate; 3c-phosphoadenosine 5c-phosphosulfate

Pap smear Papanicolaou test

PAR post-anesthesia room; preferred arrival route

par. paragraph; parallel; parenthesis; parish

Par. Paraguay; Paraguayan

para paragraph

PARC [Xerox Corporation's] Palo Alto Research Center

PARCA Patient Access to Responsible Care Act

paren. parenthesis

Parl. Parliament

parsec parallax second

part. participle; particle; partitive

part. aeq. *Latin* partes aequales (in equal parts)

part. vic. *Latin* partes vicibus (in divided doses)

PAS para-aminosalicylic acid; periodic acid-Schiff stain; pseudo aircraft simulation

PASA para-aminosalicylic acid

pass. passage; passenger; *Latin* passim (throughout); passive; passively

PAT point after touchdown

pat. patent

pa. t. past tense

PATCH planned approach to community health

patd. patented

PATH Program for Appropriate Technology in Health

path. pathological; pathology

pathol. pathological; pathology

PATOS payment at time of service

pat. pend. patent pending

PATV public access television

PAU Pan American Union

PAYE pay as you earn; pay as you enter

payt. payment

pb paperback [book]

Pb lead

PB paperback; peanut butter; petabyte

P.B. passbook; prayer book

P/B playback

PBA Professional Bowlers Association

PB&J peanut butter and jelly

PBB polybrominated biphenyl

PBG porphobilinogen

PBGC Pension Benefit Guaranty Corporation

PBI protein-bound iodine

PBIS Performance Based Incentive System

PBJ peanut butter and jelly [sandwich]

PBL planetary boundary layer; preamble (shortwave transmission)

PBM prescription benefit manager

PBO paperback original

PBOT Philadelphia Board of Trade

PBR Pabst Blue Ribbon [beer]; photobioreactor

PBS Public Broadcasting Service; Public Buildings Service

PBX private branch exchange

PC partly cloudy; personal computer; photoconductive; political correctness; politically correct

pc parallax second

pc. piece

p.c. percent; *Latin* post cibum (after meals)

P.C. Past Commander; penal code; police constable; post commander; Privy Council; professional corporation

p/c petty cash; prices current

PCA Paperweight Collectors Association; patient-controlled analgesia; Permanent Court of Arbitration

PCAST President's Council of Advisors on Science and Technology

PCB polychlorinated biphenyl; printed circuit board

PCC Panama Canal Commission; patient care coordinator

PCCAL Pharmacy Consortium for Computer Aided Learning

PCCU postcoronary care unit

PCD polycrystalline diamond

PC-DOS Personal Computer Disk Operating System

PCE perchloroethylene

pcg. picogram

PCGRIDS Personal Computer Gridded Interactive Display and Diagnostic System

PCI Peripheral Component Interconnect; prophylactic cranial irradiation

PCIS patient care information system

PCL [Hewlett-Packard Laserjet] Printer Control Language

PCM pulse code modulation

PCMB p-chloromercuribenzoate

PCMCIA Personal Computer Memory Card International Association

PCMI President's Council on Management Improvement

PCN personal communication network; primary care network

PCOD polycystic ovary disease

PCON *Primary Care Optometry News*

PCOS Polycystic Ovarian Sydrome

PCP personal care physician; phencyclidine; pneumocystis pneumonia; primary care physician; primary care provider; Progressive-Conservative Party

PCPM per contract per month

PCR physician contingency reserve; polymerase chain reaction

PCS personal communications service; predefined command sequence; programmable character set

PCSD President's Council on Sustainable Development

PCT patient care technician; post coital test

pct. percent

PCU power control unit; progressive care unit

PCVS Professional Credentials Verification Service

PCWP pulmonary capillary wedge pressure

Pd palladium

PD plumbing damage; police department; position description; program director; public defender; pulse Doppler [radar]

pd. paid

p.d. per diem

P.D. Police Department; postal district; potential difference; public defender

PDA personal digital assistant; public display of affection

PDAS photodiode array spectrophotometer

PDB project data base

Pd.B. *Latin* Pedagogiae Baccalaureus (Bachelor of Pedagogy)

PDC preexisting condition

PDD pervasive developmental disorder; program design document

Pd.D. *Latin* Pedagogiae Doctor (Doctor of Pedagogy)

PDF Parkinson's Disease Foundation; portable document file; precision direction finder; programmable data formatter

PDGF platelet-derived growth factor

PDI Periodontal Disease Index

PDL page description language

PDLL poorly differentiated lymphocytic lymphoma

Pd.M. *Latin* Pedagogiae Magister (Master of Pedagogy)

PDP program development plan

PDQ Physicians Data Query (of the NCI); pretty damn quick; pretty damn quickly

PDR *Physicians' Desk Reference*; preliminary design review

PDRY People's Democratic Republic of Yemen

PDT Pacific Daylight Time

PDU power distribution unit

PDX probable diagnosis

pe printer's error

PE physical examination; Prince Edward Island; pulmonary embolism

.pe Peru

P.E. physical education; probable error; professional engineer

P/E ratio price/earnings ratio

PEBB power electronic building block

PEBCAK problem exists between chair and keyboard

pec pectoral muscle

pecs pectoral muscles

PECUSA Protestant Episcopal Church of the United States of America

Ped pedestrian

PedNSS Pediatric Nutrition Surveillance System

pee piss

PEEP positive end-expiratory pressure

PEER Performance Efficiency Evaluation Report; Program for Extraordinary Experience Research

PEG polyethylene glycol

P.E.I. Prince Edward Island

PEL picture element

pen penitentiary

PEN [International Association of] Poets, Editors, Essayists, and Novelists

Pen. peninsula

Penn. Pennsylvania

Penna. Pennsylvania

PENS Pediatric Endocrinology Nursing Society

PEP Parkinson's Educational Program

per. period; person

Per. Persian

perc has passed soil percolation test

per cent. *Latin* per centum (by the hundred)

perf. perfect; perforated; perforation; performance; performed by; performer

perh. perhaps

peri pericardial; pericardium

PERI Pharmaceutical Education and Research Institute

perk perquisite

perm permanent; permanent wave

perm. permanent

perp perpetrator

perp. perpendicular

PERRLA pupils equal round, react to light and accommodation

pers. person; personal

Pers. Persia; Persian

PERT program evaluation and review technique

pert. pertaining

PESA percutaneous epididymal sperm aspiration

PET positron emission tomography

pet. petroleum

Pet. Peter

PETA People for the Ethical Treatment of Animals

petr. petrology

petrog. petrography

petrogr. petrography

petrol. petrology

PEU processing electronics unit

PF power factor; pianoforte; Prostatitis Foundation

pf. preferred; pfennig

.pf French Polynesia

PFC perfluorocarbon; private first class

PFD personal flotation device

pfd. preferred

PFFD proximal femoral focal deficiency

pfg. pfennig

PFLAG Parents, Families, and Friends of Lesbians and Gays

PFOB perfluorooctyl bromide

PFP Partnership for Peace

PFT pulmonary function test

PG parental guidance; pregnant

pg. page; picogram

Pg. Portuguese

.pg Papua New Guinea

P.G. paying guest; postgraduate

PGA Professional Golfers' Association

PGC professional graphics controller

PgDn page down

PGH paragraph (shortwave transmission)

PGP prepaid group practice; pretty good privacy

PGR psychogalvanic response

PGT preimplantation genetic testing

PG-13 parental guidance for children under 13

PgUp page up

PGY post graduate year

pH potential of hydrogen (0 to 14 scale—0, very acidic; 7, neutral; 14, very alkaline)

Ph Philippians

PH penthouse; public health; Purple Heart

ph. phase; phone number

.ph Philippines

PHA Public Housing Administration

P.H.A. potentially hazardous asteroid

phar. pharmaceutical; pharmacist; pharmacopoeia; pharmacy

Phar.B. *Latin* Pharmaciae Baccalaureus (Bachelor of Pharmacy)

Phar.D. *Latin* Pharmaciae Doctor (Doctor of Pharmacy)

pharm. pharmaceutical; pharmacist; pharmacology; pharmacopoeia; pharmacy

Phar.M. *Latin* Pharmaciae Magister (Master of Pharmacy)

Pharm.D. Doctor of Pharmacy

PHA's Public Housing Agencies

Ph.B. *Latin* Philosophiae Baccalaureus (Bachelor of Philosophy)

Ph.C. pharmaceutical chemist

PHCSG Primary Health Care Specialist Group

PHD pulse height discriminators

Ph.D. *Latin* Philosophiae Doctor (Doctor of Philosophy)

phenom phenomenal person

PHERP Public Health Education and Research Program

PHF Public Health Foundation

Ph.G. Graduate in Pharmacy

PHID Project for Health Information Dissemination

phil. philological; philology; philosopher; philosophical; philosophy

Phil. Philippians; Philippines

Phila. Philadelphia

Phil. I. Philippine Islands

Phil. Is. Philippine Islands

Philly Philadelphia

philol. philological; philology

philos. philosopher; philosophical; philosophy

PhilSp. Philippine Spanish

Phl Philippians

PHLI Public Health Leadership Institutes

Phlm. Philemon

PHLS Public Health Laboratory Service

PHLX Philadelphia Stock Exchange

Phm Philemon

Ph.M. *Latin* Philosophiae Magister (Master of Philosophy)

PHN Public Health Network

PHO physician-hospital organization

phon. phonetic; phonetics; phonology

phonet. phonetic; phonetically; phonetics

phono phonograph

phonol. phonology

photo. photograph

photog. photograph; photographic; photography

photogr. photography

photom. photometry

photo op photographic opportunity

PHP Parents Helping Parents; prepaid health plan

PHPES Program for Health Policy in Economies under Stress

PHPPO Public Health Practice Program Office

phr. phrase

phren. phrenology

phrenol. phrenology

PhRMA Pharmaceutical Research and Manufacturers of America

PHS Public Health Service

PHS&T packaging, handling, storage, and transportation

PHSS Population Health Summary System

PHTM Public Health and Tropical Medicine

PHTN Public Health Training Network

p.h.v. *Latin* pro hac vice (for this purpose)

phy ed physical education

phys. physical; physician; physicist; physics; physiological; physiology

phys ed physical education

physiol. physiological; physiology

PHz petahertz

Pi inorganic phosphate

PI performance indicator; primary infertility; principal investigator; private investigator

p.i. politically incorrect

P.I. present illness

PIA practicably irrigable acreage

pic [motion] picture

PIC Public Information Center

PICO Polio Information Center Online

PICS Platform for Internet Content Selection

PID pelvic inflammatory disease; Poisons Information Database

PIE Proto-Indo-European

PIF program information file

PIGLET Personalized Intelligently Generated Explanatory Text

PIGS passive infrared guidance system

PIH prolactin-inhibiting hormone

PIK payment in kind

PIL publishing interchange language

PILOT phased integrated laser optics technology

PIM personal information manager

PIN personal identification number

PING Packet Internet Groper

PINS persons in need of supervision

pinx. *Latin* pinxit (he or she painted it)

pion pi-meson

PIP picture [with]in picture; program implementation plan

PIPES piperazine diethanesulfonic acid

PIP$_2$ phosphatidylinositol 4,5-bisphosphate

PIREPS pilot reports

PIRG Public Interest Research Group

PIS psychiatric information services

PITA pain in the ass

PITC phenylisothiocyanate

PITI principal, interest, taxes, and insurance

pix pictures

pixel picture element

pixelsat picture element satellite

pizz. pizzicato

P.J. presiding justice

PJ's pajamas

PK preacher's kid; psychokinesis

pk. park; peak; peck

.pk Pakistan

pkat picokatal

pkg. package; parking

pkt. packet

PKU phenylketonuria

pkV peak kilovoltage

Pkwy parkway

Pky parkway

PKZIP Phil Katz's Zip (file compression and/or archiving program)

PL partial loss; private line

pl. plate; plural

Pl. place

.pl Poland

P.L. Public Law

plat. plateau; platoon

PLBB Patent Licensing Bulletin Board

PLC public limited company

PLCO [National Cancer Institute] Prostate, Lung, Colorectal, and Ovarian [Cancer Screening Trial]

plf. plaintiff

PLI paternal leukocyte immunization

PLLO phase-locked loop oscillators

PLM payload module

PLMD periodic limb movements disorder

pln. plain

PLO Palestine Liberation Organization

PLOKTA press lots of keys to abort

PL/1 Programming Language 1

PLP pyridoxal 5c-phosphate; parathyroid hormonelike protein

PLS please (shortwave transmission)

pls. please

PLSS portable life-support system; public land survey system

plu. plural

plur. plural

pm phase modulated; phase modulation

pM picomolar

Pm promethium

PM past master; police magistrate; postmaster; postmenopausal; postmistress; postmortem; prime minister; provost marshal

pm. premium; premolar

.pm Saint Pierre and Miquelon

p.m. *Latin* post meridiem (after noon)

P.M. *Latin* post meridiem (after noon)

PMA Photo Marketing Association

PM & R physical medicine and rehabilitation

PMC Pacific Marine Center; permanently manned capability

PMCIA Personal Computer Memory Card International Association

PME personnel management evaluation

PMEL Pacific Marine Environmental Laboratory

PMF probable maximum flood; product master file

PMFJI pardon me for jumping in

PMG postmaster general; primary medical group

PMH past medical history

PMI private mortgage insurance

PMJI pardon my jumping in

pmk. postmark

PML progressive multifocal leukoencephalopathy

PMMW passive millimeter wave

pmol picomole

PMP parts, material, and process; previous menstrual period

PMPM per member per month

PMR proportional mortality ratio

PMRA Physical Medicine and Rehabilitation Alliance

PMS premenstrual syndrome

PMSA Primary Metropolitan Statistical Area

PMSG pregnant mare's serum gonadotropin

PMT photo multiplier tube

pmt. payment

PMW position mode wavelength

PN practical nurse; pseudo noise

.pn Pitcairn

p.n. promissory note

P/N part number; promissory note

PNAs polynuclear aromatic hydrocarbons

pneum. pneumatic; pneumatics

PNG portable network graphics

p.n.g. *Latin* persona non grata (undesirable person)

PNHP Physicians for a National Health Program

PNMT phenylethanolamine N-methyltransferase

PNP psychogenic nocturnal polydipsia

PNPB positive-negative pressure breathing

PNS peripheral nervous system

PNSS Pregnancy Nutrition Surveillance System

PNTY pantry

pnxt *Latin* pinxit (he or she painted it)

po putout

Po polonium

PO personnel officer; petty officer; physician organization; postal order; purchase order

p.o. *Latin* per os (by mouth)

P.O. post office

P/O police officer

POA plan of action

POB post office box

POC particulate organic carbon; point of compliance; port of call; product of combustion

POD probability of detection; proton omnidirectional detector

P.O.D. payable on delivery; post office department

p.o.'d pissed off

PODS pools of doctors

POE point-of-entry; port of entry

POES Polar-Orbiting Operational Environmental Satellite

poet. poetic; poetical; poetry

POF premature ovarian failure

POGO Polar Orbiting Geophysical Observatories

POHI physically and otherwise health impaired

pol politician

POL petroleum, oil, and lubricants; physician office laboratories

pol. polite; political; politics

Pol. Poland; Polish

POLAR Polar Plasma Laboratory

poli sci political science

polit. political; politician; politics

po. lo. suo. *Latin* ponit loco suo (puts in his place)

poly polyester fiber

poly(A) polyadenylic acid

poly(U) polyuridylic acid

POM particulate organic matter; public order member

POMC pro-opiomelanocortin

pomo postmodern; postmodernism

POMP Purinethol, Oncovin, Methotrexate, and Prednisone

POMR problem-oriented medical record

POMS Polar Operational Meteorological Satellite

PON particulate organic nitrogen

pon. pontoon

pop popular

PoP point of presence

POP Post Office Protocol; proof of purchase

pop. popular; popularly; population

POPIN [United Nations] Population Information Network

Pop. L Popular Latin

POPLINE Population Information Online

POR problem-oriented record

por. portrait

p.o.r. pay on return; price on request

porn pornography

porno pornographic; pornography

port. portable; portrait

Port. Portugal; Portuguese

POS point of sale; point of service; polar orbiting satellite

pos. position; positive

POSH prevention of sexual harassment; probability of severe hail; (the claim that POSH stands for "port out, starboard home" is without foundation)

POSNA Pediatric Orthopaedic Society of North America

poss. possession; possessive; possible

possess. possessive

POSSLQ person of the opposite sex sharing living quarters

POST power-on self test

post. posterior

post-mod post-modern

post-obit. *Latin* post obitum (after death)

post-op post-operative

POSW privately owned stored water

pot. potential

POTS plain old telephone service

POTUS President of the United States

POU point of use

POV point of view; privately owned vehicle

POW prisoner of war

pp pianissimo; partly paid

PP postpartum; prepositional phrase

pp. pages; prepaid; postpaid

p.p. parcel post; past participle; *Latin* per procurationem (by proxy); postpaid

P.p. punctum proximum

P.P. *Latin* propria persona (in his own person)

PPA phenylpropanolamine; preferred provider arrangement

p.p.a. per power of attorney

PPAC Practicing Physicians Advisory Council

PPAG Pediatric Pharmacy Advocacy Group

ppb parts per billion

PPB paper, printing, and binding

PPBS Planning, Program, and Budgeting System

PPCA proserum prothrombin conversion accelerator

PPCF plasmin prothrombins conversion factor

PPCP PowerPC platform

PPD purified protein derivative (of tuberculin)

ppd. postpaid; prepaid

P.P.E. Personal Protection Equipment

PPFA Planned Parenthood Federation of America

p-p factor pellagra-preventing factor

PPG primary provider group

PPH primary pulmonary hypertension

pph. pamphlet

PP^i inorganic pyrophosphate

PPI plan position indicator; producer price index

P.P.I. policy proof of interest

ppl participial

ppl a. participial adjective

pple participle

PPLO pleuropneumonia-like organism

ppm page per minute; parts per million

PPMC physician practice management company

ppmv parts per million by volume

PPO preferred provider organization

PPP Point to Point Protocol; purchasing power parity

PPRC Physician Payment Review Commission

PPRibp 5-phospho-α-D-ribosyl 1-pyrophosphate

Pps pulses per second

PPS prospective payment system; prospective pricing system; protected payments system

P.P.S. *Latin* post postscriptum (additional postscript)

ppt parts per thousand; parts per trillion; precipitate

pptn. precipitation

PPV positive pressure ventilation

PQ Parti Québecois; Quebec (two-letter postal code); photosynthetic quotient

p.q. previous question

PQI personal quality improvement

PQ-9 plastoquinone-9

pr preferences

Pr praseodymium; propyl; Proverbs

PR payroll; proportional representation; public relations; Puerto Rico

pr. pair; present; printed; printing; pronoun

.pr Puerto Rico

P.r. *Latin* punctum remotum (far point)

PRA plasma renin activity

PRAM parameter random access memory

PRAMS Pregnancy Risk Assessment Monitoring System

PRB Population Reference Bureau

PRC People's Republic of China; Postal Rate Commission

PRCA Professional Rodeo Cowboys Association

PRD presidential review directive

preamp preamplifier

prec. preceding

pred. predicate; predicative; predicatively

pred. a. predicative adjective

preemie prematurely born infant

pref. preface; preferred; prefix

prefab prefabricated

prelim preliminary; preliminary examination

prem. premium

pre-med pre-medical college undergraduate major

premie prematurely born infant

PR enzyme phosphorylase-rupturing enzyme; photoreactivating enzyme

pre-op pre [sex-change] operation; pre-operative

prep preparatory

PREP Pediatrics Review and Education Program

prep. preposition; prepositional
prepd. prepared
prepn. preparation
preppie a student at or a graduate of a preparatory school
preppy a student at or a graduate of a preparatory school
pres. present; president
Presb. Presbyterian
Presby. Presbyterian
pres. ppl present participial
pres. pple present participle
pres. t. present tense
pret. preterit
prev. previous; previously
PREVLINE Prevention Online
prexy president
prez president
PRF pulse recurrence frequency; pulse repetition frequency
prf. proof
PRH prolactin-releasing hormone
PRI Public Radio International
prim. primary; primitive
prin. principal; principle
print. printing
priv. private; privative
PRK photorefractive keratotomy
prkg. parking
PRL Polar Research Laboratory; prolactin
PRN printer
p.r.n. *Latin* pro re nata (as the situation demands)
pro professional; prostitute
PRO professional review organization; pronoun; public relations officer

pro. pronoun
prob. probable; probably; probate; problem
proc. proceeding; proceedings; process
PROCAARE Program for Collaboration Against AIDS and Related Epidemics
procto proctoscopy
prod. produce; produced; product; production
Prof professional
prof. professional
Prof. Professor
Prof'l professional
prog. program
proj project; projector
Project DARE Drug Abuse Resistance Education
prole proletarian
prom a dance (from "promenade")
PROM programmable read-only memory
prom. promontory
ProMED Program for Monitoring Emerging Diseases
promo promotional announcement
pron. pronominal; pronoun; pronounced; pronunciation
pronunc. pronunciation
prop propeller
prop. proper; property; proposition; proprietor; proprietress
ProPAC Prospective Payment Assessment Commission
propr. proprietor; proprietress
prop. reg. proposed regulation

pro rat. aet. *Latin* pro ratione aetatis (according to [patient's] age)

pros. prosody

Pros. Atty. prosecuting attorney

Prot. Protestant

protec. protectorate

pro tem *Latin* pro tempore (for the time being)

prov. province; provisional; provost

Prov. Provençal; Proverbs

prox. *Latin* proximo [mense] (next [month])

PrP prion protein

PRP potentially responsible party

prp. present participle

PRPP 5-phospho-α-D-ribosyl 1-pyrophosphate

PRS price reporting system

PRT personal rapid transit; platinum resistance thermometers

PRTC priority real time command

Pruss. Prussian

Prv Proverbs

prvt private

prwr prewar (usually before World War II)

ps picosecond

PS photosystem; PostScript; point source (of pollution)

Ps. Psalm; Psalms

p.s. passenger steamer

P.S. police sergeant; postscript; public school; public statutes

PSA prostate-specific antigen; public service announcement

Psa. Psalms

PSAP Pharmacotherapy Self-Assessment Program

PSC Pisces; polar stratospheric cloud

PSCU Private Sector Casemix Unit

PSDA Patient Self-Determination Act

PSE Pacific Stock Exchange; please (shortwave transmission); power supply electronics

psec. picosecond

PSEF Plastic Surgery Educational Foundation

pseud. pseudonym

PSF point spread function

psf. pounds per square foot

PSG platoon sergeant

psi pounds per square inch

psia pounds per square inch absolute

psid pounds per square inch, differential

psig pounds per square inch gauge

PSIMPLE Problem Solving in Medical Physiology, Logically Explained

PSIS Plastic Surgery Information Service

PSK phase shift keying

PSM project security manager

PSO physician services organization

PSP Paralytic Shellfish Poisoning; phenolsulfonphthalein; program segment prefix; progressive supranuclear palsy

PSPA Physician Services Practice Analysis

PSR Physicians for Social Responsibility; premature separation and rupture; program status review; pulsar

PSRO professional standards review organization

PST Pacific Standard Time

PSU power supply unit

PSVT paroxysmal supraventricular tachycardia

psych psychoanalyze

psych. psychiatric; psychiatry; psychological; psychologist; psychology

psycho psychopath

psychol. psychological; psychologist; psychology

psywar psychological warfare

pt [hospital] patient

Pt Peter; platinum

PT Pacific Time; patrol torpedo; physical therapist; physical therapy; physical training; proficiency testing

pt. part; payment; pint; preterit

Pt. point; port

.pt Portugal

p.t. pro tempore

P.T. prick teaser

P/T part time; psychotherapist

PTA Parent-Teacher Association; prior to [hospital] admission

pta. peseta

PTAH phosphotungstic acid hematoxylin

PTC phenylthiocarbamide

PTCA percutaneous transluminal coronary angioplasty

PtCT patient care technologies

Ptd phosphatidyl

PtdCho phosphatidylcholine

PtdEth phosphatidylethanolamine

PtdIns phosphatidylinositol

PtdSer phosphatidylserine

PTE pulmonary thromboembolism; pulmonary thromboendarterectomy

PTEA pulmonary thromboendarterectomy

PTF plasma thromboplastin factor

ptg. printing

PTH parathyroid hormone

PTHC percutaneous transhepatic cholangiography

PTI previously taxed income

P.T.I. pretrial intervention

PTL Praise the Lord

PTMA phenyltrimethylammonium

PTMPY per thousand members per year

PTO Parent-Teacher Organization; Patent and Trademark Office; power takeoff

p.t.o. please turn over

PTR problem trouble report; program technical report

PTSA Parent-Teacher-Student Association

PTSD posttraumatic stress disorder

PTSO Parent-Teacher-Student Organization

PTT partial thromboplastin time

PTU propylthiouracil

PTV pay television; public television

pty. proprietary

Pu plutonium

PU pickup

P.U. Used to indicate a bad or offensive smell (from "phew")

pub. public; publication; published; publisher

publ. publication; published; publisher

P.U.C. Public Utilities Commission

PUD peptic ulcer disease; planned unit development

PUL pulmonary metastases

pulm. pulmonary

pulv. *Latin* pulvis (powder)

PUO pyrexia of unknown/uncertain origin

Pur purine

P.U.R. *Public Utility Reports*

PUSH People United to Serve Humanity

PV photovoltaic; polyvinyl; potential vorticity

PVA polyvinyl acetate

PVC permanent virtual circuit; polyvinyl chloride

PVL parameter value language

PVM parallel virtual machine

PVO private voluntary organization

PVP polyvinylpyrrolidone

PVT private

pvt. private

PW puncture wound

.pw Palau

P/W prewar (usually before World War II)

PWA People with AIDS [Coalition]; person with AIDS; Public Works Administration

P-wave pressure wave

PWBA Pension and Welfare Benefits Administration

PWC [National Organization of] Physicians Who Care

PWM pokeweed mitogen

PWR power (shortwave transmission); pressurized water reactor

pwr. power

PWS public water system; public water supply

PWSA Prader-Willi Syndrome Association

pwt. pennyweight

px medical prognosis

PX Post Exchange

pxt. *Latin* pinxit (he or she painted it)

.py Paraguay

PYO pick your own

Pyr pyrimidine

pyro. pyrotechnics

PZM pressure zone microphone

PZT piezoelectric transducer

Q

q charge

Q quarter; queen

q. quart; quarter; quarterly; question; quintal; quire

Q. quarto

QA quality assurance

.qa Qatar

QAE Quality Assurance Engineer

QALY quality-adjusted life years

q and a question and answer

QB quarterback; queen's bishop

Q.B. Queen's Bench

Q.B.D. Queen's Bench Division

QBO quasi-biennial oscillation

QC quality circle; quality control

Q.C. Queen's Counsel

q.c.f. *Latin* quare clausum fregit (wherefore he broke the close, that is, trespass)

QCPP quality control program plan

q.d. *Latin* quaque die (every day)

Q.D. *Latin* quasi dictat (as if he should say)

QED Quality, Efficiency, Dependability; quantitative evaluative device; quantum electrodynamics

Q.E.D. *Latin* quod erat demonstrandum (which was to be demonstrated)

Q.E.F. *Latin* quod erat faciendum (which was to have been done)

Q.E.I. *Latin* quod erat inveniendum (which was to be found out)

Q.E.N. *Latin* quare executionem non (wherefore execution [should] not [be issued])

QF quick-firing

q.h. *Latin* quaque hora (every hour)

QI quality improvement

QIC quarter-inch cartridge

q.i.d. *Latin* quater in die (four times a day)

QK quick (shortwave transmission)

QKt queen's knight

ql. quintal

Qld. Queensland

qlty. quality

QM quartermaster

q.m. *Latin* quoque matutino (every morning)

Q.M. *Latin* quaque mane (every morning)

QMAS Quality Measurement Advisory Service

QMB qualified Medicare beneficiary

QMC quartermaster corps

QMG quartermaster general

QMR Quick Medical Reference

qn. question

QNB quinuclidinyl benzilate

QNS quantity not sufficient

q.____h. *Latin* quaque hora (every ____ hours)

Qo Qoheleth

Qoh. Qoheleth

QP queen's pawn

q.p. *Latin* quantum placet (as much as you please)

qq. questions

Qq. quartos

qq.v. *Latin* quae vide (which [things] see)

QR queen's rook

qr. quarter; quarterly; quire

q.r. *Latin* quantum rectum (however much is correct)

q.s. *Latin* quantum sufficit (as much as suffices)

Q.S. quarter sessions

QSO quasi-stellar object

qt quart

q.t. quiet

Q.T. *Latin* qui tam (who sues)

Q-TIP trust qualified terminal interest property trust

Qto. quarto

qtr. quarter

qty. quantity

qu. query; question

quad quadraphonic; quadriceps (thigh muscle); quadruplet

Quad quadrangle

quad. quadrangle; quadrant; quadrilateral; quadrillion

quads quadriceps (thigh muscles)

qual. qualitative

quant. quantitative

quar. quarter; quarterly

quart. quarterly

quasar quasi-stellar object

Que. Quebec

ques. question

quint quintuplet

quot. quotation

quot. op. sit. *Latin* quoties opus sit (as often as necessary)

q.v. *Latin* quod vide (which see)

QWERTY standard computer and typewriter keyboard (from the first six keys of the top row of letters)

QWIP quantum well infrared photodetector

QWL quality of work life

R

r correlation coefficient; radius; resistance

R gas constant; radical; rain; range; Réaumur; receiver; registered [trademark]; Republican; response; restricted (children under 17 must be accompanied by a parent or guardian); right; roentgen; rook; run

r. rare; recto; reigned; retired; rod; rubber; ruble; rupee

R. patented; rabbi; received as transmitted (shortwave transmission); rector; registered; *Latin* rex (king); *Latin* regina (queen); river

Ra radium

RA research assistant; research associate; resident advisor; resident assistant; right atrium; route analysis

Ra. range

R.A. rear admiral; regular army; residence assistant; right ascension; Royal Academy

R/A room air

RAAF Royal Australian Air Force

racon radar beacon

rad radian; radiation absorbed dose; *Slang* radical (that is, excellent)

RAD Royal Academy of Dancing

rad. radical; radius; radix

radar radio detecting and ranging

RADM rear admiral

RAE right atrial enlargement

RAES retail automated execution system

RAF Royal Air Force

RAI radioactive iodine

RAID redundant array of inexpensive disks

RAM radar absorbing material; random-access memory; rarely adequate memory; Royal Academy of Music

RAMDAC random-access memory digital-to-analog converter

RAND research and development

R & B rhythm and blues

R & D research and development

R & M reliability and maintainability

R and R rest and recreation

RAO right anterior oblique

rap. rapid

RAPD rapid analysis of polymorphic deoxyribonucleic acid

RAPS radiologists, anesthesiologists, pathologists; regulated all-paper system

RAR revenue agent's report

RARR range and range rate

RAS reticular activating system; Royal Astronomical Society

RASC Royal Astronomical Society of Canada

RASER research and seeker emulation radar

RASS radio acoustic sounding system

RAT right anterior thigh

RAV Rous-associated virus

RAWIN radar wind sounding

Rb rubidium

RB reciprocal beneficiary; running back

RBC red blood cell; red blood cell count

RBE relative biological effectiveness

RBF renal blood flow

RBI runs batted in

RBMA Radiology Business Management Association

RBRVS resource based relative value scale

RC Red Cross; Roman Catholic

R.C. rolls of court

R/C radio-controlled

RCAF Royal Canadian Air Force

RCC Regional Climate Center

R.C. Ch. Roman Catholic Church

RCD received (shortwave transmission)

rcd. received

RCE reaction control equipment

R.C.L. ruling case law

RCMP Royal Canadian Mounted Police

RCN Royal Canadian Navy

RCP respiratory care practitioner; Royal College of Physicians

RCPC Royal College of Physicians of Canada

RCP(E) Royal College of Physicians (Edinburgh)

RCP(I) Royal College of Physicians (Ireland)

rcpt. receipt

RCR registered commodity representative

RCRA Resource Conservation and Recovery Act

RCS radar cross section; reaction control system; Royal College of Surgeons

RCSC Royal College of Surgeons of Canada

RCS(E) Royal College of Surgeons (Edinburgh)

RCS(I) Royal College of Surgeons (Ireland)

RCT randomized controlled trial

rct. recruit

RCVR receiver (shortwave transmission)

rd rod; Rutherford

RD reference document; registered dietitian; rural delivery

Rd. road

RDA recommended daily allowance; Rural Development Administration

RDB Rare Disease Database

RDBMS relational database management system

RDF radio direction finder

RDFS ratio of decayed and filled surfaces

RDFT ratio of decayed and filled teeth

RDH Registered Dental Hygienist

rDNA ribosomal deoxyribonucleic acid

RDS respiratory distress syndrome

RDU remote data uplink

Re earth radii; rhenium

RE repair escrow [required]; reproductive endocrinologist; right end

Re. Rupee

.re Réunion

R.E. real estate

REA Rural Electrification Administration

reb rebel

rebar reinforcing bar

rec. receipt; record; recording; recreation

recap recapitulation

recce reconnaissance

recd. received

recip. reciprocal; reciprocity

recon reconnaissance

rec. sec. recording secretary

rect. receipt; rectangle; rectangular; rectified; rector; rectory

red. reduced; reduction

redox. reduction oxidation

redupl. reduplicated; reduplication

ref referee

REF refer to (shortwave transmission)

ref. reference; referred

re. fa. lo. *Latin* recordari facias loquelam (cause the plaint to be recorded)

refash. refashioned; refashioning

REFCORP Resolution Funding Corporation

refl. reflection; reflective; reflex; reflexive

refr. refraction

refrig refrigerating; refrigeration

reg regulation

reg. regent; regiment; region; register; registered; registration; registrar; registry; regular; regularly; regulation

regd. registered

reg. gen. *Latin* regula generalis (a general rule [of court])

reg. jud. *Latin* registrum judiciale (the register of judicial writs)

reg. pl. *Latin* regula placitandi (rule of pleading)

regs regulations

regt. regent; regiment

rehab rehabilitation

REIT real estate investment trust

rel. related; relating; relative; relatively; released; religion; religious

relig. religion

relo relocation

rem roentgen equivalent in man

REM rapid eye movement; remark

rem. remittance

REMIC real estate mortgage investment conduit

renov renovated

ren. sem. *Latin* renovetur semel (shall be renewed [only]) once)

rep repertory; repetition; representative; reputation

rep. repair; repetition; report; reporter; represent; representative; reprint; republic

Rep. representative; republic; Republican

repl. replace; replaced; replacement; replacing

REPNZ repeat [while] not zero

repo repossessed merchandise or property; repossession of merchandise or property; repurchase agreement

repr. representative; represented; representing; representation; reprint; reprinted

repro reproduction

rept. report

Repub. Republic; Republican

REPZ repeat [while] zero

req. require; required; requisition

reqd. required

reqmt. requirement

RES reticuloendothial system

res. reservation; reserve; reservoir; residence; resolution

Res. reservation; reservoir

resid residual

resp. respective; respectively

RESPA Real Estate Settlement Procedures Act

respirs respirations

ret. retired; return

retd retained; retired; returned

RETRF Rural Electrification and Telephone Revolving Fund

retro *French* rétro (French clipping for rétrospectif, that is, retrospective)

retro. retroactive

re-up re-sign up, that is, to enlist again

rev. revenue; reverse; reversed; review; revised; revision; revolution

Rev Reverend

Rev. Revelation; Reverend

rev'd. reversed

reverb reverberation

rev'g. reversing

rev. proc. revenue procedure

rev. rul. revenue ruling

Rev. Ver. Revised Version

rew rewind

Rf rutherfordium

RF radio frequency; rheumatic fever; right field; right fielder

rf. reef; refund

RFA Radio Free Asia; request for applications; right frontoanterior (position)

RFC request for comment; river forecast center

R.F.C. Reconstruction Finance Corporation

R.F.C.A. Reconstruction Finance Corporation Act

RFCM radio frequency countermeasure

RFD rural free delivery

RFDU radio frequency distribution unit

RFE Radio Free Europe

rfi radio frequency interference

RFI request for information

RFLP restriction fragment length polymorphism

RFP request for proposal; request for proposals; right frontoposterior (position)

RFQ request for quotation; request for quotations

RFT registered floor trader (stock market); [IBM's] Revisable Format Text; right frontotransverse (position)

RFQ request for quote; request for quotes

RG relational grammar; retrograde; right guard; Rio Group

R.G. *Latin* regula generalis (general rule, or order [of a court])

RGB red, green, blue

rh rheumatic

Rh Rhesus factor; rhodium

RH relative humidity; releasing hormone

r.h. relative humidity; right hand

Rha. L-rhamnose

rhbdr. rhombohedron

RHCC Rural Health Care Corporation

RHCS regional health care system

RHD rheumatic heart disease

rheo. rheostat

rhet. rhetoric; rhetorical; rhetorically

R-hFSH recombinant human follicle stimulating hormone

RHIN Regional Health Information Network

rhino rhinoceros

rhinos. rhinoceros

RHIP rank has its privileges

RHIS REUTERS Health Information Services

rhomb. rhombic

rhp rated horsepower

RHP Rainforest Health Project

RI reproductive immunologist; Rhode Island

R.I. Rhode Island

RIA radioimmunoassay; Research Institute on Addictions

RIATT Research Institute for Assistive and Training Technologies

RICHS Rural Information Center Health Service

RICO Racketeer Influenced and Corrupt Organizations [Act of 1970]

RID radial immunodiffusion; Registry of Interpreters for the Deaf

ridic ridiculous

RIF reduction in force; resistance-inducing factor

RIG station equipment (short-wave transmission)

rIL-2 recombinant interleukin-2

RIO radar intercept officer

RIP raster image processor; reproductive immunophynotype

R.I.P. *Latin* requiescat in pace (may he or she rest in peace); *Latin* requiescant in pace (may they rest in peace)

RISA radioiodinated serum albumin

RISC reduced instruction set computer

RIST radioimmunosorbent test

RIT Rochester Institute of Technology

rit. ritardando

riv. river

RJ radial jerk (reflex); road junction

RJE remote job entry

RJOS Ruth Jackson Orthopaedic Society

RK radial keratectomy; radial keratotomy

RL Radio Liberty; real life (that is, as opposed to virtual reality, as on the Internet)

R.L. revised laws; Roman law

R>L right greater than left

RLE right lower extremity; run-length encoded

RLG ring laser gyro

RLL right lower lobe; run length limited

RLN remote local area network node

R.L.O. Returned Letter Office

RLQ right lower quadrant

RLS restless legs syndrome; Robert Louis Stevenson

Rm Romans

RM reconfiguration module; reichsmark; room

rm. ream; room

RMA reliability-maintainability-availability; right mentoanterior (position)

RMB *Chinese* renminbi (people's currency)

RMCL recommended maximum containment level

rmdr remainder

RMI Republic of the Marshall Islands

RML right middle lobe

RMMS remote maintenance monitoring system

RMN Richard Milhous Nixon

RMP right mentoposterior (position)

rms root mean square

RMS Railway Mail Service; remote manipulator system; Royal Mail Service; Royal Mail Steamship

RMT right mentotransverse (position)

RMV respiratory minute volume

Rn radon

RN registered nurse; Royal Navy

RNA ribonucleic acid

RNAase ribonuclease

RNase ribonuclease

RNase D ribonuclease D

RNC Republican National Committee

rnd around

rnd. round

RNP ribonucleoprotein

RNS Respiratory Nursing Society

RNZAF Royal New Zealand Air Force

RO read only

ro. recto; rood

.ro Romania

R.O. revenue officer

R/O receiver only

r-o run-on

ROA return on assets; right occipitoanterior (position)

ROC Republic of China (Taiwan); rest of Canada (other than Quebec)

ROE residue on evaporation; return on equity

ROFL rolling on floor laughing

r.o.g. receipt of goods

ROI return on investment

ROK Republic of Korea (South Korea)

rom roman

ROM range of motion; range of movement; read-only memory

Rom. Roman; Romance; Romania; Romanian; Romans

ROM BIOS read-only memory basic input/output system

roo kangaroo

ROP record of production; right occipitoposterior (position); run of paper; run of press

r.o.r. release on own recognizance

ROS review of systems

Ros. Roscommon

ROT registered options trader; right occipitotransverse (position)

rot. rotating; rotation

ROTC Reserve Officers' Training Corps

ROTF rolling on the floor

ROTFL rolling on the floor laughing

ROTFLMAO rolling on the floor laughing my ass off

ROTFLOL rolling on the floor laughing out loud

ROTM right on the money

roto rotogravure

ROV remotely operated vehicle; rover

ROY G. BIV red, orange, yellow, green, blue, indigo, violet (the colors of the spectrum)

rp reduced principal

RP repairs in progress

R.P. Received Pronunciation

RPB recognized professional body

RPC remote procedure call

RPF renal plasma flow

RPG report program generator; role playing game

RPh Registered Pharmacist

RPI retail price index

RPL recurrent pregnancy loss

rpm revolutions per minute

RPN reverse Polish notation

RPO railway post office

RPR remote procedure request

rps revolutions per second

RPT repeat; I repeat (shortwave transmission)

rpt. repeat; report

RPV remotely piloted vehicle

R.Q. respiratory quotient

RR railroad; respiration rate; rural route

R.R. [hospital] recovery room; right reverend

RRB Railroad Retirement Board

RRC residency review committee

rRNA ribosomal RNA

RRS Radiation Research Society

RRT Registered Respiratory Therapist

Rs Solar Radius

RS recording secretary; Royal Society

R.S. Revised Statutes

RSA recurrent spontaneous abortion; Rehabilitation Services Administration

RSC residual sodium carbonate; Royal Shakespeare Company

RSD reflex sympathetic dystrophy

RSFSR *Russian* Rossijskaja Sovetskaja Federativnaja Sotsialisticheskaja Respublika (Russian Soviet Federated Socialist Republic)

RSI relative strength indicator; repetitive strain injury; repetitive stress injury

RSN radio supernova; real soon now (sometimes sarcastic); record sequencing number

RSNA Radiological Society of North America

RSP right sacroposterior (position)

RSPA Research and Special Programs Administration

RSR rotating shadowband radiometer

RSS root sum square

RST right sacrotransverse (position)

RSV Revised Standard Version

RSVP *French* répondez s'il vous plaît (respond if you please—that is, a response is expected)

RSWC right side up with care
Rt Ruth
RT radiation therapy; radio technician; radiotelephone; respiratory therapist; response time; return ticket; right tackle; room temperature
rt. right
Rt. route
R/T real-time
RTA ready to assemble; renal tubular acidosis
RTB Rural Telephone Bank
RTC Resolution Trust Corporation
Rte. route
RTECS Registry of Toxic Effects of Chemical Substances
RTF [Microsoft's] Rich Text Format
RTFFAQ read the fucking FAQ
RTFM read the fucking manual
RTG radioisotope thermal generator
RtH right-handed
Rt. Hon. Right Honorable
RTK Net The Right-To-Know Network
RTM read the manual
rTMP ribothymidylic acid
r-TPA recombinant tissue plasminogen activator
RT-PCR reverse transcriptase-polymerase chain reaction
RTOG Radiation Therapy Oncology Group
Rt. Rev. Right Reverend
RTSMP real-time symmetric multiprocessor

RTTY radio-teletype
RTU remote terminal unit
RTW ready-to-wear
rty. rarity
Ru Ruth; ruthenium
.ru Russian Federation
RUC rapid update cycle
RUE right upper extremity
RU-486 Roussel-Uclaf-486 (mifepristone)
RUG resource utilization group
RUL right upper lobe
Rum. Rumania; Rumanian
RUQ right upper quadrant
Rus. Russia; Russian
Russ. Russia; Russian
RUST Remote User Scheduling Terminal
RV recreational vehicle; reentry vehicle; Revised Version; right ventricle
R/V Research Vessel
Rv. Revelation
RVE right ventricular enlargement
RVH right ventrical hypertrophy
RVS relative value scale
RVU relative value unit
RW radiological warfare
.rw Rwanda
R.W. Right Worshipful; Right Worthy
R/W read/write
R.W.E. Ralph Waldo Emerson
RWJF The Robert Wood Johnson Foundation
RWM read write memory
RWR radar warning receiver
rwy. railway

Rx *Latin* recipe (take), that is, a medical prescription; remedy

RX receive

ry. railway

S

s second; second; split; stere; strange quark

S entropy; safety; Samuel; satisfactory; Saturday; Senate; send (shortwave transmission); sentence; sexual [situations] (television rating); siemens; single (as in personal ads); small; smoking section; soprano; south; southern; straight (as in personal ads); strike; sulfur; Sunday; sunny; superior

s. shilling; singular; sire; solo; son; substantive

S. saint; sea; signature; signor; signore; statute

Sa Saturday

SA seaman apprentice; semen analysis; sex appeal; solar array; subject to approval

.sa Saudi Arabia

s.a. *Latin* sine anno (without year—that is, undated)

S.A. Salvation Army; seasonally adjusted; *Spanish* Sociedad Anónima (Corporation); South Africa; South America; South Australia

S-A sinuatrial

SAA solar azimuth angle; [IBM's] System Application Architecture

SAAAPA Student Academy of the American Academy of Physician Assistants

SAARC South Asian Association for Regional Cooperation

SAB spontaneous abortion

Sab. Sabbath

SAC Strategic Air Command

sac. sacrifice

SACEUR Supreme Allied Commander, Europe

SACT sinoatrial conduction time

SACU Southern African Customs Union

SAD seasonal affective disorder

SADC Southern African Development Community

SADCC Southern African Development Coordination Conference

SADD Students Against Drunk Driving

SADHA Student's American Dental Hygienists Association

SAE seasonal application efficiency; self-addressed envelope; Society of Automotive Engineers

SAEM Society for Academic Emergency Medicine

saf safety

SAF single Asian female; soon as feasible (shortwave transmission)

SAFE simulation analysis of financial exposure; Smokefree Air for Everyone

SAFER spectral application of finite element representation

SAFETY Sun Awareness for Educating Today's Youth

SAFPA Society of Air Force Physician Assistants

S. Afr. South Africa; South African

SAG Sagittarius; Screen Actors Guild

SAGE Russian-American Gallium Experiment, (formerly Soviet-American Gallium Experiment)

SAGRI Substance Abuse, Growth, and Recovery Institute

SAH Society of Automotive Historians

SAIDI spaced antenna imaging Doppler interferometer

SAIF Savings Association Insurance Fund

SAL semiactive laser

sal. salary

SALT Strategic Arms Limitation Talks; Strategic Arms Limitation Treaty

SAM single Asian male; surface-to-air missile

Sam. Samuel

SAMBA Society of Ambulatory Anesthesia

SAMDS Serbian American Medical and Dental Society

S. Amer. South America; South American

SAMHSA Substance Abuse and Mental Health Services Administration

Saml. Samuel

sAMP adenylosuccinic acid

san sanatorium

S & H shipping and handling

S & L savings and loan association

S & M sadomasochism

S & P 500 Standard and Poor's 500-Stock Price Index

S & T science and technology

sanit. sanitary; sanitation

S-A node sinoatrial node

SAO Smithsonian Astrophysical Observatory

Sa02 arterial oxygen saturation

SAP soon as possible (shortwave transmission)

s.ap. apothecaries' scruple

SAPA Society of Army Physician Assistants

Sar sarcosine

SAR search and rescue; sodium adsorption ratio; Sons of the American Revolution; special access required; synthetic aperture radar

SAREC Science of Anticipation Recognition Evaluation Control [of Health Risks]

SARSAT search and rescue satellite-aided tracking

SART sinoatrial recovery time; Society of Assisted Reproductive Technology

SAS Scandinavian Airline Systems; Society for Applied Spectroscopy; soil absorption system; space activity suit; space adaptation syndrome; Statistical Analysis System

SASE self-addressed stamped envelope

Sask. Saskatchewan

sat saturated

SAT a trademark used for a set of standardized college entrance examinations (originally, Scholastic Aptitude Test)

sat. saturate; saturated; saturation

Sat. Saturday

SATA Society for Advanced Telecommunications in Anesthesia

satbot satellite robot

SATCOM satellite communication

satd. saturated

SATH Society for the Advancement of Travel for the Handicapped

sat. sol. saturated solution

sat. soln. saturated solution

S. Aust. South Australia

SAV state-of-the-atmosphere variables

SAVE Systematic Alien Verification for Entitlement

SAWS Silent Attack Warning System

sax saxophone

Sax. Saxon

Sb antimony

SB sedimentation basin; simultaneous broadcast; stolen base; southbound

sb. substantive

.sb Solomon Islands

S.B. *Latin* Scientiae Baccalaureus (Bachelor of Science); [United States] Senate bill

SBA Small Business Administration

SBAA Spina Bifida Association of America

SBD silent but deadly [flatulent emission]

SbE south by east

SBE subacute bacterial endocarditis

SBF single Black female

S.B.I.C. Small Business Investment Company

SBIR small business innovative research

SBIRS space-based infrared system

SBL space-based laser

SBM single Black male; Society of Behavioral Medicine

SBN Standard Book Number

SBP Society of Biological Psychiatry

SBR sequencing batch reactors

SBS sick building syndrome

SBUV solar backscatter ultraviolet

SbW south by west

Sc scandium

SC Security Council; South Carolina; Supreme Court

sc. scale; scene; *Latin* scilicet (that is to say); scruple; *Latin* sculpsit (carved by)

Sc. Scotch; Scots; Scottish

.sc Seychelles

s.c. small capital (letter); subcutaneous; subcutaneously

S.C. Sisters of Charity; South Carolina

S/C spacecraft

SCA Sexual Compulsives Anonymous; shuttle carrier aircraft; Society for Commercial Archeology; Society for Creative Achronisms

Scand. Scandinavia; Scandinavian

SCAR Society for Computer Applications in Radiology

S.Car. South Carolina

SCARD Society of Chairmen of Academic Radiology Departments

SCAT School and College Ability Test; special crimes action team; supersonic commercial air transport

SCATA Society for Computing and Technology in Anaesthesia

SCATT scatterometer

SCBNP Society for the Collecting of Brand-Name Pencils

Sc.B. *Latin* Scientiae Baccalaureus (Bachelor of Science)

SCBT/MR Society of Computed Body Tomography and Magnetic Resonance

SCC serial communications controller; storage connecting circuit

SCCA Sports Car Club of America

SCCCPMA Society for Computing in Critical Care, Pulmonary Medicine, and Anesthesia

SCCM Society of Critical Care Medicine

Sc.D. *Latin* Scientiae Doctor (Doctor of Science)

SCET spacecraft event time

SCF satellite control facility

ScGael. Scottish Gaelic

sch. school

schizo a schizophrenic person

sci. science; scientific

SCI *Science Citation Index*

SCIA Society for Computers in Anesthesia

SCID severe combined immunodeficiency; spacecraft identification

sci-fi science fiction

scil. *Latin* scilicet (surely, to wit)

SCLC small cell lung cancer; Southern Christian Leadership Conference

SCLK spacecraft clock

SCM supply chain management

Sc.M. *Latin* Scientiae Magister (Master of Science)

SCO Scorpio

SCORIF stimulated cycle oocyte retrieval in [office] fertilization

Scot. Scotch; Scotland; Scottish

SCP single-cell protein

SCPO senior chief petty officer

SCR skin conductance response; standard class rate; stripchart recorder

scr. scruple

SCRES [United States] Senate concurrent resolution

script. manuscript; prescription

Script. Scriptural; Scripture

SCS Soil Conservation Service

SCSI small computer system interface

SCT Society for Clinical Trials

S.Ct. *Supreme Court Reporter*

sctd scattered

scuba self-contained underwater breathing apparatus

sculp. sculptor; sculptress; sculpture

SCV Sons of Confederate Veterans

SCVIR Society of Cardiovascular and Interventional Radiology

SCVP Society for Cardiovascular Pathology

sd said; sewed

SD should (shortwave transmission); sight draft; software development; South Dakota; special delivery; standard deviation

sd. sound

Sd. sound

.sd Sudan

s.d. *Latin* sine die (without day, indefinitely)

S.D. *Latin* Scientiae Doctor (Doctor of Science); South Dakota; Southern District

SDA specific dynamic action

S.Dak. South Dakota

SDB Society for Developmental Biology

S/D B/L sight draft, bill of lading attached

SDBP Society for Developmental and Behavioral Pediatrics

SDD software design document

SDEV standard deviation

SDH subdural hematoma

SDI Strategic Defense Initiative

SDILINE Selective Dissemination of Information Online

SDLC synchronous data link control

SDMS Society of Diagnostic Medical Sonographers

S. Doc. Senate Document

SDP software development plan

SDPA Society of Dermatology Physician Assistants

SDR sensor data record; special drawing rights; system design review

SDRAM synchronous dynamic random access memory

SDS Students for a Democratic Society; Synchronous Data Set; System Design Specification

SDT small-diameter timber; system design team; systems development team

SDWA Safe Drinking Water Act

Se selenium

SE southeast; southeastern; split end; stock exchange; system engineer

.se Sweden

SEA solar elevation angle

SEAHP Southeast Asian Health Project

SEAL sea, air, land [team]

SEAS Shipboard Environmental Data Acquisition System

SEATO Southeast Asia Treaty Organization

SEbE southeast by east

SEbS southeast by south

sec secant; second; secretary

SEC Securities and Exchange Commission; security deposit

sec. second; secretary; section; sector; *Latin* secundum (according to); security

sech hyperbolic secant

SECSG Southeastern Cancer Study Group

sect. section; sectional

secy. secretary

SED said (shortwave transmission)

sed. sediment; sedimentation

SEER surveillance, epidemiology, and end results

SEI systems engineering and integration

seismol seismology

SEIU Service Employees International Union

SEL Space Environment Laboratory

sel. select; selected; selectivity

SELA *Spanish* Sistema Económico Latinoamericana (Latin American Economic System)

SEM scanning electron microscope

sem. seminary

Sem. Semitic

semi semifinal; semitrailer

SEMI subendocardial myocardial infarction

semilog semilogarithmic

semipro semiprofessional

SEMPA Society of Emergency Medicine Physician Assistants

sen. senate; senator; senior

SENFAS Support and Education Network for Fetal Alcohol Syndrome [Parents and Caregivers]

SEOS synchronous earth observatory satellite

SEP simplified employee pension

sep. separate; separation

Sep. September

sepd. separated

sepn. separation

SEPP Society for the Education of Physicians and Patients

Sept. September

seq. sequel; *Latin* sequens (the following)

seqq. *Latin* sequentia (the following [things])

SER somatosensory evoked response

ser. serial; series; sermon

Serb. Serbia; Serbian

SERC Smithsonian Environmental Research Center

SERE survival, evasion, resistance, escape

Serg. sergeant

Sergt. sergeant

SERHOLD Serials Holdings

SERLINE Serials Online

SERM selective estrogen receptor modulator

serv. service

servo servomechanism; servomotor

SES says (shortwave transmission); socioeconomic status; speech extraction system

SESAP Surgical Education and Self-Assessment Program

SESPA Scientists and Engineers for Social and Political Action

sess. session

SET Secure Electronic Transaction

SETI Search for Extraterrestrial Intelligence

SETS Statistical Export and Tabulation System

SEU single event upset

7 & 7 [Seagram's] Seven Crown whiskey and Seven-Up

17-KS 17-ketosteroids

73 best regards/kisses (short-wave transmission)

sf sforzando; square feet

SF sacrifice fly; San Francisco; scarlet fever; science fiction; single female; sinking fund

SFAIAA so far as I am aware

SFC sergeant first class

SFDU standard formatted data unit

SFE supercritical fluid extraction

SFHA special flood hazard area

SFIP standard flood insurance policy

SFMR stepped frequency microwave radiometer

SFN Society for Neuroscience

SFO San Francisco airport code; subfornical organ

SFRY Socialist Federal Republic of Yugoslavia

s.f.s. *Latin* sine fraude sua (without fraud on his or her part)

SFSR Soviet Federated Socialist Republic

SFTAH Society for the Autistically Handicapped

sfz sforzando

sg specific gravity

Sg seaborgium; Song of Songs

SG senior grade; solicitor general; Surgeon General

sg. singular

.sg Singapore

sgd. signed

SGI Silicon Graphics Inc.

SGIM Society of General Internal Medicine

SGLI Servicemen's Group Life Insurance

SGML Standard Generalized Markup Language

SGN suprachiasmatic nuclei

SGNA Society of Gastroenterology Nurses and Associates

SGO Society of Gynecologic Oncologists

S.G.O. Surgeon General's Office

SGOT serum glutamic-oxaloacetic transaminase

SGP southern Great Plains

SGPT serum glutamic-pyruvic transaminase

SGR Sagittarius; Society of Gastrointestinal Radiologists

SGSS solar generator subsystem

Sgt. sergeant

Sgt.Maj. sergeant major

SH social history

sh. share; sheet

.sh Saint Helena

Shak. Shakespeare

Shakes. Shakespeare

SHAPE Supreme Headquarters Allied Powers, Europe

SHARP Skinheads Against Racial Prejudice

SHAZAM Solomon–wisdom of, Hercules–strength of, Atlas–stamina of, Zeus–power of, Achilles–great courage of, Mercury–speed of [from original Cap'n Marvel]

SHBG sex hormone-binding globulin

SHCA Society for Healthcare Consumer Advocacy

shd should

SHEA Society for Healthcare Epidemiology of America

SHEiiBA Safety, Health, and Environment Intra Industry Benchmarking Association

Shet. Shetland

SHF single Hispanic female; superhigh frequency

SHH speech/hearing handicapped

SHHH Self Help for Hard of Hearing People

shipt. shipment

SHM single Hispanic male

SHMO social health maintenance organization

SHO Showtime

shoran short-range navigation

shp shaft horsepower

shpt. shipment

SHR significant hydrologic resources

shr. share

SHRS School Health Resource Services

SHS Society for Human Sexuality

SHSRR Society for Health Services Research in Radiology

sht. sheet

shtg. shortage

SHU Scoville Heat Unit

Shy Shy-Drager syndrome

sI 6-mercaptopurine ribonucleoside

Si silicon; Wisdom of Jesus, the Son of Sirach

SI secondary infertility; Smithsonian Institution; *French* Système International [d'Unités] (International System of Units)

.si Slovenia

Sia sialic acids

SIADH syndrome of inappropriate secretion of antidiuretic hormone

sib. sibling

Sib. Siberia; Siberian

SIC standard industry classification

Sic. Sicilian; Sicily

SICP Society of Invasive Cardiovascular Professionals

SICU surgical intensive care unit

SID state inpatient database; sudden ionospheric disturbance

SIDS sudden infant death syndrome

SIECUS Sexuality Information and Education Council of the United States

SIF somatotropin release-inhibiting factor

SIG signal (shortwave transmission); signature (shortwave transmission); special interest group

sig. signal; signature

Sig. *Latin* signa (mark or label); signature; *Latin* Signetur (let it be marked or labeled); signor; signore

sigill. *Latin* sigillum (seal)

SIH somatotropin release-inhibiting hormone

SIL sister-in-law

SIM simulator; Society for the Internet in Medicine; solar irradiance monitor

SIMM single in-line memory modules

simp simpleton

SIMS stable isotope mass spectrometer

simsubs simultaneous submissions

SIMV spontaneous intermittent mandatory ventilation, synchronized intermittent mandatory ventilation

sin sine

SINE sign, that is, operator's personal initials (shortwave transmission)

SINES short interspersed elements

sing. singular

sinh hyperbolic sine

SIOP Society for Industrial and Organizational Psychology

si op. sit *Latin* si opus sit (if needed)

SIP single in-line package; system implementation plan

SIPC Securities Investors Protection Corporation

SIPP single in-line pin package

SIR shuttle imaging radar

Sir. Wisdom of Jesus, the Son of Sirach

SIS [National Library of Medicine] Specialized Information Services

sitcom situation comedy

SITD still in the dark

SITES Smithsonian Institution Traveling Exhibition Service

6cyl six cylinder

6-PTS 6-pyruvoyltetrahydropterin synthase

.sj Svalbard and Jan Mayen Islands

S.J. Society of Jesus

S.J.D. *Latin* Scientiae Juridicae Doctor (Doctor of Juridical Science)

SJF single Jewish female

SJM single Jewish male

SK Saskatchewan

sk. sack

.sk Slovakia

SKED schedule (shortwave transmission)

Skr. Sanskrit

SKS seeks

Skt. Sanskrit

SL salvage loss; sea level; sign language [interpretation]; source language; south latitude; SpaceLab; sublingual

sl. slightly; slow

.sl Sierra Leone

s.l. *Latin* sine loco (without place [of publication])

S.L. session laws

SLA second language acquisition; Symbionese Liberation Army

s.l.a.n. *Latin* sine loco, anno, vel nomine (without place, year, or name of publication)

slanguage slangy language

SLAPP Strategic Lawsuit Against Public Partnerships

SLAR sideways-looking airborne radar

Slav. Slavic; Slavonic

SLBM submarine-launched ballistic missile

SLAR sideways-looking airborne radar

Slav. Slavic

SLC space launch complex

SLCM submarine-launched cruise missile

SLCS software life cycle support

sld. sailed; sealed; sold

SLE systemic lupus erythematosus

slimnastics sliming gymnastics

SLIP Serial Line Internet Protocol

SLMA Student Loan Marketing Association

slo-mo slow motion

SLORC State Law and Order Restoration Council (of Myanmar)

SLP sea-level pressure

slpr sofa sleeper sofa

SLR sea-level rise; single-lens reflex camera; straight leg raising

SLS Saint Lawrence Seaway [Development Corporation]

SLSI super-large-scale integration

SLT single lung transplantation

SLV standard launch vehicle

SLW supercooled liquid water

Sm samarium; Samuel

SM sensor module; sergeant major; service mark; single male; Soldier's Medal; stage manager; stationmaster; structural model

sm. small

.sm San Marino

S.M. *Latin* Scientiae Magister (Master of Science)

S/M sadomasochism

S-M sadomasochism

SMA sergeant major of the army

sma. small

S-mail United States Postal Service mail (from "snail mail")

S.Maj. sergeant major

SMB server message block

SMC small Magellanic cloud; system maintenance console; system manager console

sm. cap. small capital (letter)

SMC-GUI system manager's console graphical user interface

SMCL secondary maximum contaminant level

SMDM Society for Medical Decision Making

SMG something (shortwave transmission)

SMI severely mentally impaired

SMMC system maintenance monitoring console

SMMR scanning multichannel microwave radiometer

SMN seaman

smog smoke and fog

SMP symmetric multiprocessing

SMR Society of Magnetic Resonance

SMS synchronous meteorological satellite

SMSA standard metropolitan statistical area

S.M.Sgt. senior master sergeant

SMT surface mount technology

SMTP Simple Mail Transfer Protocol

SMU Southern Methodist University

SMV slow-moving vehicle

Sn snow; tin

SN serial number; soon (short wave transmission); stock number; supernova

.sn Senegal

s.n. *Latin* sine nomine (without name)

S/N ratio signal-to-noise ratio

SNA systems network architecture

SNACC Society for NeuroAnesthesia and Critical Care

snafu situation normal all fouled up; situation normal all fucked up

SNC since (shortwave transmission)

SNCC Student Nonviolent Coordinating Committee

SNE subacute necrotizing encephalomyelopathy

SNF skilled nursing facility

SNG substitute natural gas; synthetic natural gas

SNL Sandia National Laboratory; *Saturday Night Live*

SNM Society of Nuclear Medicine

SNMP Simple Network Management Protocol; Small Network Management Packet

SNOMED Systematized Nomenclature [of Human and Veterinary] Medicine

SNR signal-to-noise ratio; supernova remnant

SNRI serotonin and norepinephrine reuptake inhibitor

snRNA small nuclear RNA

SNU solar neutrino units

SO seller's option; significant other; strikeout; symphony orchestra

so. south; southern

.so Somalia

s.o. seller's option; strikeout

SOA S-band omni antenna

SoAfr. South Africa, South African

SOAP Society for Obstetric Anesthesia and Perinatology;

Spectrometric Oil Analysis Program

SOB Senate Office Building; shortness of breath; son of a bitch

SOBP Society of Biological Psychiatry

SOC synthetic organic chemical

soc. social; socialist; society; sociology; socket

Soc. Socialist; society

SOCAP Society of Consumer Affairs Professionals [in Business]

sociol. sociologist; sociology

SOD superoxide dismutase

So.Dak. South Dakota

SOF sound on film; Special Operations Forces

sofar sound fixing and ranging

S. of Sol. Song of Solomon

SOFT Society of Forensic Toxicologists

SOG Special Operations Group

SoHo South of Houston [Street] (a neighborhood in New York City)

SOHO Solar and Heliospheric Observatory

SOI severity of illness; solar oscillations imager

SOL shit out of luck

sol. soluble; solution

Sol. Is. Solomon Islands

soln. solution

SOLP standards of laboratory practice

SOLRAD solar radiation

Som. Somalia; Somalian; Somersetshire

sonar sound navigation and ranging

SONET synchronous optical network

SOP standard operating procedure

sop. soprano

soph. sophomore

SorG straight or gay

SORSI Sacro Occipital Research Society International

SOS a signal of distress in Morse code; chipped beef on toast (from "shit on a shingle"); same old shit

s.o.s. *Latin* si opus sit (if needed)

SOT Society of Toxicology

sou. south; southern

SOV subject-object-verb

sov. sovereign

Sov. Soviet

SOW statement of work

Sp Spanish

SP scalable processing; self-propelled; shore patrol; single pole; specialist; speech pathologist; speech pathology; standard playback; submarine patrol

sp. species; specimen; spelling

Sp. Spain; Spanish

s.p. *Latin* sine prole (without issue—that is, childless)

S.P. same point; same principle

SPA Society for Physicians in Administration; Software Publishers Association; sperm penetration assay

spac spacious

SPAN Small Publishers of North America; standard portfolio analysis of margin

Span. Spanish

Spanglish Spanish and English mixture

SPAR *Latin* Semper Paratus (always ready—motto of the United States Coast Guard); a member of the women's reserve of the United States Coast Guard

SPARC scalar processor architecture

Sparteca South Pacific Regional Trade and Economic Cooperation Agreement

SPC South Pacific Commission; space; specific fuel consumption

SPCA Society for the Prevention of Cruelty to Animals; Spark Plug Collectors of America

SPCC Society for the Prevention of Cruelty to Children

SPD Standardized Position Description

spd. speed

S.P.D.R.'s Standard and Poor's depositary receipts

SPDT single pole, double throw

S.P.E. Society for Pure English

S.P.E.B.S.Q.S.A. Society for the Preservation and Encouragement of Barber Shop Quartet Singing in America

spec speculation; write specifications for

spec. special; specialist; specific; specifically; specification; speculation

spec grav specific gravity

spec house a house built on speculation that a buyer will be found

specif. specific; specifically

specs specifications; spectacles (eyeglasses)

SPECT single photon emission computed tomography

sped *Offensive* special education

SPF single professional female; sun protection factor

sp gr specific gravity

sph. spherical; spherical lens

SPHCOM Society for the Preservation of Historical Coin-Operated Machines

sp ht specific heat

Spiders Standard and Poor's depositary receipts

SPIE Society of Photo-Optical Instrumentation Engineers

SPL sound pressure level; special (shortwave transmission); split phase level

SPLC Southern Poverty Law Center

spm suppression and mutation (of mutants that are unstable)

SPM single professional male; software programmers manual; suspended particulate matter

SPMC Society of Paper Money Collectors

SPN shared processing network; Society of Pediatric Nurses

SPNT Society for the Promotion of Nutritional Therapy

SPO status postoperative

SP1 stimulatory protein 1

spool simultaneous peripheral operation online

SPOT satellite positioning and tracking

SPP Sequenced Packet Protocol; Society for Pediatric Pathology

spp. species

SPQR *Latin* Senatus Populusque Romanus (the Senate and the people of Rome)

SPR Society for Pediatric Radiology

spr. spring

sps symbols per second

SPS solar power satellite; standby power system

s.p.s. *Latin* sine prole superstite (without surviving issue—that is, no living children)

SPSS Statistical Package for the Social Sciences

SPST single pole, single throw

spt. seaport

SPU signal processing unit; Society for Pediatric Urology

SPVS Society of Practicing Veterinary Surgeons

SPX sequenced packet exchange

SQ subcutaneous

sq. squadron; square

Sq. square

sq. ft. square feet

sq km square kilometer

SQL structured query language

sq mi square mile

SQUID superconducting quantum intereference device

sr steradian

Sr showers; strontium

SR scanning radiometer; software review; solar radiation; special relativity; surgical removal

sr. senior

Sr. Senior; Señor; Sister

.sr Suriname

SRA scanning radar altimeter

Sra. Señora

SRAM static random access memory

SRB solid rocket booster

SRDC State Rural Development Councils

SRE Society for Radiological Engineering

SREH storm-relative environmental helicity

S. Rept. Senate Report

S. Res. Senate Resolution

SRF somatotropin-releasing factor

SRF-A slow-reacting factor of anaphylaxis

SRH somatotropin-releasing hormone

SRI sorry (shortwave transmission)

SRIF somatotropin release-inhibiting factor

SRM solid rocket motor

sRNA soluble ribonucleic acid

SRO self-regulatory organization; single room occupancy; standing room only

SROA Society for Radiation Oncology Administrators

SROM spontaneous rupture of membranes

SRP signal recognition particle; soluble reactive phosphate; soluble reactive phosphorus

SRS Scoliosis Research Society; Sleep Research Society; slow-reacting substance

SRS-A slow-reacting substance of anaphylaxis

SRT speech reception threshold

Srta. Señorita

ss sentence structure; single-stranded, steady state

SS saints; saline solution; Saturday-Sunday; *German* Schutzstaffel (protection echelon—the elite quasimilitary unit of the Nazi party); shortstop; short stories; snow showers; social security; Song of Solomon; steamship; Sunday school; suspended solids

ss. *Latin* scilicet (that is to say, namely); sections; *Latin* semis (one half)

s/s same size

SSA Sinatra Society of America; Social Security Administration; sole source aquifer

SSAT Society for Surgery of the Alimentary Tract

SSB small smart bomb

SSBR Social Statistics Briefing Room

SSC stainless steel crown (dentistry)

SSCI *Social Science Citation Index*

SSCP Society for a Science of Clinical Psychology

SSD solid state detector; sudden sniffing death

SSDD single sided, double density

SSDI *Social Security Death Index*

SSE south-southeast

SSF Society for the Study of Fertility

S.Sgt. staff sergeant

SSI small-scale integration; Supplemental Security Income; Supplemental Security Income Program

SSIEM Society for the Study of Inborn Errors of Metabolism

SSIES special sensor for ions, electrons, and scintillations

SSME space shuttle main engine

SSM/I special sensor microwave/imager

SSM/T special sensor microwave/temperature

SSN Social Security number; Space Surveillance Network

SSNR Society for the Study of Neuronal Regulation

SSO Society of Surgical Oncology

SSP shameless self-promotion

ssp. subspecies

SSPA solid-state power amplifier

SSPE subacute sclerosing panencephalitis

SSPM software standards and procedures manual

SSR solid state recorder; Soviet Socialist Republic

SSRC Social Science Research Council

SSRI selective serotonin reuptake inhibitor

SSRT single stage rocket technology

SSS Selective Service System

SST sea surface temperature; spectroscopic survey telescope; supersonic transport

SSTA sea surface temperature anomaly

SSTT small satellite thermal technologies

SSU stratospheric sounding unit

SSW south-southwest

SSWAHC Society for Social Work Administrators in Health Care

ST standard time; stratosphere-troposphere

st. stanza; state; statute; stet; stitch; stone; strophe

St. saint; state; strait; street

.st Sao Tome and Principe

s.t. short ton

STA scheduled time of arrival; Society for Technology in Anesthesia

sta. station; stationary

stalkerazzi stalking paparazzi

staph staphylococcus

START strategic arms reduction talks

stat immediately (from *Latin* statim); statistics

STAT stratospheric tracers of atmospheric transport

stat. statistic; statistics; statuary; statute

Stat. *United States Statutes at Large*

stats statistics

STB set-top box; Surface Transportation Board

S.T.B. *Latin* Sacrae Theologiae Baccalaureus (Bachelor of Sacred Theology); *Latin* Scientiae Theologicae Baccalaureus (Bachelor of Theology)

stbd. starboard

STC satellite test center

STCC Shirley Temple Collectors Club

STD scheduled time of departure; sexually transmitted disease

std. standard

S.T.D. *Latin* Sacrae Theologiae Doctor (Doctor of Sacred Theology)

STE septic tank effluent; suite

Ste *French* sainte (female saint)

STEL short-term exposure limit

sten. stenographer; stenography

steno stenographer; stenography

stenog. stenographer; stenography

STEP Space Test Experiment Platform

ster. sterling

stereo stereophonic

St. Ex. Stock Exchange

STFM Society of Teachers of Family Medicine

stg. sterling

st'g strong

stge. storage

STH somatotropic hormone

S3T sequentially sampling sediment trap

stip. stipend; stipulation

stk. stock

St.L. St. Louis

S.T.L. *Latin* Sacrae Theologiae Licentiatus (Licentiate of Sacred Theology)

STM short-term memory

S.T.M. *Latin* Sacrae Theologiae Magister (Master of Sacred Theology)

STN station (shortwave transmission)

STOL short takeoff and landing

stoolie stool pigeon

STOP Safe Tables Our Priority

stor. storage

storg. storage

STOVL short takeoff and vertical landing

StP St. Paul [Minnesota]

STP Scientifically Treated Petroleum; shielded twisted pair [of wires for electrical transmission]; standard temperature and pressure

str straight; strength

STR synchronous transmitter receiver

str. steamer; strait; string; stringed; strings; strong; strophe

Str. strait

Strad Stradivarius violin

strep streptococcus

stry story

STS shuttle transport system; Society of Thoracic Surgeons; space transportation system; star tracker sensor

ST-SAS septic tank soil absorption system

STSG split-thickness skin graft

STSs sequence-tagged sites

STT small tactical terminal

STTR Small Business Technology Transfer Program

stu studio

STU scan timing unit; standard time unit

stud. student; studio

STV subscription television

Su Sunday

SU sulfonylurea

SUA serum uric acid

sub submarine; substitute

sub. subaltern; suburb; suburban

SUBCOM subcommutator

subd. subdivision

subdeb subdebutante

subdiv. subdivision

subj. subject; subjective; subjunctive

subjunct. subjunctive

subord. subordinate

sub-q subcutaneous

subs. subscription

subsec. subsection

subsp. subspecies

subst. substantival; substantive; substitute

substand. substandard

Sud. Sudan

suf. suffix

suff. suffix
Suff. Suffragan
SUI stress urinary incontinence
SUM software users manual
SUMER solar ultraviolet measurements of emitted radiation
Sun. Sunday
SUNA Society of Urologic Nurses and Associates
SUNY State University of New York
SUP Society for Ultrastructural Pathology
sup. superior; superlative; supine; supplement; supplementary; supply; *Latin* supra (above)
Sup.Ct. superior court; Supreme Court
super superintendent; supernumerary
super. superior
superl. superlative
supp. supplement; supplementary
suppl. supplement; supplementary
supr. supreme
Supt. superintendent
supvr. supervisor
SUR Society of Uroradiology
sur. surface; surplus
Sur. Suriname; Surinamese
SURFRAD surface radiation
surg. surgeon; surgery; surgical
Surg. Gen. Surgeon General
surr. surrender
surv. survey; surveying; surveyor

sus. per coll. *Latin* suspendatur per collum (let him or her be hanged by the neck)
Suss. Sussex
SUV sport utility vehicle
sux. suction
SUZI subzonal insertion
sv sailing vessel; saves
Sv sievert
SV simian virus; sludge volume
.sv El Salvador
s.v. *Latin* sub verbo (under the word); *Latin* sub voce (under the word)
svc. service
svce service
SVD spontaneous vaginal delivery
SV40 simian vacuolating virus 40
SVGA super video graphics array
svgs. savings
SVI sludge volume index
SVL several (shortwave transmission)
SVM service module
SVMB Society of Vascular Medicine and Biology
SVN Society for Vascular Nursing
SVO subject-verb-object
sw short wave
SW software; southwest; southwestern
sw. switch
Sw. Sweden; Swedish
S/W software
SWAK sealed with a kiss

SWAP severe weather avoidance procedures

SWAT special weapons and tactics; special weapons attack team

Swaz. Swaziland

SWB short wheelbase

swbd. switchboard

SWbS southwest by south

SWbW southwest by west

SWC Space Warfare Center

SWCD [United States Department of Agriculture] Soil and Water Conservation District

SWCS Soil and Water Conservation Society

SWE snow water equivalent

Swed. Sweden; Swedish

sweetie sweetheart

SWF shortwave fading; single White female

SWG standard wire gauge

SWIM solar wind interplanetary measurements

Switz. Switzerland

SWM single White male

SWON Social Work Oncology Network

S-word shit

SWP Socialist Workers Party; Swiss water process

SWS Sturge Weber Syndrome

SWZ Swaziland

sx symptoms

SXI solar x-ray imager

.sy Syria

syl. syllable

syll. syllable

sym. symbol; symmetrical; symphony

syn. synonym; synonymous; synonymy

sync synchronized; synchronization

synch synchronized; synchronization

synd. syndicate

synon. synonymous

synth. synthesizer; synthetic

synthespian synthetic thespian (computer-generated virtual actor)

syph syphilis

syr *Latin* syrupus (syrup)

Syr. Syria; Syrian

sys. system

sysadmin system administrator

sysop system operator

syst. system

sz size

Sz seizures

.sz Swaziland

SZA Solar Zenith Angle

T

t tense (grammar); [long] ton; top quark

T temperature; tenor; tesla; thunderstorms; Thursday; thymine; time reversal; [United States] Treasury; tritium; true; T-shirt; Tuesday

t. tare; teaspoon; teaspoonful; *Latin* tempore (in the time of); time; ton; transitive; troy

T. tablespoon; tablespoonful; township

Ta tantalum

TA teaching assistant; teaching associate

TAANOS The American Academy of Neurological and Orthopedic Surgeons

tab tablet

TAB timing and acquisition bit

tab. table

TAC Tactical Air Command; total allowable catch

TACAN tactical air navigation

tach tachometer

tach. tachycardia

TACOM [United States Army] Tank-Automotive Command

TACT total audit concept technique

TAF tumor angiogenic factor

TAG Thalassemia Action Group; The Adjutant General

Tag. Tagalog

TAH total abdominal hysterectomy

TAlk total alkalinity

tan tangent

TAN teeny area network

Tan. Tanzania

T & A time and attendance; tits and ass; tonsillectomy and adenoidectomy; tonsils and adenoids

T & E test and evaluation

T and E travel and entertainment

T & G tongue and groove

T & M time and materials

T & T tympanotomy and tube [placement]

tangelo tangerine pomelo cross

tanh hyperbolic tangent

TANJ there ain't no justice

TANSTAAFL There ain't no such thing as a free lunch!

TAP take a picture; Trans-Alaskan Pipeline

TAPI telephony applications programming interface

TARDEC [United States Army] Tank-Automotive Research, Development and Engineering Center

tarfu things are really fouled up; things are really fucked up

tarp tarpaulin

TAS telephone answering system; true airspeed

Tas. Tasmania; Tasmanian

TASC The American Surrogacy Center

taser teleactive shock electronic repulsion [temporary immobilizer]

TAT Thematic Apperception Test; Transatlantic Telephone

TATCA terminal air traffic control automation

TATRC Telemedicine and Advanced Technology Research Center

TAU Taurus

TAV transatmospheric vehicle

taxi taxicab

taxon. taxonomy

tb tablespoon; tablespoonful

Tb terbium; Tobit

TB terabyte; tuberculosis

t.b. trial balance; tubercle bacillus

TBA to be announced; to be answered

TBC thermal barrier coating; to be confirmed

TBCF The Breast Cancer Fund

TBD to be defined; to be delivered; to be designed; to be determined; to be developed; to be documented

TBG thyroxine-binding globulin

TBH to be honest

TBHQ tertiary butylhydroquinone

T-bill United States Treasury bill

TBINET The Brain Injury Information Network

TBIRD Traumatic Brain Injury Resource Directory

tbl. table

TBM tactical ballistic missile

tBoc tert-butyloxycarbonyl

T-bond United States Treasury bond

TBP thyroxine-binding protein

TBPA thyroxine-binding prealbumin

TBR to be read; to be resolved

TBS talk between ships; to be supplied; Turner Broadcasting System

tbs. tablespoon; tablespoonful

tbsp. tablespoon; tablespoonful

TBSR total business systems review

TBV total blood volume

TBW total body water

TByte terabyte

tc tetracycline

Tc technetium

TC teachers college; telecommand; terra-cotta; till countermanded; total carbon

tc. tierce

.tc Turks and Caicos Islands

T.C. [United States] Tax Court

TCCA Tin Container Collectors Association

TCDD tetrachlor dibenzo dioxin

TCE thermal control electronics; trichloroethylene

T cell thymus-derived cell

TCG time compensation gain

tchr. teacher

TCI Tele-Communications Inc.

TCID tissue culture infectious dose

TCL tool command language

TCM traditional Chinese medicine; Turner Classic Movies

TCP Transmission Control Protocol

TCP/IP Transmission Control Protocol/Internet Protocol

TCS thermal control system

TCXO temperature controlled crystal oscillator

Td tetanus and diphtheria

TD tank destroyer; technical director; touchdown; Treasury Department

.td Chad

TDA tax-deferred annuity; telecommunications and data

acquisition; Trade and Development Agency

TDD telecommunications device for the deaf

TDEM time-domain electromagnetics

TDF testis-determining factor

TDM time-division multiplexing

TDMA time division multiple access

TDMS Toxicology Data Management System

TDN total digestible nutrients

TDP ribothymidine 5c-diphosphate

TDR temperature data record; test discrepancy report; time domain reflectometry; *Toxicology Desk Reference*

TDS total dissolved solids

TDWR Terminal Doppler Weather Radar

TDY temporary duty

TE tight end

T.E. textile engineer; textile engineering

TEA torque equilibrium attitude

TEAL The Electronic Anesthesiology Library

TeBG testosterone-estradiol-binding globulin

tec detective

tec. technical; technician

tech technical person

tech. technical; technician

Tech. technology

techies technologically oriented people

technol. technology

TED Thomas Edmund Dewey; total energy detector; trawl efficiency device; turtle excluder device

TEDD total end-diastolic diameter

Te Deum *Latin* Te Deum laudamus (You, God, we praise)

tee T-shirt

TEE transesophageal echocardiography

TEFL teaching English as a foreign language

Teflon polytetrafluoroethylene

TEFRA Tax Equity and Fiscal Responsibility Act

TEHIP Toxicology and Environmental Health Information Program

TEI Text Encoding Initiative

tel. telegram; telegraph; telephone

telco telephone company

telecom telecommunications

teleg. telegram; telegraph; telegraphic; telegraphy

telegr. telegraphy

teleph. telephony

TeleSCAN Telematics Services in Cancer

TELEX teletypewriter exchange

TEM transmission electron microscope; triethylenemelamine

temp temperature; temporary [employee]

TEMP test and evaluation master plan

temp. temperance; temperature; template; temporal; temporary; *Latin* tempore (in the time of)

TEN toxic epidermal necrolysis

ten. tenor; tenuto

Tenn. Tennessee

tennies tennis shoes

TENS transcutaneous electrical nerve stimulation

TEO technology executive officer

TEPA triethylene phosphoramide

TEPP tetraethylpyrophosphate

Ter. terrace; territory

TERA Toxicology Excellence for Risk Assessment

T/E ratio testosterone/epitestosterone ratio

TERIS Teratogen Information System

term. terminal; termination

Terr. terrace; territory

terry terry cloth

TESA testicular sperm aspiration

TESD total end-systolic diameter

TESL teaching English as a second language

TESOL Teachers of English to Speakers of Other Languages

TEST Telemedicine and Education Support Team

test. testator; testatrix; testimony

Test. Testament

TET tubal embryo transfer

Teut. Teuton; Teutonic

TeV tera-electron volts

Tex. Texas

Tex-Mex Texas-Mexican

TF true/false

.tf French Southern Territories

T.F. Territorial Force

TFA Thyroid Foundation of America

T.F.A. totally fucking awesome

TFCS Treasury Financial Communication System

TFG transfer frame generator

TFM traffic flow management

tfr. transfer

TFT thin film transfer; thin film transistor

TFTP Trivial File Transfer Protocol

TG transformational grammar; transgender

.tg Togo

t.g. type genus

TGC time-varied gain control; time-gain compensation

TGE transmissible gastroenteritis of swine

TGF transforming growth factor

TGFα transforming growth factor α

TGFβ transforming growth factor β

TGH telegraph (shortwave transmission)

TGIF thank God it's Friday

TGR together (shortwave transmission)

T group training group

TGS timeline generation system

tgt. target

TGV *French* Train à Grande Vitesse (high-speed French train)

Th Thessalonians; thorium; Thursday

TH townhouse

.th Thailand

THAAD Theater High Altitude Area Defense [missile system]

Thai. Thailand

Th.B. *Latin* Theologiae Baccalaureus (Bachelor of Theology)

THC tetrahydrocannabinol; thermohaline circulation

Th.D. *Latin* Theologiae Doctor (Doctor of Theology)

theat. theater; theatrical

theatr. theatrical

theol. theologian; theological; theology

therap. therapeutic; therapeutics

therm. thermometer

Thes. Thessalonians

Thess. Thessalonians

THF tetrahydrofolate

THIC The Heart Institute for Children

THIR temperature humidity infrared radiometer

30 no more, the end (as used in press releases)

Th.M. *Latin* Theologiae Magister (Master of Theology)

THMs trihalomethanes

tho though

ThOD theoretical oxygen demand

thoro thorough

Thos. Thomas

thou thousand

thp thrust horsepower

THR total hip replacement

3-D three dimensional

3Hyp 3-hydroxyproline

3M Minnesota Mining and Manufacturing Company

three R's reading, writing, and arithmetic

thrombo thrombophlebitis; thrombosis

thru through

Thu. Thursday

Thur. Thursday

Thurs. Thursday

Thy thymine

THz terahertz

Ti titanium; Titus

TI time (shortwave transmission)

TIA thanks in advance; transient ischemic attack

TIAA Teachers Insurance and Annuity Association

Tib. Tibetan

TIC tongue in cheek; total inorganic carbon

t.i.d. *Latin* ter in die (three times a day)

TIE Telemedicine Information Exchange; Treatment Improvement Exchange

TIF tax increment financing

TIFF tagged image file format

TILS tumor-infiltrating lymphocytes

TIM technical interchange meeting

Tim. Timothy

TIMS theoretical indicative margin system; Tuberculosis Information Management System

TIN taxpayer identification number; total inorganic nitrogen

TINA Truth in Negotiations Act

tinc. tincture

tinct. tincture

TINWIS that is not what I said

TIP technology investment plan; total inorganic phosphate

Tip. Tipperary

TIPPSA Technical Industrial Pharmacists and Pharmaceutical Scientists Association

TIROS Television and Infrared Operational Satellite; Television Infrared Observation Satellite

tit. title

Tit. Titus

TITh 3,5,3c-triiodothyronine

tix tickets

TJ triceps jerk (reflex)

.tj Tajikistan

TJR total joint replacement

Tk toolkit

TK take (shortwave transmission)

tk. truck

.tk Tokelau

TKE turbulent kinetic energy

TKO technical knockout; to keep [vein] open

TKR total knee replacement

tkt. ticket

Tl thallium

TL target language (that is, language being learned); tubal ligation

t.l. total loss

TLA three-letter acronym

TLC tender loving care; The Learning Channel

TLE temporal lobe epilepsy; thin-layer electrophoresis

TLM telemetry

t.l.o. total loss only

tlr. tailor

TLV threshold limit value

Tm thulium; Timothy

TM telemetry; them (shortwave transmission); trademark; transcendental meditation; tympanic membrane

.tm Turkmenistan

t.m. true mean

T.M. *Tax Magazine*

TMA Toy Manufacturers of America

T-man [United States] Treasury man

TMC The Movie Channel

TMD temporomandibular joint dysfunction

TMET treadmill exercise test

TMI Three Mile Island; trainable mentally impaired; tympanic membrane intact

TMJ temporomandibular joint

TMO telegraph money order

TMOD Treatment and Management of Ocular Disease

TMOT trust me on this

TMP ribothymidylic acid; trimethoprim

T.M.R. *Trademark Reports*

TMW tomorrow (shortwave transmission)

TN Tennessee

tn. ton; town; train

.tn Tunisia

TNC The Nature Conservancy

TNF tumor necrosis factor

tng. training

TNK think (shortwave transmission)

TNM tumor-node-metastasis; tumor-node-metastases

TNN The Nashville Network

T-note United States Treasury note

Tnpk. turnpike

TNR *The New Republic*

TNS Transcultural Nursing Society

TNT trinitrotoluene; Turner Network Television

TNTC too numerous to count

TNX thanks

TO table of organization; telegraph office; tubo-ovarian

.to Tonga

t.o. turnover; turn over

Tob. Tobit

TOC total organic carbon

Toch. Tocharian

TOCP triorthocresyl phosphate

TOD top of descent

TOEFL Test of English as a Foreign Language

TOF top of file

tol. tolerance

TOMS total ozone mapping spectrophotometer

TON threshold odor number

TONE Trial of Nonpharmacologic Interventions in the Elderly

tonn. tonnage

TOP temporarily out of print

topo. topographic; topographical

topog. topography

TOPS Take Off Pounds Sensibly; transparent operating system

TORI totally obvious rapid information

TOS terms of service

TOT time of travel; time over target

tot. total

TOXLINE Toxicology [Information] Online

TOXLIT Toxicology Literature

TOXNET Toxicology [Data] Network

TP title pending; triple play

Tp. township

.tp East Timor

t.p. title page; toilet paper

tPA tissue plasminogen activator

TPA third party administrator; tissue plasminogen activator

Tpk. turnpike

Tpke. turnpike

TPL total path length

TPN triphosphopyridine nucleotide

TPNH triphosphopyridine nucleotide, reduced form

TPN+ triphosphopyridine nucleotide, oxidized form

TPP thiamin pyrophosphate

TPR temperature, pulse, and respiration

TPS thermal protection system

tps. townships; troops

TPTB the powers that be

TQI total quality improvement

TQM total quality management

TR Theodore Roosevelt; transmit-receive

tr. tape recorder; transitive; translated; translation; translator; transpose; transposition; treasurer; trust; trustee; turnover rate

.tr Turkey

T.R. tons registered (of a ship)

T/R transmit/receive

trach. tracheal; tracheotomy

TRACON terminal radar approach control

trag. tragedy; tragic

trans. transaction; transitive; translated; translation; translator; translator; transportation; transpose; transposition; transverse

transf. transfer; transferred

transl. translated; translation

transp. transportation

TRASOP Tax Reduction Act Stock Ownership Plan

trav. traveler; travels

TRC Transportation Research Center

T.R.E. *Latin* Tempore Regis Edwardi (in the time of King Edward)

treas. treasurer; treasury

TRF thyrotropin-releasing factor

TRH thyroid-releasing hormone; thyrotropin-releasing hormone

TRI Toxic Release Inventory

trib. tributary

trig trigonometry

trigon. trigonometric; trigonometry

trike tricycle

TRIO Transplant Recipients International Organization

tripl. triplicate

TRIPP Teaching Resource for Instructors in Prehospital Pediatrics

Tris tris(hydroxymethyl)aminomethane; tris(hydroxymethyl)-methylamine

trit. triturate

TRK tracking

TRLR trailer

tRNA transfer RNA

T.R.O. temporary restraining order

troch trochiscus

trop. tropic; tropical

trou trousers

trp. troop

TRPSA transponder assembly

TRR test readiness review

TRT testosterone replacement therapy; thoracic radiotherapy

TRU through (shortwave transmission)

trvl travel

Try tryptophan

TS this (shortwave transmission); total solids; transsexual

ts. typescript
t.s. tough shit
T.S. tensile strength
TSA Technical Support Alliance; Tourette Syndrome Association
TSC Transportation Systems Center
TSCA Toxic Substances Control Act
TSCATS Toxic Substances Control Act Test Submissions [Database]
TSE Thomas Stearns Eliot
T.Sgt. technical sergeant
TSH thyroid-stimulating hormone
TSH-RF thyroid-stimulating hormone-releasing factor
TSI timber stand improvement; Transportation Safety Institute
TSP trisodium phosphate
tsp. teaspoon; teaspoonful
TSPI time-space-position-information
TSR terminate and stay resident
TSS total suspended solids; toxic shock syndrome; twin-screw steamer
tss. typescripts
T'storm thunderstorm
T-strm thunderstorm
Tt Titus
TT telegraphic transfer; teletypewriter; that (shortwave transmission); time-tagged; transit time; trust territory
.tt Trinidad and Tobago
TTAD Telemedicine Technology Area Directorate

TTB time-tagged buffer
TTBOMK to the best of my knowledge
TTC The Triplet Connection
TTFN ta ta for now
TTH Tuesday/Thursday
TTHMs total trihalomethanes
TTL transistor-transistor logic
TTO transtracheal oxygen
T Town Tulsa
TTP ribothymidine 5c-triphosphate
TTP-HUS thrombotic thrombocytopenic purpura and hemolytic uremic syndrome
TTT that the (shortwave transmission)
TTX tetrodotoxin
TTY teletypewriter
TTYL talk to you later
TTYS talk to you soon
Tu Tuesday
TU thank you (shortwave transmission); transport unit
T.U. trade union; transmission unit
TUC Trades Union Congress
'tude attitude
Tue. Tuesday
Tues. Tuesday
TUFT transuterine fallopian transfer
Tun. Tunisia; Tunisian; Tunisian
turbo turbocharger
Turk. Turkey; Turkish; Turkmenistan
TURP transurethral resection of prostate
turps turpentine

TUU transureteroureterostomy

tux tuxedo

TV television; transvestite

.tv Tuvalu

T/V thermal/vacuum

TVA Tennessee Valley Authority

TV-14 strong caution for children under 14 (television rating)

TV-14-D strong caution for children under 14, possible intensely suggestive dialogue (television rating)

TV-14-L strong caution for children under 14, possible strong coarse language (television rating)

TV-14-S strong caution for children under 14, possible intense sexual situations (television rating)

TV-14-V strong caution for children under 14, possible intense violence (television rating)

TVG time-varied gain

TV-G for general audience (television rating)

TVH transvaginal hysterectomy

TVI television interference (shortwave transmission)

TV-MA mature audience only (television rating)

TV-MA-L mature audience only, possible crude indecent language (television rating)

TV-MA-S mature audience only, possible explicit sexual activity (television rating)

TV-MA-V mature audience only, possible graphic violence (television rating)

TVP textured vegetable protein

TV-PG parental guidance suggested (television rating)

TV-PG-D parental guidance suggested, possible suggestive dialogue (television rating)

TV-PG-L parental guidance suggested, possible infrequent coarse language (television rating)

TV-PG-S parental guidance suggested, possible sexual situations (television rating)

TV-PG-V parental guidance suggested, possible moderate violence (television rating)

TVS tornado vortex signature

TV-Y for all children (television rating)

TV-Y7 for children age 7 and older (television rating)

TV-Y7-FV for children age 7 and older, possible intense fantasy violence (television rating)

TW tomorrow (shortwave transmission)

.tw Taiwan

T/W thrust to weight ratio

TWA Trans World Airlines

twack twelve pack

24-7 twenty-four hours a day, seven days a week (that is, constantly)

TWI two-way interface

twnhs townhouse

2 to

2 x 4 two inch by four inch board size

2DAY today

twofer two for [one]

2,4,5-T (2,4,5-trichlorophe-noxy) acetic acid

201Tl thallium-201

2-PAM 2-pralidoxime

Twp. township

TWTA traveling-wave tube am-plifier

TWX teletypewriter exchange

TX transmit

TXR transmitter

TXT text (shortwave transmis-sion)

TY they (shortwave transmis-sion)

tymp. tympanotomy

typ. typographer; typography

typo typographical [error]

typo. typographer; typography

Tyr. Tyrone

TYVM thank you very much

Tx transmit; treatment

TX Texas

.tz Tanzania

TZA Tanzania

U

u up quark

U internal energy; [residential] unit; units; uracil; uranium; you

u. unit; units; upper

U. uncle; University; unsatisfac-tory

UA United Artists; urinalysis

.ua Ukraine

UAE United Arab Emirates

UAPD Union of American Physi-cians and Dentists

UAR United Arab Republic

UARS upper atmosphere re-search satellite

UART universal asynchronous receiver transmitter

UAV unmanned aerial vehicle; unmanned aerospace vehicle

UAW United Automobile Work-ers

UB uniform billing

U.B. upper bench

UBI United Bar Code Industries

UBIC unrelated business income

UB2 you be too

uc uppercase (letter)

UC ulcerative colitis; user com-munity; uterine contraction

U.C. Upper Canada

UCAID University Corporation for Advanced Internet Develop-ment

U.C.C. Uniform Commercial Code

U.C.C.C. Uniform Consumer Credit Code

U.C.C.J.A. Uniform Child Cus-tody Jurisdiction Act

UCE unsolicited commercial e-mail

UCHI usual childhood illnesses

UCM unresolved complex mix-ture

UCMJ Uniform Code of Military Justice

UCP *Uniform Customs and Practice [for Commercial Documentary Credits]*

UCPA United Cerebral Palsy Association

UCR usual, customary, and reasonable

U.C.R. Uniform Crime Reports (compiled by the Federal Bureau of Investigation)

UCS universal character set

UCT Universal Coordinated Time

UDAG Urban Development Action Grant

UDC universal decimal system

UDEAC *French* Union Douanière des États de l'Afrique Centrale (Central African Customs and Economic Union)

UDITPA The Uniform Division of Income for Tax Purposes Act

UDP uridine 5c-diphosphate; User Datagram Protocol

UDPG uridine diphosphoglucose

UDPGal uridine diphosphogalactose

UDPGlc uridine diphosphoglucose

UDP-GlcUA uridine diphosphoglucuronic acid

UE upper extremities

UEF user ephemeris file

UFA unesterified free fatty acid

U.F.C. Ultimate Fighting Championship

UFCA Uniform Fraudulent Conveyance Act

UFO unidentified flying object

UFTA Uniform Fraudulent Transfer Act

.ug Uganda

UGI upper gastrointestinal

UGT urgent

UHF ultrahigh frequency

UHMS Undersea and Hyperbaric Medical Society

UHR ultra high resolution

UI unemployment insurance

UIC underground injection control

UICC International Union Against Cancer

UIP usual interstitial pneumonia [of Liebow]

UIS Unemployment Insurance Service

UK United Kingdom

uke ukulele

UL unimproved land; urban legend

U.L. Underwriters Laboratories Inc.

U/L uplink

ULA uniform laws or acts

U.L.A. *Uniform Laws Annotated*

ULF ultra low frequency

ULSI ultra-large-scale integration

ult. ultimate; ultimately; *Latin* ultimo (last month)

ultim. ultimately

.um United States Minor Outlying Islands

UMA upper memory area

UMB upper memory block

umb. umbilical

UMGA Unified Medical Group Association

UMLS Unified Medical Language System

ump umpire

UMSLG University Medical School Librarians Group

UMTRCA Uranium Mill Tailings Radiation Control Act

UMW United Mine Workers

UMWA United Mine Workers of America

un unit

UN United Nations; until (shortwave transmission)

UNA United Nations Association

UNAIDS [Joint] United Nations Program on HIV/AIDS

UNAMIR United Nations Assistance Mission for Rwanda

unan. unanimous

UNARIUS [Academy of Science] Universal Articulate Interdimensional Understanding of Science

UNAVEM III United Nations Angola Verification Mission III

unb. unbound

unbd. unbound

unc. uncirculated

UNCF United Negro College Fund (now called "The College FUND/UNCF")

UNCRO United Nations Confidence Restoration Operation in Croatia

UNCTAD United Nations Conference on Trade and Development

UNDCP United Nations [International] Drug Control Program

UNDOF United Nations Disengagement Observer Force

UNDP United Nations Development Program

Une unnilennium

UNEP United Nations Environment Program

UNESCO United Nations Educational, Scientific, and Cultural Organization

unexpl. unexplained

UNFDAC United Nations Fund for Drug Abuse Control

UNFICYP United Nations Force in Cyprus

UNFPA United Nations Fund for Population Activities

ung *Latin* unguentum (ointment)

UNGA United Nations General Assembly

Unh unnilhexium

UNHCR United Nations Office of the High Commissioner for Refugees

UNI United Nurses International; Univision

UNICEF United Nations Children's Fund, (formerly United Nations Children's Emergency Fund)

UNIDO United Nations Industrial Development Organization

UNIENET United Nations International Emergency Network

UNIFIL United Nations Interim Force in Lebanon

UNIKOM United Nations Iraq-Kuwait Observation Mission

Unit. Unitarian; Unitarianism

UNITAR United Nations Institute for Training and Research

univ. universal; university

Univ. Universalist

UNIVAC Universal Automatic Computer

unkn. unknown

UNMIH United Nations Mission in Haiti

UNMOGIP United Nations Military Observer Group in India and Pakistan

UNMOT United Nations Mission of Observers in Tajikistan

Uno unniloctium

UNOMIG United Nations Observer Mission in Georgia

UNOMIL United Nations Observer Mission in Liberia

UNOMOZ United Nations Operation in Mozambique

UNOMUR United Nations Observer Mission Uganda-Rwanda

UNOSG United Nations Office of the Secretary General

UNOS United Network for Organ Sharing

UNOSOM II United Nations Operation in Somalia II

Unp unnilpentium

unp. unpaged; unpaginated

UNPREDEP United Nations Preventive Deployment [Force]

UNPROFOR United Nations Protection Force

Unq unnilquadium

UNRISD United Nations Research Institute for Social Development

UNRRA United Nations Relief and Rehabilitation Administration

UNRWA United Nations Relief and Works Agency

Uns unnilseptium

uns. unsymmetrical

UNTAC United Nations Transitional Authority in Cambodia

UNTSO United Nations Truce Supervision Organization

UNU United Nations University

U/O urinary output

UOA United Ostomy Association

UP underproof; Upper Peninsula [of Michigan]

up. upper

UPA Uniform Partnership Act

UPC Universal Product Code

UPDRS unified Parkinson disease rating scale

upgd. upgrade; upgraded

UPI United Press International

UPIN Unique Physician Identifier Number

UPJ ureteropelvic junction

UPPP uvulopalatopharyngoplasty

UPPR upper

UPR user preferred routing

upr. upper

UPS uninterruptible power supply; United Parcel Service

UP3 uvulopalatopharyngoplasty

UPU Universal Postal Union

UR utilization review; your (shortwave transmission)

U.R. *Latin* uti rogas (be it as you desire)

Ura uracil

URA Urban Renewal Administration

URAC Utilization Review Accreditation Committee

Urd uridine

URESA Uniform Reciprocal Enforcement of Divorce Act

URF unidentified reading frame; uterine relaxing factor

URI upper respiratory infection

URL uniform resource locator; (*sometimes* universal resource locator)

URN universal resource name

urol. urological; urology

URTI upper respiratory tract infection

Uru. Uruguay; Uruguayan

US ultrasound; unconditioned stimulus; Uniform System; United States; United States [highway]

.us United States of America

u.s. *Latin* ubi supra (where mentioned above); *Latin* ut supra (as above)

U.S. Uncle Sam; united service; United States

USA United States Army; United States of America; USA (cable television network)

USACD United States Arms Control and Disarmament Agency

USACE United States Army Corps of Engineers

USACHPPM United States Army Center for Health Promotion and Preventive Medicine

USADSF United States of America Deaf Sports Federation

USAF United States Air Force

USAFA United States Air Force Academy

USAFE United States Air Forces in Europe

USAFI United States Armed Forces Institute

USAFSAM United States Air Force School of Aerospace Medicine

USAID United States Agency for International Development

USAKF United States of America Karate Federation

USAN United States Adopted Name

USAR United States Army Reserve

USAREUR United States Army, Europe

USARIEM United States Army Research Institute of Environmental Medicine

USB Universal Serial Bus

USBOC United States Bureau of the Census

USBR United States Bureau of Reclamation

USC. United States Code

USCA United States Croquet Association

USC.A. United States Code Annotated; United States Court of Appeals

USCAP United States and Canadian Academy of Pathology

USC.C. United States Circuit Court

USCG United States Coast Guard

USCS United States Customs Service

USC.S.C. United States Civil Service Commission

USD United States Dollars

USDA United States Department of Agriculture

USD.C. United States District Court

USDI United States Department of the Interior

USDW underground source of drinking water

userid [Internet] user identification

USES United States Employment Service

USET United States Equestrian Team

USFS United States Forest Service

USFWS United States Fish and Wildlife Service

USG United States government

USGA United States Golf Association

USGPO United States Government Printing Office

USGS United States Geological Survey

USHA United States Handball Association

USHC United Seniors Health Cooperative

USIA United States Information Agency

USITC United States International Trade Commission

USL Unix System Laboratories

USM United States Mail; United States Mint

USMA United States Military Academy

USMC United States Marine Corps

USMLE United States Medical Licensing Examination

USN United States Navy

USNA United States Naval Academy

USNCB United States National Central Bureau

USNR United States Naval Reserve

USO ultra stable oscillator; United Service Organizations

USP United States Pharmacopoeia

USPHS United States Public Health Service

USPO United States Post Office

USPS United States Postal Service

USPTO United States Patent and Trademark Office

USR. *United States Supreme Court Reports*

USRA United States Railway Association

USR.S. United States Revised Statutes

USRT universal synchronous receiver transmitter

USS United States Senate; United States ship

USSC United States Space Command

USSR Union of Soviet Socialist Republics

USTA United States Telephone Association; United States Tennis Association

UST.C. United States Tax Cases

USTTA United States Travel and Tourism Administration

usu. usually

usw. *German* und so weiter (and so forth)

UT universal time; Utah

Ut. Utah

UTC Coordinated Universal Time

UTCS universal time coordinate system

ut dict. *Latin* ut dictum (as directed)

ute utility vehicle

UTI urinary tract infection

util. utilities; utility

utl. utilities

UTM universal Turing machine

UTP uridine 5c-triphosphate

ut sup. *Latin* ut supra (as above)

Uun ununnilium

Uuu unununium

UV ultraviolet

UVA ultraviolet, long wave

UVB ultraviolet, short wave

UVC ultraviolet C

UVCS ultraviolet coronagraph spectrometer

UVEB unifocal ventricular ectopic beat

UVS ultraviolet spectrometer

UW underwriter; underwritten

ux. *Latin* uxor (wife)

UXB unexploded bomb

.uy Uruguay

.uz Uzbekistan

V

V 5; potential; vanadium; velocity; verb; very; victory; violence (television rating); vocative; volt; volume; vowel

v. verb; verse; version; verso; *Latin* versus (against); *Latin* vide (see); volume

V. venerable; very; viscount; viscountess

VA Department of Veterans Affairs; (formerly Veterans' Administration); vicar apostolic; Virginia

Va. Virginia

.va Vatican City State

V/A visual acuity

V-A ventriculoatrial

VAB voice answer back

VAC ventriculoatrial conduction

vac. vacuum

VACM vector averaging current meter

vactor virtual actor
VAD velocity-azimuth display
V.Adm. vice admiral
VAFB Vandenberg Air Force Base
VAFSTF Vaccine Associated Feline Sarcoma Task Force
vag. vagina; vaginal; vagrant
VAI ventilator-assisted individual
val. valentine; value; valued
Val. valley
VAMC Veterans Affairs Medical Center
vamp vampire
van caravan; vanguard
VAN value-added network
V & V verification and validation
VAP value-added process
Va/Q alveolar ventilation/perfusion ratio
VAR value-added reseller; value-added retailer
var. variable; variant; variation; variety; various
vas. vasectomy
VAT value-added tax
Vat. Vatican
VATS video-assisted thoracic surgery; video-assisted thoracoscopic surgery
VB vertebral body
vb. verb; verbal
<vbg> very big grin
vbl verbal
vbln. verbal noun
vBNS very high performance Backbone Network Service
VBT vertebral body tenderness

VC vice chancellor; vice consul; Victoria Cross; Vietcong; virtual channel
.vc Saint Vincent and the Grenadines
V/C vector control
V.C.C. vice-chancellor's court
VCD vocal cord dysfunction
VCE variable cycle engine
VCID virtual channel identification
VCO voltage controlled oscillator
VCPI virtual control program interface
VCR video cassette recorder
VCS Veterinary Cancer Society
VCUG voiding cystourethrogram
VCXO voltage controlled crystal oscillator
VD venereal disease
v.d. vapor density; various dates
V-day victory day
VDC volts DC
VDE visual development environment
VDISK virtual disk
VDRL Venereal Disease Research Laboratories
VDS virtual data set
VDSL very high bit-rate digital subscriber line
VDT video display terminal
VDU visual display unit
VE virtual environment
.ve Venezuela
V.E. *Latin* venditioni exponas (a sale must be exposed, that is, made)

VEBA voluntary employee benefit account

V-E Day Victory in Europe Day

VEE Venezuelan equine encephalomyelitis

veep vice president

veg. vegetable; vegetarian; vegetate

V.E.G.F. vascular endothelial growth factor

veggie vegetable; vegetarian

vel. vellum; velocity

Ven. venerable; Venezuela; Venezuelan

VER visual evoked response

ver. verse; version

Veronica very easy, rodent-oriented netwide index to computerized archives

vers versed sine

vert. vertebrate; vertical

VESA Video Electronics Standards Association

VESL Vocational English as a Second Language

vesp. *Latin* vesper (evening)

vet veteran; veterinarian; veterinary

veter. veterinary

vet. med. veterinary medicine

VETS Veterans' Employment and Training Service

VF vicar forane; video frequency; visual field

VFD volunteer fire department

VFIT visual field intact

VFR visual flight rules

VFW Veterans of Foreign Wars

VG vicar general

.vg [British] Virgin Islands

v.g. *Latin* verbi gratia (for the sake of example)

VGA video graphics array

VGL very good-looking

VGLI Veterans Group Life Insurance

VHA Voluntary Hospitals of America

VHDL very high density lipoprotein

VHF very high frequency

VHPCC very high performance computing and communication

VHRR very high resolution radiometer

VHS video home system

VHSIC very high speed integrated circuit

VI Vancouver Island; Virgin Islands; volume indicator

.vi [U.S.] Virgin Islands

v.i. verb intransitive; *Latin* vide infra (see below)

V.I. Vancouver Island; Virgin Islands

VIA Vaccine Information and Awareness

vibe vibration

vibes vibraphone

vic. vicinity

Vic. Vicar; Victoria

Vict. Victorian

VID vehicle identification [number]

vid. video

videorazzi video camera paparazzi

Viet. Vietnam; Vietnamese

vig vigorish
VIL vertically integrated liquid
vil. village
VIN vehicle identification number
VIP very important person
VIR Virgo
VIRGO variability of [solar] irradiance and gravity oscillations
vis. visibility; visible; visual
Vis. viscount; viscountess
Visct. viscount; viscountess
VISSR visible-infrared spin-scan radiometer
VISTA Volunteers in Service to America
vit vitamin
vitals vital signs (pulse rate, temperature, respiratory rate)
viz. *Latin* videlicet (that is, namely)
VJ video jockey
V-J Day Victory over Japan Day (WWII)
VL Vulgar Latin
VLA very large array
VLBA very long baseline array
VLBI very long baseline interferometry
VLCC very large crude oil carrier
VLDL very low-density lipoprotein
VLF very low frequency
VLMF very low magnetic field
VLSI very large scale integration
VLT very large telescope
VM virtual memory
VMA vanillylmandelic acid
V-mail video mail; voice mail

VMC visual meteorological conditions; void metal composite
VMCM vector measuring current meter
V.M.D. *Latin* Veterinariae Medicinae Doctor (Doctor of Veterinary Medicine)
VMI Virginia Military Institute
V-MI Volpe-Manhold Index
VMM virtual memory manager
VMS vertical motion simulator; virtual memory system
.vn Vietnam
VNA Visiting Nurse Association
VNAA Visiting Nurse Associations of America
VNC Virtual Nursing College
VO verbal order; voiceover
vo. verso
VOA Voice of America
VOC volatile organic chemical; volatile organic compound
voc. vocational; vocative
vocab. vocabulary
vol. volcano; volume; volunteer
VOM volt-ohm milliameter
V-1 *German* Vergeltungswaffe 1 (vengeance weapon 1)
VOR very high frequency omnidirectional radio range
VOS verb-object-subject; vessel of opportunity; voluntary observing ship; volunteer observing ship
vou. voucher
VP variable pitch; verb phrase; vice president
VPD vacuum photo diode
VPG virtual proving grounds

VPOTUS Vice President of the United States

VPS volume performance standard

VR virtual reality

VRA very high frequency real-time antenna

VRAM video random access memory

v. refl. reflexive verb

VRTC Vehicle Research Test Center

VRM variable-rate mortgage

VRML virtual reality modeling language

vry very

VS very superior; veterinary surgeon; vital signs (pulse rate, temperature, respiratory rate)

vs. verse; *Latin* versus (against)

v.s. vide supra

VSAT very small aperture terminal

VSCP Vital Statistics Cooperative Program

VSM volcano system monitor

VSO verb-subject-object; very superior old

VSOP very superior old pale

VSP Vessel Sanitation Program

VSS vital signs stable

vss. verses; versions

V/STOL vertical short takeoff and landing

VT vacuum tube; variable time; Vermont

Vt. Vermont

v.t. verb transitive

VTB vestibular test battery

VTE venous thromboembolic event

VTF vacuum test fixture

VTHL vertical takeoff, horizontal landing

VTOL vertical takeoff and landing

VTR videotape recorder

VTVL vertical takeoff, vertical landing

V-2 *German* Vergeltungswaffe 2 (vengeance weapon 2)

VTX very high frequency real-time transmitter

VU volume unit

.vu Vanuatu

Vul. Vulgate

vulg. vulgar

Vulg. Vulgate

VUS views

vv. verbs; verses; violins; volumes

v.v. vice versa

VVSOP very, very superior old pale

VW *German* Volkswagen (people's car)

V/W vaporware

VxD virtual device driver

VY very (shortwave transmission)

VZR varicella zoster (chicken pox)

W

w weight; width; work

W tungsten; watt; Wednesday; week; Welsh, west; western;

White (as in personal ads); widowed (as in personal ads); with (shortwave transmission)

w. wife; with

w/ with

WA Washington; with average; word after (shortwave transmission)

WAAC Women's Army Auxiliary Corps

WAAF Women's Auxiliary Air Force

WAC Women's Army Corps

WACMA World Arnold-Chiari Malformation Association

WADB West African Development Bank

WADEM World Association for Disaster and Emergency Medicine

WADR with all due respect

WAF Women in the Air Force

WAFS World Area Forecast System

WAGICS Women and Genetics in Contemporary Society

WAIS Wechsler Adult Intelligence Scale; wide area information server

WAM wave model

WAN wide area network

WAPA Western Area Power Administration

WAPD World Association of Persons with Disabilities

war. warrant

Ward X the morgue

WARF Wisconsin Alumni Research Foundation

Wash. Washington

Wasp White Anglo-Saxon Protestant

WASP World Association for Social Psychiatry

Wat. Waterford

WATS Wide Area Telecommunications Service

W. Aust. Western Australia

WAV wavetable synthesis

WAVES Women Accepted for Volunteer Emergency Service

Wb weber

WB westbound; word before (shortwave transmission)

w.b. water ballast; waybill

W.B. weather bureau

WBA World Boxing Association

WBC white blood cell; white blood count; World Boxing Council

WBF wood-burning fireplace; World Bridge Federation

wbfp. wood-burning fireplace

WBMOD wide band [scintillation] model

WbN west by north

WbS west by south

WBS work breakdown structure

WC water closet; wind chill; without charge; worker's compensation; workmen's compensation

WCA World Chiropractic Alliance

W.C. and Ins. Rep. *Workmen's Compensation and Insurance Reports*

WCF White Christian female

WCI Wound Care Institute

WCL World Confederation of Labor

WCM White Christian male

WCTF World Children's Transplant Fund

WCTU Women's Christian Temperance Union

wd when distributed

Wd widowed (as in personal ads)

WD War Department; water damage; well-developed; white dwarf; word (shortwave transmission); would (shortwave transmission)

wd. wood; word

W/D washer and dryer

WDC washer/dryer connection; World Data Center

WDCGG World Data Center for Greenhouse Gases

WDDES World Digital Database for Environmental Sciences

WDLL well-differentiated lymphocytic lymphoma

WDV water dilution volume

wdy wordy

We Wednesday

webarian web designer; web-using librarian

webliography bibliography on the World Wide Web

Webs world equity benchmark shares

Wed. Wednesday

WEDI Workgroup on Electronic Data Interchange

Wedn. Wednesday

Wednes. Wednesday

WEE western equine encephalomyelitis

WEFAX weather facsimile

WEU Western European Union

wf wrong font

WF White female; wood floors

.wf Wallis and Futuna Islands

WFC World Food Council

WFCS World's Fair Collectors Society

WFH World Federation of Hemophilia

WFIem. Western Flemish

WFMH World Federation for Mental Health

WFO Weather Forecast Office

WFP World Food Program

WFris. West Frisian

WFS Women for Sobriety

WFTU World Federation of Trade Unions

WFWG Windows for Workgroups

WG wrong (shortwave transmission)

w.g. wire gauge

WGAS who gives a shit

WGmc West Germanic

WH watt-hour; which (shortwave transmission)

wh. white

WHA World Hockey Association

WHAM! Women's Health Action and Mobilization

WHCA White House Communications Agency

WHERE Women for Healthcare Education, Reform, and Equity

whf. wharf

WHMIS Workplace Hazardous Materials Information System

WHO World Health Organization

Whodb White House Office Database

WHOI Woods Hole Oceanographic Institution

WHOSIS WHO Statistical Information System

WHPA wellhead protection area

W-hr watt-hour

WHS Washington Headquarters Services

whs. warehouse

whse. warehouse

whsle. wholesale

wht. white

wi when issued

WI will (shortwave transmission); Wisconsin

W.I. West Indian; West Indies

W/I walk-in

WIA weather-impacted airspace; wounded in action

WIBC Women's International Bowling Congress

WIC Women, Infants, and Children (supplemental food program)

wid. widow; widower

wilco will comply

WIMC Women in Managed Care

WIMP window, icon, menu, pointing [device]; window, icon, mouse, pull-down [menu]

WIN Weight-control Information Network; within (short-wave transmission); Work Incentive program

wind. windowed

W Indies West Indies

WINK windowed eat-in kitchen

WIPO World Intellectual Property Organization

WIPP [United States] Waste Isolation Pilot Plant

Wis. Wisconsin; Wisdom of Solomon

Wisc. Wisconsin

Wisd. Wisdom

WIT witness (shortwave transmission)

wiz wizard

WK week (shortwave transmission)

wk. weak; week

WKD worked (shortwave transmission)

WKG working (shortwave transmission)

wkly. weekly

wk vb weak verb

WL water line; wavelength; well (shortwave transmission)

WLA wasteload allocation

WLC wavelength calibration

WLU work load unit

WM White male

wm. wattmeter

WMA World Medical Association

wmk. watermark

WMO World Meteorological Organization

WN well-nourished; when (shortwave transmission)

WNBA Women's National Basketball Association

WNL within normal limits

WNW west-northwest

WNWD well-nourished and well-developed

WO warrant officer; who (shortwave transmission)

w/o without

w.o.c. without compensation

WOCN Wound, Ostomy, and Continence Nurses Society

WODC World Ozone Data Center (also **WO3DC**)

WoMS World of Multiple Sclerosis

WONDER Wide-ranging Online Data for Epidemiologic Research

WORM write once, read many [times]

WOTAN weather observation through ambient noise

WOW World Ocean Watch

WP weather permitting; word processing; word processor

WPA Work Projects Administration; World Psychiatric Association

WPBA World Professional Billiards Association

wpc watts per channel

WPF White professional female

WPI Wholesale Price Index

WPL Wave Propagation Laboratory

wpm words per minute

WPM White professional male

wpn. weapon

WR were (shortwave transmission); western range; wide receiver

W.r. Wassermann reaction

Wra Wright antigens

WRAC Women's Royal Army Corps

WRAF Women's Royal Air Force

WRAMC Walter Reed Army Medical Center

WRAPD World Rehabilitation Association for the Psycho-Socially Disabled

writ. writer; written by

WRIPS Wave Rider Information Processing System

WRNS Women's Royal Naval Service

wrnt. warrant

WROS with rights of survivorship

WRT with respect to

WRVS Women's Royal Voluntary Service

WS was (shortwave transmission); West Saxon; William Shakespeare; Wisdom of Solomon; working storage; workstation

.ws Samoa

WSA wilderness study area; Williams Syndrome Association

WSFO Weather Service Forecast Office

WSMR White Sands Missile Range

WSTA World Societies for Technology in Anaesthesia

WSW west-southwest

wt warrant

WT watertight; what (shortwave transmission)

wt. weight

wtd wanted

WTF what the fuck

WTFIGO What the fuck is going on?

WTG way to go

WTH what the hell

WTO World Tourism Organization; World Trade Organization (formerly, **GATT**)

WToO World Tourism Organization

WTrO World Trade Organization

W/U workup

WUD would (shortwave transmission)

WV West Virginia

W.Va. West Virginia

WVI World Veterinary Index

WVR Within Visual Range

WVS Women's Voluntary Service

w/w wall-to-wall

WW widowed (as in personal ads)

WWAF widowed Asian female

WWAM widowed Asian male

WWBF widowed Black female

WWBM widowed Black male

WWF World Wildlife Fund

WWHF widowed Hispanic female

WWHM widowed Hispanic male

WWI World War I

WWII World War II

WWJD What Would Jesus Do

WWJF widowed Jewish female

WWJM widowed Jewish male

WWMCCS Worldwide Military Command and Control System

WWNWS Worldwide Navigational Warning Service

WWW World Weather Watch; World Wide Web

WWWF widowed White female

WWWM widowed White male

WX weather

WY why (shortwave transmission); Wyoming

Wyo. Wyoming

WYSIAYG what you see is all you get

WYSIWYG what you see is what you get

XYZ

x abscissa; by; times (that is, multiplication)

X adult audiences only; Christ; Christian; experimental; extra; reactance; 10

x. *Latin* ex (not including, without)

Xan xanthine

XBT expendable bathythermograph

XC cross-country

XCP expendable current profiler

XD ex dividend

x-div. ex dividend

XDR external data representation

Xe xenon

Xerox PARC Xerox Palo Alto Research Center

XFER transfer

XFCN external function

XGA extended graphics array

XI ex interest

XIDB extended integrated data base

XING crossing

XL ex-library; extra large; extra long

Xmas Christmas

XML Extensible Markup Language

XMM x-ray multi mirror

XMP xanthosine 5c-monophosphate

XMS extended memory specification

XMT transmit

XMTR transmitter

Xn. Christian

Xnty. Christianity

XO extra old

XPNDR transponder

XPS Xeroderma Pigmentosum Society

Xref cross-reference

XRF x-ray fluorescence

XS extra small

x-sect cross section

XSU cross strap unit

XT crosstalk; extended technology

xtal crystal

XTP xanthosine 5c-triphosphate

xtr extra

XUV extreme ultraviolet

XW ex warrants

XX double strength ale; 20

XXL extra extra large

XXX pornographic; triple strength ale

Xy xylose

Xyl xylose

XYL wife (shortwave transmission)

y yen

Y admittance; hypercharge; year; YMCA; YMHA; YWCA; YWHA; young; yttrium

y. year

YA yesterday (shortwave transmission); yet another; young adult

YAC yeast artificial chromosome

YAG yttrium aluminum garnet

YAP young aspiring professional

YAR Yemen Arab Republic

Yb ytterbium

YB yearbook

YCC Youth Conservation Corps

yd. yard

YDT Yukon Daylight Time

.ye Yemen

yel. yellow

yeo. yeoman; yeomanry

YHVH Jehovah; Yahweh

YHWH Jehovah; Yahweh

YHz yottahertz

Yinglish Yiddish influenced English

yippie Youth International Party [member]

YL young lady (shortwave transmission)

YMCA Young Men's Christian Association

YMHA Young Men's Hebrew Association

YMMV your mileage may vary

yng. young

YO years old

YOB year of birth

Yorks. Yorkshire

YPLL years of potential life lost

yr. year; your

yrbk. yearbook

YRBS Youth Risk Behavior Survey

yrd yard

yrly. yearly

Yrs. Yours

ys yoctasecond

ysec yoctasecond

YSO young stellar object

YST Yukon Standard Time

Y.T. Yukon Territory

YTD year to date

YTM yield to maturity

Y2K problem year 2000 problem

.yu Yugoslavia

Yug. Yugoslavia; Yugoslavian

Yugo. Yugoslavian

yuppie young urban professional

YWCA Young Women's Christian Association

YWHA Young Women's Hebrew Association

Z atomic number; impedance; zenith distance

z. zero; zone

.za South Africa

Zach. Zacharias

ZAF South Africa

ZAN we can receive absolutely nothing (shortwave transmission)

ZAP acknowledge please (shortwave transmission)

ZB zero beat

ZBB zero-based budgeting

ZBR zone bit recording

Zc Zechariah

ZC zoning change

Z-CAV zoned constant angular velocity

ZCG local receiving conditions good (shortwave transmission)

ZCP local receiving conditions poor (shortwave transmission)

ZCS cease sending (shortwave transmission)

ZD zero defect

z.d. zenith distance

ZDV Denver Air Route Traffic Control Center; zidovudine

Zech. Zechariah

ZEEP zero end-expiratory pressure

Zeph. Zephaniah

ZETA zero energy thermonuclear assembly

ZEV zero emissions vehicle

ZFB your signals are fading badly (shortwave transmission)

ZFS your signals are fading slightly (shortwave transmission)

ZFW Fort Worth Air Route Traffic Control Center

ZG zero gravity

ZGS your signals are getting stronger (shortwave transmission)

ZGW your signals are getting weaker (shortwave transmission)

ZHC how are your receiving conditions? (shortwave transmission)

ZHz zettahertz

ZI zonal index; zone of interior

ZID zone of initial dilution

ZIF zero insertion force

ZIFT zygote intrafallopian transfer

zin zinfandel

'zine an inexpensively produced, usually underground, usually photocopied fan magzine (from "magazine")

zip compressed file

ZIP zone improvement plan; Zone Information Protocol

Zl zloty

ZLB give long breaks (shortwave transmission)

ZLS we are suffering from a lightning storm (shortwave transmission)

zm. zeptometer

.zm Zambia

ZMO stand by a moment (shortwave transmission)

ZMQ stand by for... (shortwave transmission)

Zn zinc

ZOC zone of contribution

ZOI zone of influence

ZOK we are receiving OK (shortwave transmission)

zoo zoological garden

zool. zoological; zoology

ZOT zone of transport

Zp Zephaniah

ZPG zero population growth

ZPRSN Zurich Provisional Relative Sunspot Number

Zr zirconium

ZRO are you receiving OK? (shortwave transmission)

zs zeptosecond

Z's sleep

zsec zeptosecond

ZSF send faster (shortwave transmission)

ZSH static is heavy here (shortwave transmission)

ZSR your sigs strong readable (shortwave transmission); zeta sedimentation ratio

ZSS send slower (shortwave transmission)

ZST zone standard time

ZSU your signals are unreadable (shortwave transmission)

ZT zone time

ZTH send by hand (shortwave transmission)

ZVS signals varying in intensity (shortwave transmission)

.zw Zimbabwe

ZWO send words once (shortwave transmission)

ZWR your sigs weak but readable (shortwave transmission)

ZWT send words twice (shortwave transmission)

zzz sleep

zzzz snore